W9-ADB-085

IDEAS OF THE RESTORATION IN
ENGLISH LITERATURE, 1660-71

PR
437
.J67
1984

IDEAS OF THE RESTORATION IN ENGLISH LITERATURE 1660–71

Nicholas Jose

Harvard University Press
Cambridge, Massachusetts
1984

Salem Academy and College
Gramley Library
Winston-Salem, N.C. 27108

Copyright © 1984 by Nicholas Jose

All rights reserved

Printed in Hong Kong

Library of Congress Cataloging in Publication Data

Jose, Nicholas, 1952–
  Ideas of the Restoration in English Literature,
  1660–1671.

  Bibliography: p.
  Includes index.
  1. English literature — Early modern, 1500–1700 —
History and criticism. 2. Politics and literature —
Great Britain.   3. Great Britain—History—Restoration,
1660–1688. I. Title.
PR437.J67   1983   820′.9′004   82-21292
ISBN 0 674 44276 8

For my parents

Contents

Abbreviations   viii

Preface   xi

1 The State Chaos   1

2 New Order   17

3 Ideas of Restoration I : The Panegyric Task   31

4 Ideas of Restoration II : Looking Back and Looking Forward   44

5 Ideal Restoration and the Case of Cowley   67

6 The Poetry of the Second Dutch War   97

7 Theatrical Restoration   120

8 *Samson Agonistes:* The Play Turned Upside Down   142

9 Conclusion : Artifice and Scrutiny   164

Notes   175

Index   200

Abbreviations

The following abbreviations have been used for works frequently cited. Unless otherwise stated, the place of publication is London. The original spelling and punctuation of the editions cited have been followed in all cases, except for some slight alteration of capitalisation of minor words in seventeenth-century titles.

Carey and Fowler
> *The Poems of John Milton*, ed. John Carey and Alastair Fowler (1968). All quotations from Milton's poems are from this edition.

Cowley, *Essays*
> Abraham Cowley, *Essays, Plays and Sundry Verses*, ed. A.R. Waller (Cambridge, 1906).

Cowley, *Poems*
> Abraham Cowley, *Poems: Miscellanies, The Mistress, Pindarique Odes, Davideis, Verses Written Upon Several Occasions*, ed. A.R. Waller (Cambridge, 1905). All quotations from Cowley, unless otherwise stated, are from Waller's editions.

CSPD
> Calendar of State Papers, Domestic Series.

Davies
> Godfrey Davies, *The Restoration of Charles II, 1658-1660* (San Marino, 1955).

DNB
> *Dictionary of National Biography.*

Evelyn
> *The Diary of John Evelyn*, ed. E.S. de Beer (6 vols, Oxford, 1955).

Kinsley
> *The Poems of John Dryden*, ed. James Kinsley (4 vols, Oxford, 1958). All quotations from Dryden's poems are from this edition unless otherwise stated.

Margoliouth
> *The Poems and Letters of Andrew Marvell*, ed. H.M. Margoliouth, revised by Pierre Legouis with the collaboration of E.E. Duncan-Jones (2 vols, Oxford, 1971). All quotations from Marvell are from this edition unless otherwise stated.

Masson
> David Masson, *The Life of John Milton: Narrated in Connexion with the Political, Ecclesiastical, and Literary History of His Time* (6 vols, and index, 1880-94).

Milton, *Complete Prose*
> *Complete Prose Works of John Milton*, general ed., Don M. Wolfe (7 vols, New Haven and London, 1953-74).

Ogg
> David Ogg, *England in the Reign of Charles II* (2 vols, Oxford, 1934).

Pepys
> *The Diary of Samuel Pepys*, ed. Robert Latham and William Matthews (11 vols, 1970-).

POAS
> *Poems on Affairs of State: Augustan Satirical Verse*, 1660-1714, general ed., George de F. Lord (7 vols, New Haven and London, 1963-75).

STC
> *Short-Title Catalogue of Books Printed in England, Scotland, Ireland, Wales, and British America and of English Books Printed in Other Countries, 1641-1700*, compiled by Donald Wing (3 vols, New York, 1945-51).

Preface

At several key places in his poetry Alexander Pope refers to the
Restoration. The references, though judicious, are unflattering.
Pope found it hard to admire the reign of the merry monarch. The
Restoration was a classic example of Pope's perception that artistic
and social decadence were reflected in each other.

> In Days of Ease, when now the weary Sword
> Was sheath'd, and Luxury with Charles restor'd;
> In every Taste of foreign Courts improv'd,
> 'All by the King's Example, liv'd and lov'd.'
> Then Peers grew proud in Horsemanship t'excell,
> New-market's Glory rose, as Britain's fell;
> The Soldier breath'd the Gallantries of France,
> And ev'ry flow'ry Courtier writ Romance.
> Then Marble soften'd into life grew warm,
> And yielding Metal flow'd to human form:
> Lely on animated Canvas stole
> The sleepy Eye, that spoke the melting soul.
> No wonder then, when all was Love and Sport,
> The willing Muses were debauch'd at Court;
> On each enervate string they taught the Note
> To pant, or tremble thro' an Eunuch's throat.
> But Britain, changeful as a Child at play,
> Now calls in Princes, and now turns away.
> Now Whig, now Tory, what we lov'd we hate;
> Now all for Pleasure, now for Church and State;
> Now for Prerogative, and now for Laws;
> Effects unhappy! from a Noble Cause.
>   (*Imitations of Horace*, Ep.II i, 139-60)[1]

Yet Pope's regretful tone reveals another dimension to his vision of
the Restoration. It was impossible to deny the direct continuity
between the earlier age and his own, and it was necessary to
recognise a debt. The Augustan ideals which so inspired — and
disturbed — Pope and many of his contemporaries were first
established in English terms, politically, socially and culturally, at
the Restoration. The Stuart line was re-established at the
Restoration : its splendid swansong was to come in Pope's own
time with Anne, when 'Peace and Plenty tell, a STUART reigns'
(*Windsor Forest*, 42). The poet laureate of the Restoration was John
Dryden, Pope's acknowledged master. Johnson reports that Pope,
less than twelve-years-old, 'persuaded some friends to take him to
the coffee-house which Dryden frequented, and pleased himself
with having seen him'.[2] Later Pope was to take a rather more
superior attitude towards Dryden, but, if he hinted that Dryden
could be bettered, he always admitted that Dryden had dictated
the terms:

> Waller was smooth; but Dryden taught to join
> The varying verse, the full resounding line,
> The long majestic march, and energy divine.
> Tho' still some traces of our rustic vein
> And splay-foot verse, remain'd, and will remain.
> Late, very late, correctness grew our care,
> When the tir'd nation breath'd from civil war.
> (*Imitations of Horace* : Ep.II i, 267-73)

Pope's attitude to the Restoration was complex. If its aspirations
provided him with a set of standards, its shortcomings gave him a
warning, and both were relevant to his own world. Above all the
Restoration intensified Pope's conviction that a society's art was a
measure of its moral vitality. When he created his visionary
indictment of his own society the Restoration offered an additional
frame of reference. Colley Cibber, the imperial king of Dulness,
'the Antichrist of wit', is proclaimed in an echo of that passage in
the *Aeneid* (VI, 791-4) which Dryden recalled when trumpeting
Charles in *Astraea Redux* 1660 (320-3):

> This, this is he, foretold by ancient rhymes:
> Th'Augustus born to bring Saturnian times.
> (*The Dunciad*, III, 319-20)

When in Book IV the poet contemplates the terrifying bond between 'Arbitrary Sway' and Dulness, he is once again drawn to a Stuart motif ' "The RIGHT DIVINE of Kings to govern wrong" ' (IV, 175-88). Finally, when the curtain of universal darkness falls, we witness the ultimate mocking apotheosis of imperial renovation:

> Lo! thy dread Empire, CHAOS! is restor'd;
> Light dies before thy uncreating word....
>   (IV, 653-4)

Behind this moment of restoration lies the force of Pope's fascinated terror and despair at historical dreams.

The Restoration has remained a focal point for considering the connexion between social and cultural ill-health. In his *Essay on Criticism* Pope attacked the corruptive power of court-condoned pornography in Charles's reign (534-49), and still in recent times the debate has continued to rage about Restoration comedy.[3] When Lord Macaulay came to deliver his verdict on the age, he did so, following Pope, in terms of its moral conduct: 'scarcely any rank or profession escaped the infection of the prevailing immorality'. Macaulay found a direct link between the political exigencies of the age and its immorality: 'it is an unquestionable and a most instructive fact that the years during which the political power of the Anglican hierarchy was in the zenith were precisely the years during which national virtue was at the lowest point'. And he found such depravity not merely reflected in but promoted by literature: 'poetry stooped to be the pandar of every low desire'.[4] Macaulay's most vivid engagement with the period occurred when he turned to Restoration drama. He observed there a kind of life he deemed hardly worthy of even the remotest corners of the Empire: 'we find ourselves in a world in which the ladies are like very profligate, impudent and unfeeling men, and in which the men are too bad for any place but Pandaemonium or Norfolk Island'. 'In the whole dramatic literature of the generation which followed the return of Charles the Second' Macaulay found a 'systematic attempt to associate vice with those things which men value most and desire most and virtue with every thing ridiculous and degrading.' He regarded this 'systematic attempt' almost as a political programme, and raised his literary evaluation of the plays to an indictment of the age: 'it must, indeed, be acknowledged, in justice to the writers of whom we have spoken thus severely, that they were to a great extent the creatures of their age'. And finally Macaulay, like Pope, laid the blame for the age on the social irresponsibility of the government: 'to punish public outrage on morals and religion is unquestionably within the competence of rulers'.[5]

Both Pope and Macaulay simplified the Restoration for their own purposes, but the degree of distortion is instructive. They were unable to separate a literary from an historical assessment and in consequence a courtly literary caricature came to stand for social reality. It is instructive because our approach to the period is still so often similar. The idea of the Restoration conjures up lively images of sultry buxom women in dishabillé, of heavy-lidded Rochesterian rakes, of braying bewigged fops with floppy cuffs, of sluggish beefy politicians (like those members of the Lauderdale family in the Ham House portrait gallery) and shrewd operators (like Samuel Pepys with his troubled philandering), all presided over by Dryden's Charles — 'with a greater gust' — to the dark strains of Purcell. Such a view is, of course, a one-sided confection, even if at times we may happily forget it. But sorting through the fictions is difficult. The literature of the Restoration is tied to its society so intimately and so peculiarly that our sense of the period historically is always mediated by our literary experience of it, just as the literature is unintelligible, unpalatable and even dismissible unless informed by historical knowledge, interest and imagination. The Restoration is an extraordinary instance of the relationship between culture and society.[6] Facts and necessities gave rise to the age's various self-images — complex sets of ideas, forms and styles — which in turn provided a medium for the explorations of writers and artists: from whose achievements we in our turn draw our richest sense of the age. This book traces a few only of the lineaments of the relationship between what was happening and what people made of it in literature. The concentration is on the early years of Charles's reign, the Restoration in 1660 and its immediate aftermath, which set the tone for the next quarter-century or so. The literature considered is mainly, if loosely, political. For the most part I have set aside the larger view, both in terms of literary and historical developments and also in terms of the long history, before and after the Restoration decade, of the ideas which writers used in order to think about their time. The sacrifice is warranted, I believe, by the crucial and largely unexplored importance of the Restoration movement itself. Out of that crucible, formed from a compound of inherited rhetoric and quite new hopes and fears, came altered styles, altered tones, altered forms of consciousness, which led on gradually to the great distinctive achievements of the latter part of the century. But it is the initial stages of the process which interest me here; and in particular some of the ways in which a political readjustment was dealt with in literature. In order to highlight the most direct and illuminating points of contact, my coverage of both history and literature has had to be selective. The quality of the works considered varies enormously. The lesser works shed some light on the greater works; the greater works absorb into themselves and transmute the styles, attitudes and awarenesses of the lesser works. I save the greatest, *Samson Agonistes*, till last. My argument moves through the decade to that point, in a roughly chronological manner, but within that arrangement I have grouped the material so as to emphasise the very different ways Charles's return could be refracted in literature. Many people were aware of and troubled by a disparity between ideals and actuality in the period. The wording of my title is intended to point towards that disparity.

A word should be said about literary history of this kind. It is customary nowadays to dismiss literary history as a banal compilation of chronological, biographical and bibliographical facts, awkwardly wedded to a factitious postulation of influences, sources and world pictures. But a true literary history is that which recognises the continuity between literature and history, as it recognises the continuity between our lives, the life of the writer and the life of his work. History is our home, and 'history does not merely touch on language, but takes place in it'.[7] Language exists in time, not just the meanings of words and patterns of syntax, but also the ideas, forms, themes and images which people use to express themselves. To investigate a work fully, one performs an act of both historical and literary imagination. If some works are vastly more intelligent and alive than others, that judgement is properly informed by comparison, contrast and a due recognition of the continuity between a genius and his contemporaries in a shared world.

Many people have helped with my work and I am grateful to them all. I would like to thank Dr Joan Thirsk of St Hilda's College,

Oxford, for her guidance with one stage of the work, and Miss Barbara Everett, Mr Michael Gearin-Tosh, and Professor Christopher Hill for helpful suggestions. I am also grateful to the staff of the Bodleian Library and the library of Magdalen College, Oxford, for much kind co-operation; and to Mrs Jean Linnett for preparation of the typescript. I am especially happy to mention the advice and encouragement of Mr Michael Neve, Dr David Norbrook, Mr Stephen Oliver, Dr Ginny Papaioannou, Dr Jane Adamson and Miss Madeleine O'Dea. My principal acknowledgement is to Mr Emrys Jones, of Magdalen College, Oxford, for his exciting, exacting supervision of my D Phil thesis. His many comments were rigorous, yet always constructive, stimulating and suggestive. It was a privilege and a pleasure to work with him. Finally I would like to thank Professor Ian Donaldson of the Humanities Research Centre, A N U, Canberra, for his ideas, of restoration and other things, and for his interest and support over the years. For the book's shortcomings, however, I remain accountable.

The Rhodes Trust made possible my initial study in Oxford, while the kindness of the Warden of Rhodes House and Lady Williams enhanced my stay there. I am also grateful to the Myer Foundation and the Australian Academy of the Humanities for a grant towards the final stages of my research.

1 The State Chaos

The Restoration of Charles II was an event of great moment and was proclaimed, expounded, celebrated and recorded in a profusion of pageantry and panegyric, tracts, sermons, pictures, diary entries and, later on, memoirs and histories. The array of responses to Charles's return was effusive and apparently unanimous, although often clumsy or heavy-handed, and conveys a striking sense of surprise, wonder, and even shock. The king's Restoration was a mystery verging on the miraculous, as many contemporaries saw it, and had come about with almost inexplicable suddenness and ease. Poets registered the wonder of the occasion abundantly and equally in prose writings religiosity combined with loyalism to confer a peculiarly exalted significance on the event, working to achieve for the political change a heightened, near-mythical status. To remove Charles's Restoration from the shifting uncertainties of the immediate political situation required ingenuity and boldness and it is curious that what now might be regarded as a blatantly wishful way of seeing seems at the time to have been not merely convincing but inevitable and natural. Restoration panegyric was not the product of superficial time-serving alone. After twelve years of government upheaval, and after twelve months of particularly extreme instability, a fresh start which was also a return to stability was urgently desired. The chance to speak or write or see panegyrically was a chance to describe and celebrate the hoped-for renovation. It was not merely propaganda: rather it was the attempt, however partial and imprecise, to voice deeper feelings and to give a form to a social myth which was in fact already proving its power. In exploring reactions to the Restoration, panegyrical and otherwise, we observe propaganda, myth and history shaping each other as together they come into being.

On 1 May 1660 Charles's emissary came before parliament with the Declaration of Breda, a document drafted by Edward Hyde in which the king satisfied parliament as to his general clemency and

1

his willingness to submit to parliament in details of the Restoration settlement. That day parliament voted 'that the late King's death was tyrannical and illegal;...and that Charles II was the undoubted heir to the crown, and should be brought in with honour and safety'.[1] Charles was proclaimed king on 8 May. In exile he had gathered about him a large number of royalists and after his arrival at Breda in Holland more and more supporters, loyal and politic, came to join him. By the time he departed from Scheveling on 23 May, something of a mass exodus to Holland had taken place. Katherine Philips, the 'matchless Orinda', recalled the phenomenon with wonder and mock alarm, fearing that 'the gasping land/Itself [would] empty', because of the intimate magnetic bond between king and people: 'thy Presence is their home...

> As we unmonarch'd were for want of thee,
> So till thou come shall we unpeopled be.[2]

When the king arrived at Dover on the morning of 25 May, even greater exultant crowds assembled to greet him and this again gave cause for alarmed wonder. Dryden in *Astraea Redux* saw it from Charles's point of view as supernatural, as if the land itself were actually moving towards the king. Another cause for marvelling was the paradoxical storminess of the crowd's welcome to the agent of calm: 'no Calm of Peace was e'r/ Welcom'd with such tempestuous Joys', an innocent reminder of the bloodier contrast between past tempests and the newly arriving peace.[3]

Charles came in by ship. ('Coming in' is the blunt phrase for the Restoration used by Pepys, who was on board the king's landing boat.) Associations were nourished from the start between monarch, ocean and navy, and in later years the nautical connexion became crucial to Charles's image as he endeavoured to establish himself as restorer of the fleet and conqueror of the ocean for Britain. In 1660 Katherine Philips called one of her Restoration poems 'Arion on a Dolphin, To his Majesty at his passage into England'; Dryden fancied Charles making grateful offerings 'to all the Sea-Gods'; and the king was depicted as pilot of the ship of state, connected with the halcyon which brings peace when floating on its nest, and with the ark.[4] Charles's triumphal progress included a ship in full sail. In one poem, Robert Wild's slightly pre-Restoration *Iter Boreale* (1660), Charles was imagined

receiving the trident in homage from Neptune himself and the
ocean was envisaged presenting its own triumphs to the king:

> Methinks I see how those triumphant gales,
> Proud of their great employment, swell the sails;
> The joyful ship shall dance, the sea shall laugh,
> And loyal fish their master's health shall quaff.
> See how the dolphins crowd and thrust their large
> And scaly shoulders to assist the barge;
> The peaceful kingfishers are met together
> About the decks and prophesy calm weather;
> Poor crabs and lobsters have gone down to creep,
> And search for pearls and jewels in the deep;
> And when they have the booty, crawl before,
> And leave them for his welcome to the shore.[5]

Charles's homeward journey, from Scheveling to Dover, via
Canterbury to London, had particular appropriateness and
emotional power in making amends for his weary peregrinations
in exile. Although there was not time to organise much material
splendour, the scale and impressive significance of the event more
than compensated. The way to London was lined with people and
the thirteen-year-old Rochester conceived with wonder that 'loyal
Kent' was 'fencing her ways with moving groves of men'.[6] The
entry into London on 29 May, fittingly Charles's birthday, was
heralded with further celebrations. The move which had
precipitated the Restoration, Monck's ultimatum to the Rump on
11 February demanding new elections, had produced an explosion
of rejoicing, bonfires and subsequent poems. But the 'roasting of
the Rump' only hinted at London's reactions to Charles's entry
into the city, the first sure, properly constitutional royalist cause
for rejoicing since before Charles I's execution. 'The first good
omen,' Evelyn had called 11 February, but he described 29 May as
if that crucial historical moment had occurred when God
intervenes directly to raise man to that otherwise unknowable
state of bliss:

> I stood in the strand, & beheld it, & blessed God: ...it was the
> Lords doing, *et mirabile in oculis nostris*: for such a Restauration
> was never seene in the mention of any history, antient or
> modern, since the returne of the *Babylonian* Captivity, nor so

joyfull a day, & so bright, ever seen in this nation: this hapning when to expect or effect it, was past all humane policy.

This joyous mood was reaffirmed in the celebration of later occasions, including the Lord Mayor's Day, the coronation, and the arrival of Catherine of Braganza, which saw an especially spectacular water entertainment. All this rejoicing served several purposes. It was good propaganda for Charles to have the public significance of his return, coronation and marriage impressively brought home to the people, and it was useful for particular groups in the community — cities like Dover, Canterbury and Bath, guilds, areas of London — to declare their unabashed loyalty to the new king.[7] The forms of the celebrations as well, toasts, oaths and bonfires, represented a break from restrictions imposed under the rule of the saints: for Pepys, drinking the king's health was a sign of the new spirit, and Robert Wild captured the sense of liberation that accompanied bonfires, the luxury of burning wood after 'the knaves that have consum'd our land' had stolen so much of people's wood.[8] Bonfires were lit to 'exorcise' the old puritan rule:

Make Bone-fires bigger, purge th'infected air,
Least Treason like a Plague inhabit there.
Rebellion's Witchcraft, Witchlike may't expire,
And th'Land her sin thus expiate by fire.[9]

A resurgence of ancient English superstitions — bon-(good)-fires and theatrical burning at the stake — was a sign of the Restoration. On 11 February Pepys saw a real rump made a 'sacrifice' 'at the maypole in the Strand'. After the protectorate had made efforts to eradicate licentious festivities, now the folkloric significance of the May was zestfully revived: the timing of the king's entry made it something of a May celebration. 'You renew'd the expiring Pomp of *May*!' cried Dryden; 'with *Charls* was born the spring', capped another poet.[10]

The poets commenting on the pageantry of the coronation made sure its values were seen diametrically to oppose those of the saints. Rather than hinting at a New Jerusalem, the coronation triumphs declared most strongly that London was a new Rome, or even greater than Rome in its self-glorification and by implication its empire. Carew Reynel, describing the 'speaking Arches', claimed:

The *Triumphs* of the *Antients* mean appear,
If we compare them with our *Splendour* here...

and Henry Bold wrote:

A *Roman Triumph* is, compar'd to *This*,
A *Whitson Ale*: A meer *Parenthesis*...

The pageantry was triumphantly monarchist:

Old sullen *Cato* gladly would have made
His gay appearance in your Cavalcade... .[11]

The protectorate had been uneasy about pageantry. Important state occasions had become increasingly ceremonial, and Oliver Cromwell's funeral was full of 'ghastly splendours', in Masson's hostile words, 'all the sombre gorgeousness that could be devised from a study of the greatest royal funerals on record'.[12] While decidedly welcome to some, such luxurious idolatry was opposed by many. In Edmund Ludlow's opinion, Cromwell had betrayed the good old cause partly by his increased attention to forms, 'deluding the simple with a shew of religion'. Ludlow scorned Restoration pageantry — 'this tedious cavalcade' — with the same word, 'cavalcade', that pro-Restoration poets exploited so positively.[13] Restoration triumphal forms proclaimed the new regime by their very existence.[14] For this reason the panegyrical writings of 1660-62 were so remarkably uniform. They enjoyed a brief efflorescence within a closely circumscribed set of assumptions. Panegyrists found it difficult to make refined points, so overwhelming and all-important was the obvious evidence of the mere existence of their works. Pepys admiringly and at length described the coronation spectacle (23 April 1661) then commented wearily, his discarded puritanism re-emerging:

Now after all this, I can say that besides the pleasure of the sight of these glorious things, I may now shut my eyes against any other objects, or for the future trouble to see things of state and shewe, as being sure never to see the like again in this world.

The Restoration triumph was a short-lived moment that drew its life from the supposed unanimity of the English people and from the sudden unleashing of new ways of seeing and celebrating. The pervading tone of sudden wonder, of uniform and patently irrational marvelling, to a considerable extent explains how the king, once invited back, could return without conditions:

> Upon this King's most happy Restoration, there was seen from all parts his loyal Subjects contending how to express their Gratitude to Heaven...every Man striving who should first pay the humble Oblation of their Duties, which really proceeded from Hearts full of Reverence and Obedience to his sacred Person....[15]

The ecstatic tone of this typical royalist memoir suggests much of how it seemed in retrospect, and how it was possible for Charles to return 'on the crest of a great wave', as David Ogg saw it in his classic modern study, sweeping away 'every vestige of republicanism or political experiment'.[16]

But the wonder with which so many people greeted the Restoration suggests that Charles's return took the nation by surprise, unexpected even if welcome, and this poses a problem. Evidence indicates that support for the royalist cause did not become vigorous or widespread until the very last minute. Yet if the king's return had not been keenly desired for some time, coming gradually to seem inevitable and right, how then could it summon up so much apparently spontaneous and sincere jubilation? It seems that Charles's Restoration provided *an* answer, of sorts, and once it had occurred, people could hardly resist investing it with the force of their desperate optimism. The Restoration could well be supported in a general, rapturous, unquestioning way, because one workable answer was better than a myriad unanswerable questions. But an important distinction must be made, and the discrepancy noticed, between the powerful emotional forces which supported the Restoration after the event and the specific political factors which led, first, to the Restoration happening as it did and, second, to the details of the settlement. The situation was complicated indeed and even panegyrists registered something of the evasiveness and complex scepticism involved. To appreciate this more precisely, it is necessary to look at the elusive so-called causes of the Restoration, beginning with a brief narrative of the preceding months.

The uneasily regal ceremony of Oliver Cromwell's late

protectorate suggests something of the problems that Richard Cromwell faced when he succeeded as Protector in September 1658.[17] His 'succession' was derived from his father's death-bed nomination, and although there was not even firm evidence that Cromwell had chosen his son as his successor, it was generally deemed politically expedient that Richard should take over. Coming to power by virtue of a family relationship, he was even more like a king than his father had been, yet he was still unable to gain acceptance from die-hard royalists or constitutional monarchists. Furthermore, although he did not arouse the hatred accorded to Oliver, he had none of his father's prestige as conqueror, nor his charisma, nor his ability. In retrospect he was cast as a pitiful and petty tyrant, a Richard the Fourth. Nonetheless, a calm of resignation accompanied Richard's accession and moderate men were prepared to reconcile themselves to the fact that God had not been conspicuously active to restore the old royal line. People at this stage were willing to adopt the pragmatic viewpoint that conquest — the usurpation of power by whatever means — of necessity bestowed the right to govern. Such an adjustment of belief was required to ensure peace.

The period of calm was short-lived. On 22 April 1659 Richard was forced by a military *coup d'etat* to dissolve parliament, effectively losing most of his power to the army grandees. By 25 May his abdication was accepted. The last flush of anti-monarchical forms of government had begun. Clarendon wrote, looking back, that 'the return of the government into these men's hands again seemed to all men to be the most dismal change that could happen, and to pull up all the hopes of the King by the roots'.[18] On 19 May the Rump had constituted the Council of State as its chief administrative body and more or less assumed sovereignty, although its position was anomalous: it was indispensable only to republicans and either 'a free election or the readmission of the members excluded earlier by Pride's Purge would immediately place the Rumpers in a hopeless minority'.[19] In any case unrest increased. In July and August royalists led by Sir George Booth staged a series of conspicuously unsuccessful uprisings, and at the same time numerous other schemes were current proposing alternative forms of government. James Harrington's *Oceana* was much talked of in this period and associated with troublesome unrest thereafter in the minds of some: 'Old *England* welcome from *Oceana*' proclaimed one poet on Charles's return.[20]

The hostilities among army officers and members of the Rump finally culminated on 13 October. The parliament had transferred control of the army from one group (including some prominent Cromwellian officers) to another group of commissioners of their own choosing, who in turn ordered two regiments to guard the Palace of Westminster. These regiments were confronted there by Lambert and the majority of the other regiments, who took possession of the field and effectively interrupted parliament once more. A new Committee of Safety was formed to govern, which, in its close relationship to the General Council of Officers, was predominantly military in character. It was too dangerous to eject parliament so the Committee of Safety began proceedings for the drafting of a new constitution. But by this stage (October) General George Monck in Scotland had emerged as the upholder of the parliamentary authority. In London there was much restlessness, with minor insurrections and demands for a free parliament. The army was unruly for want of pay. The Committee of Safety was faced with increasing popular hostility. In December the General Council of Officers agreed that a new parliament should be elected. The authority of the Committee of Safety collapsed and by the end of the year a mounting desire for the king's return had surfaced. In desperation the remnants of the old Council of State acted to recall the Rump, which began its sitting on 26 December. On 1 January Monck, with Thomas Fairfax as an ally, commenced his increasingly triumphal *iter boreale* towards London. He entered London on 3 February and on 9 February the Rump ordered him to make a display of his power over the City of London. He then reversed his allegiance to side with the City and on 11 February he declared for a free parliament. Finally on 21 February he stage-managed the secluded members' return, thus ensuring new elections and the gradual certainty of Charles's Restoration. From now on the main issue was whether or not the king would be brought in with conditions, with his prerogative constitutionally delimited: but this consideration did not worry most people unduly.

The complexity of the course of events from Richard's accession onwards suggests that there was no mass movement towards the Restoration, and the myriad alternative possibilities of government put forward in this period confirm the lack of such a trend. When Richard's protectorate collapsed, because of what

Austin Woolrych calls its 'contingent weaknesses', the only chance of a stable non-Stuart regime was lost.[21] But at this stage in 1659-60 the royalist cause was in disarray and the reinstatement of Charles was no more realistic a proposition than those other proposals for alternative governments which abounded in the period, confused, inadequately based, inevitably precarious. Booth's apparently royalist uprising was described — by a cavalier — as the work of 'rash, vaine, giddy people'.[22] Many of Booth's supporters had been drawn by propaganda, or sought primarily a free parliament rather than Charles's right. Even the support for Monck later, as he marched southward, came predominantly from the gentry or was deliberately fanned by royalist politicians and did not express spontaneous feeling. Nor did Monck pay much heed to the petitions he received. As yet there was no irresistible wave of royalism.[23]

What in fact favoured the Rump in this period was the sheer unacceptability of other alternatives. In itself the Rump was not popular with large sections of 'the mob', nor was a commonwealth actively desired by many. But no broad-based remedy was available. 'The Nation is... made the maygame of fortune', wrote the royalist Sir Philip Warwick, 'such a spirit of giddiness appears, that our government seems to have the twisting of the gutts', and he commented on the inevitable brevity of governments not based on providence (without mentioning any movement *for* the king in 1659).[24] Fear of the king's revenge further discouraged the contemplation of Charles's recall. Monck was still required, even when the Rump had sat again in December, to articulate the real impasse in which the Rump found itself: he sent back the secluded members and thus created an implicitly royalist parliament.[25]

The trend among political groups in 1659 was towards increased divisiveness, the 'giddiness' that was a prelude to apparent Restoration unanimity. To a considerable extent what inspired this extreme divisiveness after the collapse of Richard's protectorate was a movement away from restored monarchy and back towards the values of the good old cause. But inevitably, although the direction was common, the individual details, proposals, reforms and aspirations of this movement were manifold and irreconcilable, in the spirit of the good old cause's stress on individual conscience. Through much of the debate of this period, writes Woolrych, 'ran the leitmotif of the good old cause, seldom explicitly defined, but always appealing emotionally to memories of a time when the Lord had lent his presence to all who fought his battles....'[26] Such emotional and frequently millenarian fervour carried over into the subsequent rejoicing at the Restoration, although the two kinds of excitement were quite distinct in origin. Large and unspecific psychological forces ebbed and flowed at a remove from strict political allegiances, while the men at the top struggled for power in the most tortuously politic ways. Their politicking was often sordid in its confusion, desperation and selfishness, and ultimately defenceless against stronger forces such as the City of London and Monck. Nor could any unanimous royalist opposition be singled out. The enemy for these men lay in the factions arising within themselves and only the shrewdest few risked even a tacit about-face to the king's cause.[27] Among politicians and in the mass of the people there was increasing restlessness, but only after the Rump had sat again in December 1659 and Monck had suppressed London's resistance to parliament could this unease be focused in a concerted desire for restoration of the old order, in the person of Charles Stuart.

Thus it came to appear that Monck had turned the tide. Contemporaries certainly explained the change in this way, casting Monck as the agent of providence. In *Astraea Redux* Dryden wrote:

> 'Twas MONCK whom Providence design'd to loose
> Those real bonds false freedom did impose.

Panegyrics were written to or about him both before and after the Restoration, and it is interesting to observe how he was praised. Cowley in his *Ode Upon His Majesties Restoration and Return* (1660) gave Monck almost pride of place and made a distinction between Monck and Charles that ennobled Monck all but at the king's expense. Monck had refused all offers of the crown and such proper disregard for worldly power was as praiseworthy as monarchy itself. To panegyrists Monck represented something different from Charles. John Collop in *Itur Satyricum* (1660), making the obvious pun, saw Monck as the man who had reconverted the country to true religion:

> One *English Monck* hath here converted more,
> Then all your *Moncks* perverted heretofore.

As harbinger of the true state church, Monck was a figure of John the Baptist or, with a patriotic twist revivifying an old legend, St George who had relieved 'the Church... the daughter of the King'. Collop's poem is rare among Restoration panegyrics for its intense Christianity, and a simple sense of Christian history such as is seldom found in royalist writings of the period. Monck could be generously praised because his work had furthered history's true Christian ends. The attitudes in Collop's poem accord with what we know of Collop the man, ardent for toleration in religion, critical of cavalier excesses, unwilling to promote Charles's return with arms.[28] Robert Wild's *Iter Boreale* was published before the Restoration (but as late as 23 April 1660) and has almost none of the grandiose rhetoric of kingship that became *de rigueur* in panegyrics to the restored Charles. Wild's merry muse is coarse, vividly dramatic in a 'satyrical' vein very different to the elevated, monumental style adopted for similar themes a month or so later. Dryden called Wild a Leveller in poetry and Wild's tone does betray a spirit at odds with Caroline courtliness. He was a loyal presbyterian clergyman who welcomed the Restoration, but his religious convictions subsequently overwhelmed his adherence to the new king's policies and he was evicted from his living under the Act of Uniformity in 1662. In this context his poem in praise of Monck (also a man of strong presbyterian sympathies) looks like a tactical evasion of praising Charles. Indeed Monck himself was similarly evasive when before the Commons on 21 February 1660 he declared for moderate presbyterianism against the prelatical church which monarchy would imply. Wild sees Monck as he who 'sav'd the lamb' and 'redeem'd' religion's life:

> Monck! the great Monck! that syllable outshines
> Plantagenet's bright name or Constantine's.

But claiming for Monck the credit of having restored religion —the thing that really mattered — was concomitant with doubts about the larger sweep of the Restoration settlement.[29]

In its different treatment of the same material Davenant's poem to Monck confirms that Collop, Wild and Cowley have made special use of their stress on the General. 'To His Excellency the Lord General Monck' appeared in March 1660, after the ultimatum had been delivered to the Rump but before they had voted the king's recall.[30] Monck is praised for his 'growing Arts of

Salem Academy and College
Gramley Library
Winston-Salem, N.C. 27108

Peace' (the very Arts Marvell's Cromwell had left behind in the *Horatian Ode*) in contrast to the reckless, illusory strength of the fanatic sectarians. Monck has restored 'truths fair Nakedness' in matters of scriptural language, but Davenant does not praise him for anything as momentous as the restoration of religion. For Davenant, as a thorough royalist, the true work was yet to come — 'Yet greater work ensues' — and his poem testifies to the uncertain pre-Restoration mood. Far from revealing an overwhelming thrust of royalism, the poem is crabbed and restrained, as if to say that a change has occurred without resolving anything, leaving the poet in a strange vacuum between the sectarians and Monck's dark policies. It was convenient for Wild and Collop to praise Monck as the executor of the Restoration, for this served to remind the English people that technically, and actually in the person of Monck, the people had recalled its king. For Davenant, on the other hand, the king's return itself was the object of glorification, because under his more absolutist concept of kingship, it was only in the return of the king's person that civic virtue could be restored to the land. Monck was merely a providential tool. But in any case Monck's manoeuvres were cast by the poets into a large-scale historical scheme which completely obscured his time-serving equivocation.

Clarendon wrote that Monck lacked 'wisdom to foresee', Pepys called him 'a dull, heavy man' and modern historians have generally stripped the General of his prophetic role. Cautious and empirical, he would not commit himself until he could gauge a situation accurately. His power was that of a General, diplomatic in a blunt unflashy manner to the point of deception, concealing 'something of the wisdom of the serpent' in order to preserve his reputation for honesty. That he is remembered as 'honest George Monck' is a tribute to his success as this kind of politician. The royalist agent John Mordaunt reported to Henrietta Maria that Monck was 'so dark a man... that no perspective can looke through him, and it will be like the last sceane of some excellent play, which the most juditious cannot positively say how it will end'. The theatrical metaphor here points up the inflated, unreal nature of the image of Monck as far-seeing providential hero. In truth he was simply able to grasp that, given the quarrelling between the army leaders, only the readmission of the secluded members to the Rump would offer a practical solution. This sufficiently concurred with the mood as perceived in London and as created by rallying supporters on Monck's march south to enable him to act with positive results. In this way he precipitated the Restoration, the trappings of which included the willingness and the technique to convert his actions into something of heroic, mythic status. Looking back over the events contemporaries 'were naturally inclined to interpret Monck's actions in the light of what had come to pass'. But Monck only brought about the Restoration because he was in a position to take advantage of a situation set up, on the one hand by nearly a year's political chaos, and on the other hand by a restive, flexible public mood. We must now turn to this confusion itself to seek a more comprehensive explanation of why the Restoration happened.[31]

Undoubtedly somewhere between the temporary calm after Richard Cromwell's accession and the jubilant welcome of Charles into London over eighteen months later a huge change occurred, 'one of those silent revolutions of public opinion, so widespread and, within the central body of neutral opinion, so general that at first it proved irresistible'.[32] The majority of public opinion, as far as it could be voiced, strongly supported Charles's return by the time it came about, but this support represented an immense and sudden alteration. People marvelled at the Restoration partly because they were so surprised at the massive change in themselves. No uniform direction of opinion or political tendency could be observed until the very eve of the Restoration and only after Monck had restored the secluded members in February 1660 did royalist feeling gather its extraordinary momentum. Given the short-term motivation of Monck's actions, the origins of fully-orchestrated royalism must be sought in the anarchy and insecurity of the months just before. The total collapse of order at the end of 1659 ('nothing but the face of confusion appeares' wrote one news-writer[33]) was only the extremity of a year's instability. Throughout the period the country was on the verge of intestine violence, not worthy the name of civil war along the grand old divisions of Cavalier and Roundhead. Now fighting threatened between a host of divided groups: army, parliamentarians, presbyterians, moderates, extremists, as well as monarchists constitutional and absolutist. 'We shiver in a thousand Rents,/ Of querulous Sects, and unappeased intents', wrote Martin Lluelyn in 1660.[34]

On top of this perpetual fear, people resented the army's power and were hostile towards the soldiers, who were themselves desperate for pay. The various ruling bodies throughout 1659 were disliked and were considered repressive, representative only of extreme minority interests. People of property were particularly frightened and feared that if the rule of law broke down property rights themselves would collapse. Indeed at the end of 1659 the few judges left closed their courts. Charles's Secretary Nicholas wrote in February 1660:

> nor can any man be secure of anything he possessed while the Army rules all for silent *leges inter arma*, and where law takes not place, there is no such thing as property.[35]

Such fears were perhaps greater in 1659-60 than in previous years because by then parliament's redistribution of private lands, such as it was, was more or less complete and royalists had by and large managed to regain their lands. Related to anxiety about property was the decline of trade that produced the severe depression of 1659, affecting everyone. Some people realised that no optimism could be expected when 'a comfortable Subsistence' was lacking.[36] Worry about material things was complemented, at the same time, by fears about matters of conscience. The saints feared for their religious liberty, as well as fearing the king's vengeance (rightly it proved), and some were even prepared to accept a military dictatorship if their consciences could be assured of freedom. Religious enthusiasm was still explosive, a divisive, frightening phenomenon to many moderates. Most powerful of all, however, was the disillusion, coupled with nostalgia, at the failure of the revolution of the saints. The psychological disappointment, so eloquently expressed in Milton's tracts of the period, was intense and must have aggravated every grievance and every discomfort of these chaotic times. A combination of the fear of anarchy and weary disillusion made up the atmosphere of the immediately pre-Restoration period. For want of any other direction, this mood made possible the Restoration settlement, brought in as it were ready-made. Marchamont Nedham the journalist, forced to change sides again in 1660 in order to survive, expressed the mood of extreme disillusionment:

> Then let us chear, this merry New-year;
>   For *Charles* shall wear the crown:
> 'Tis a *damn'd Cause*, that damns the Laws,

And turns all upside down.[37]

Sir Philip Warwick expressed the sense that a state of such chaos had been reached that it must either be self-perpetuating or inevitably generate a Restoration:

> we are now come unto our last stage; and as seditious tumults overthrew our laws, so now the seditious tumultuaries, sensible of their own intanglements, are possest with generall and violent passions to be restored to such setled laws, as may free them from the disorders and miseries, which their first tumults had brought them into....[38]

Nedham's and Warwick's remarks strikingly imply that chaos itself was the effective cause of the king's return and not anything essentially bound up in the Restoration itself. Indeed, what would happen with the Restoration was from the start an unknown factor.[39]

The alarming confusion of the months before the Restoration made a powerful and lasting impression, and ideas of chaos and confusion, often with a political stance, recurred in the literature of the years following 1660. Chaos became associated with enthusiasm and unright reason, and the notion of cloudy confusion was common. In *Astraea Redux* Dryden imagined a brain-sickness causing men to chase 'fond Chymaera's'. Later he conceived of 'wit' — or creative judgement — simply as the agent needed to work against chaos and to discipline things formlessly chimerical.[40] '*Ignis fatuus*' was a royalist term of derision for the Independents' wilder schemes.[41] (Later it was to provide Rochester with a general image of the mind's stumbling through 'doubt's boundless sea' into 'endless night'.)[42] Labyrinthine confusion became a common type of dramatic plot.[43] Already in 1663 Davenant had seen the king's return as the happy resolution of one such complicated plot:

> ... *intrigues*, like *Lab'rinths*, are design'd...
> Where Expectation may *intangled* be,
> But not so long as never to *get free*....
>   (*Poem to the Kings Most Sacred Majesty*)

Life generated from a womb, light from darkness, spring from winter, fertility from drought, calm from storm, clarity from confusion: a host of associations was to gather around the basic model, summed up in an Oxford panegyrist's words to Charles:

> Most potent King, whose *FIAT* can bring day.
> From our state-Chaos, and create us light
> More glorious, 'cause from the womb of night.[44]

The Restoration was the Creation — of light, of the world, of paradise, out of formless chaos.

2 New Order

In the long term the Restoration settlement marked an important stage in the stabilisation of readjustments that had been occurring in English society for a half-century or more. Alterations principally in power and property distribution had been accelerated and clarified as a result of the civil wars. But continuous change — progress — was not welcomed as a fact of life. Despite or even because of the upheavals of the civil wars, residual conservatism was a strong element in mid-seventeenth-century England. Deep-seated monarchism was only one aspect of a surviving habit of order, patriarchal and religious, in both private and public life. The need to stabilise and fix whatever changes had occurred, while a natural enough impulse, also expressed this tendency towards order. The chaos of 1659-60, then, was the — conveniently mystifying? — intensification and temporary end of a transitional process which had begun much earlier. The solvencies of 1659-60 at once promoted and checked change in such a way that, at last, the king could be brought in as the token of a moderately rearranged society.

The need for consolidation of an altered social and economic order lay behind the much proclaimed yearning for peace and was responsible for many of the characteristic results of the Restoration. The land settlement, for example, was conservative in two opposing ways. First, it merely concurred with the land redistribution of the Interregnum by which 'royalists regained their land in all but exceptional circumstances'.[1] Second, it redressed few grievances, scarcely helping those royalists, many in difficulties anyway, who had suffered financially in supporting the king: many royalists complained about Clarendon's policy of placating the potentially dangerous at the expense of loyal allies.[2] To this degree at least the Restoration meant the accommodation of an old order to the new. But *order* it certainly was, and the social structure became more rigid than before the civil wars.

In the crudest terms Richard Stubbes expressed the sense of a social hierarchy restored in 1660. Charles II was he who

> suffer'd not our Servants still to Lord it thus,
>> But caus'd them bow their lofty crownes to us.
>>> Nor dregs to keep the upper place
>>> But made them sinke apace.

Alexander Brome represented the rebellion's upheavals in entirely socio-economic terms:

> Now public lands and private too, they share
> Among *themselves* whose mawes did never spare
> Ought they could grasp; to get the *Royal* lands,
> They in *Blood Royal* bath'd their rav'nous hands.
> ...
> In pomp, attire, and every thing they did
> Look like true *Gentry* but the *Soul*, and *Head*,
> What *Nobility*
> Sprung in an instant, from all *trades* had we!
> ...
> These were *Lord Keepers*, but of *Cows* and *Swine*,
> *Lord Coblers*, and *Lord Drawers*, not of Wine.
> Fine *Cockney-pageant* Lords, and Lords Gee-hoo,
> Lord *Butchers*, and Lord *Butlers*, *Dray*-lords too.

In a quieter vein Thomas Higgins imagined the new order when 'all Rankes of men shall be to order brought', 'nor to be rich be reck'ned an Offence'.[3]

The order enforced itself in a multitude of ways, some deliberate and others arising of their own accord from the society's recognition of the need for order. Class stratification was manifested and buttressed by the outward signs of class difference, and these, especially in the realm of language, became crucial to poetic strategies. A gulf between popular and educated speech emerged in the period; and lower-class literacy decreased (after an increase during the revolutionary decades), as Lawrence Stone has argued, partly because the upper classes feared the subversiveness of better educated people below.[4] In particular a knowledge of the classics was considered to provide a rough guide to educational level and hence, the implication ran, social standing. Milton the consummate artist used and placed his classical material with the greatest care and subtlety, but also in the hands of lesser writers the classics could take on a particular slant, allowing a royalist poet, for example, to declare allegiance to and select his audience from a supposedly educated, unfanatical group.[5] Hobbes had criticised the inheritance of classical thought for creating 'an empire of "insignificant speech" in which men were ruled by imaginary entities';[6] and although the Royal Society officially deposed Aristotle from his tyranny over knowledge, the Stuart regime made good use of the prestige and emotional power of classical ideas, for purposes of mystification. Even the other Greek could serve. 'Welcome Plato's year', cried one poet, when all things shall be, as at first they were'.[7] If stratification was enhanced by language and education, it was also promoted materially in the developing consumer society of the time. By the end of the century 'quality' was able to denote, simply, good social position independent of birth (the NED cites this usage in 1693). Goods of high quality were beginning crudely to correlate with and buy status: as industry expanded in the late seventeenth century the range of available products diversified in parallel with a process of social discrimination.[8] The basis of such distinctions was already apparent in 1660, in an atmosphere of heightened consciousness of political and social differences. Ale, for example, was the fanatical rebel's drink: the true ruling class drank wine.

> A broken *tradesman* now,
> Piec'd with Church-Lands, makes all the *vulgar* bow
> Unto his honour, and their Bonnets vail
> To's worship, that sold Petticoats, or Ale...
> ...*Lord Drawers*, not of Wine.[9]

The conservatism of the Restoration settlement, and of the society emerging from it, was backward-looking and nostalgic in spirit. Edward Hyde, first Earl of Clarendon and Lord Chancellor, is a good example of this tendency. He wished that 'his countrymen ... might never enjoy quiet or freedom' until an old-style order was re-established without compromise, 'restoring the whole Nation to its primitive Temper and Integrity of its old good Manners, its old Humour, and its old good Nature'.[10] Hyde was an accomplished politician and his behaviour did not always bear out his rhetoric, nevertheless his statement of his beliefs indicates well the values which were ideally to be embodied in the restored nation. Hyde was a constitutionalist who, for the sake of the ancient rights, would even oppose the monarch (though he was in fact a most dutiful servant of Charles). He wrote of himself that:

> He had a most zealous Esteem and Reverence for the Constitution of the Government; and believed it so equally poised, that if the least Branch of the Prerogative was torn off, or parted with, the Subject suffered by it, and that his Right was impaired: and He was as much troubled when the Crown exceeded it's just Limits, and thought it's Prerogative hurt by it....[11]

But by the Restoration such a notion of an 'equally poised' constitution seemed anachronistic, a legacy of static Caroline theory of government, Marvell's 'great Work of Time' broken irreparably by Cromwell in the long term as in the short. Hyde's conservatism, at least in theory, was inflexibly architectural; and his idea of the state depended on the existence of one unified, unifying state church. He saw the Anglican church as a perfect edifice which supported peace and gave its members moral and emotional security:

> He did really believe the Church of *England* the most exactly formed and framed for the Encouragement and Advancement of Learning, and Piety, and for the Preservation of Peace, of any Church in the World:... and that the diminishing the Lustre it had, and had always had in the government, by removing the Bishops out of the House of Peers, was a Violation of Justice; the removing a Land-mark, and the shaking the very Foundation of Government; and therefore He always opposed, upon the Impulsion of Conscience, all Mutations in the Church....[12]

If Hyde's beliefs were widely and genuinely shared by his countrymen then the restored church must indeed have been a powerful agent for maintaining order and a given social hierarchy, and for inhibiting social change. The evidence suggests that for precisely these reasons, as well as out of sentimental regard for the old church, the gentry at large were strongly committed to one Church of England.[13] The religious settlement at the Restoration was extreme because of 'the force of royalist and Anglican reaction'.[14] The story of the settlement is complicated: it now appears that Charles was sincere at Breda in 1660 when he declared his intention of leniency to 'tender consciences'. Ironically and against his will Hyde had to pursue the king's policy of a 'new model of church government' which would accommodate 'both Puritan and episcopalian elements' and make toleration of Catholics easier.[15] It is strong proof of the Cavalier parliament's determination to bring back the old Church of England wholesale — 'the zeal of the gentry ... both in the counties and at Westminster' — that the king's hopes were thwarted.[16] The backlash against the rule of the saints, and even against the moderate presbyterians who, despite their loyalism, were suspiciously regarded as instigators of the rebellion, was triumphant, forceful and authoritarian — to such an extent that it was not altogether expedient in the long run. In the severe legislation of the Clarendon Code political motives were sanctioned by ideology and nostalgia;[17] but increasingly the relationship between pragmatism and faith was to tend in the other direction, towards demystification and disbelief. The aged William Cavendish, Duke of Newcastle advised the king in 1660:

> Ceremony, though it is nothing in itself, yet it doth everything ... What is the church without ceremony and order? When that fails, the church is ruined... So that ceremony and order, with force, governs all, both in peace and war, and keeps every man and everything within the circle of their own conditions.[18]

But even in the early 1660s this was an extreme and naive view. A new age was dawning in which things were no longer so simple. The restored church supported the king's authority and hereditary right with a vengeance and restive dissenters were actively persecuted. Yet the very fierceness of this reaction pointed to the continuing vigour of opposing beliefs, even if the validity of the beliefs was only reflected in the at times hysterical insecurity of the new Cavaliers.

Large sections of the community reacted against the religious frenzies of the saints and the enormously high demands the saints made on conscience. One pamphleteer roundly designated 1660 as 'the year that the saints [were] disappointed'.[19] The Cavaliers reacted so strongly against freedom of individual consciences partly because they were unable to comprehend the religious issues at stake. If the real, ineradicable importance of ideas to the opposition had been fully understood, it is unlikely that the religious settlement would have been quite so heavy-handed and so dangerously uncompromising. By denying any sense to anti-establishment religious language the Cavaliers deafened themselves to those feelings and beliefs which were to emerge again and again as subversive of the Stuart regime. 'Disputes concerning religious forms are, in themselves, the most frivolous of any', wrote Hume, discussing the Restoration a century later, 'and merit attention only so far as they have influence on the peace and order of civil society'.[20] Hume was arguing, wrongly, that any significant divisions in the nation disappeared with Charles's return. Hume's account derives largely from Clarendon and his insensitivity to religious matters follows the elder historian's in a Tory tradition. Hume makes explicit what was often implied at the Restoration, that religion and religiosity should be enlisted in the service of policy. The poet Davenant had been pleased to realise in 1663 that Charles's crown and those 'ceremonious forms which wait on it' had been handed down like the Mosaic Law:

> Then like the law which *Moses* had from heaven,
> [The crown] seems to be imposed as well as given.
> (*Poem to the Kings most Sacred Majesty*)

The royalists' utilitarian attitude towards Anglican rhetoric and their uncomprehending scepticism about nonconformist and Independent religious rhetoric are of the utmost importance in reading poems about the king's Restoration. The religious language available to panegyrists had been unsettled and displaced by a preponderance of politial connotation. Ceremonious usage of language and form, such as the progress or the ornate pindaric ode, was undermined by an awareness of the necessary service ceremony was performing. 'Ceremony...doth everything', wrote the Duke of Newcastle, but once ceremony was seen to *do*, rather than merely *be*, much of its effect and wondrousness. was lost. Royalist ceremonious and symbolic language seems hollow unless the reader shares in its conventions, which includes concurring in the worth of its intentions. In the same way Independent religious prose, when read by someone ideologically disabled from entering into its assumptions becomes mere ranting, shaking and quaking, a kind of nonsense.

These conditions were fertile for certain kinds of poetic utterance. One popular technique was the inversion of meaning, when two sorts of language, one nonsense, the other crystalline truth, were given an inverted relationship to each other. The relationship imitated the contradictory forces bound together in the society, and set up a crude kind of dialectical engagement. One poet, for example, wrote:

> As for *Protectorship*, so call'd it is
> By an unfortunate Antiphrasis.

Another wrote, 'a Common-wealth's a common woe', another, 'the World's turn'd round; 'tis quite another thing', another, 'the Christian-seeming, Trayterous-being Crew'.[21] In a more contorted case John Collop used the same words under different perspectives within one stanza:

> Faction and treason mould in forms of Law:
> Prove th'Lawyers anagram true, that Lyers aw.
> May Royall Laws, late Common-place Book's pains
> Receive no common place as loyall gains.[22]

Here the official cant of the protectorate is set against loyal truth. Such meanings were made from an awareness that different strands of language formed distinct realms of discourse with special connotations. Some poems were shaped by the notion of a 'blessed change' that was at once an inversion of and reversion to what had gone before, a redressing of the overturning of church and state. Richard Stubbes compared the nation to a compass needle: once it had been 'turn'd about' it desired to return whence it came, to be 'turned up side down' yet again.[23]

The habit of inversion came to the fore with the rise of explicit anti-puritan verse after the Restoration. 'From 1660 onwards it became the rule in English authorship to take revenge for the past twenty years of Puritan ascendancy by every possible form of insult to whatever had worn a Puritan guise, or been implied in Puritanism, and by every possible assertion and laudation of the opposite', wrote Masson with hyperbolical succinctness.[24] Linguistic revenge whether coarse or courtly was a frequent ploy. The rewriting of history, often by inverting it, was another technique used, particularly in political drama. Daring though it at first seemed, anti-puritan satire often appeared on stage.[25] It was a curious business, because the revised historiography was so closely dependent on the old historiography which it was concerned to correct, and because panegyric, which was by no means new at the Restoration, was even more closely dependent on the forms and motifs of praise used during the commonwealth and protectorate. Masson's 'assertion and laudation of the opposite' points to the crude relationship between Restoration apologists and their remembered enemies, but omits the irony that the same providential claims and images which had been used for Cromwell surfaced again in service of Charles. Indeed, poets such as Dryden and Waller were able to mine their own Cromwellian works. But one should not be too cynical about this. If Restoration writers were not disposed to appreciate the irony of such a continuity, they were unable to avoid the challenge it presented. Cromwellian rhetoric had to be absorbed and surpassed; and, to cite one example only, the sense of momentousness and wonder Marvell had achieved in his *First Anniversary* and his poem on Cromwell's death cannot have seemed easy to match. For inspiring awe, it was hard to beat the story of Cromwell, who 'the force of scatter'd Time contracts'. If we are too cynical we miss what is special in Restoration panegyric, its keen need of a quality of newness, which was very hard to find. Motifs from Cromwellian panegyric were neither simply transferred nor strictly blocked out.[26] But royalist poets were concerned to participate in the creation of a panegyric vision which was freshly coherent in its own terms, as a means of answering and buttressing themselves against the memory of the ascendancy of the saints and republicans. The high uniformity of Restoration panegyric is partly a consequence of that memory. Despite its contradictions and hidden fragility, the new society of the Restoration was persistently shadowed forth by writers as a complete, renewed and lofty edifice, to be contrasted with the ruins of the commonwealth and protectorate.

By English standards Charles's powers were unusually great.[27] His position was reinforced by theory and by political manoeuvring on a grand scale, and the new state took on a monumental quality from which public writings (notably Dryden's *Annus Mirabilis*) derived a deliberate constructivist style. The initial wave of support for Charles was harnessed to 'reveal' the monarchy's divinely ordained foundations. Religion, mythology, law and tradition worked together to define the crown's powers, and, as Ogg observed, 'secular vocabulary provides a poor medium for a description of these powers'.[28] But a religious vocabulary is not fully appropriate either, nor even a purified, quintessentially monarchical kind of language. The panegyrical language used of Charles was discoloured by its local subservience and by its unobtrusive dishonesty. The theory of the balanced constitution could hardly be articulated in the sweeping monarchist language with which Charles was praised. Parliamentarian ideas occurred only here and there in royalist panegyrics and with little rhetorical flourish. Yet precisely these absent ideas proved an insuperable disturbance to Charles and James. Panegyrical language was guilty of a major and tactically crucial sin of omission. Hume noticed this central subterfuge in the Restoration settlement. He observed that the Cavalier parliament was 'probably sensible, that to suppose in the sovereign any ... invasion of public liberty is entirely unconstitutional; and that therefore expressly to reserve, upon that event, any right of resistance in the subject, must be liable to the same objection'.[29]

Hume continued, however, that although 'the royalists ... were very ready to signalize their victory, by establishing those high principles of monarchy which their antagonists had controverted ... when any real power or revenue was demanded for the crown, they were neither so forward nor so liberal in their concessions as the king would gladly have wished'.[30] It was simply not possible to revert to an old ideal order and stay there. The edifice of the Restoration could only be upheld by pressures which would inevitably cause its collapse: out of the flaws and cracks developed the events of the next half-century. Puritan attitudes could not be stamped out; consolidated social divisions aggravated inequity; the rapidly growing metropolis increasingly operated as a 'leveller', an agent of ferment.[31] If old religious and constitutional arrangements could be brought back, this was not the case with economic and foreign policies. In short, like it or not, admit it or not, the new society could never replicate an old order because a new era was under way.

The last attempts to hold back the clock always look peculiarly obsolete and ill-fated, a patchwork job of restoration on a building which cannot survive without radical alteration. The architectural metaphor highlights the synthetic, man-made nature of the Restoration. The unanimity of 1660 was only the

unanimity of discontent channelled towards royalism, almost like
a fashion or a craze accelerated by devices like the pamphlet *Vox
veré ANGLORUM; Or, Englands Loud Cry for their King* (1659).
Many of the so-called causes of the Restoration come to seem like
wishful thinking after the event, or else the result of a design
skilfully, half-fortuitously carried out by those with power.
Monck, for example, who had acted pragmatically from moment
to moment, was glorified as the Restoration's effective cause. He
was the hero who had acted valiantly to destroy the
republican's *artificial* commonwealth and redeem the island. The
commonwealth was frequently condemned as a falsehood, an
Oceana, a fanatic's Utopia. 'Artificiall Man made, a Leviathan'
was how the preface to *Ratts Rhimed to Death* (1660) referred to the
Rump's government. But the sense of artifice rubbed off on to
Charles's government which despite its claim to ancient
credentials seemed itself like something constructed and
manipulated. The extent of policy required for 'perfecting the
Restoration' (Masson's inspired phrase[32]) revealed the true nature
of the settlement.

The Restoration had too many roles to fill. It was simultaneously
a return to base, the tail end of the civil wars, and the start of a new
era. At its core there was an indeterminate quality, an
unfathomable ambiguity which could not be disguised completely
by assigning causes or fabricating grand political and historical
schemes. Some lines by the turncoat Marchamont Nedham,
erstwhile secretary to Cromwell, catch most perfectly the sinister
double perspective with which the new age could be regarded:

> Come let us live, and laugh away
>   The follies of this age;
> Treason breeds care; we'll sing and play
>   Like birds within a cage.
> What jolly Slaves are we![33]

Beneath this jolly Elizabethan pastiche the bitterness of
enslavement stings.

The uncertainty at the heart of the Restoration encouraged
inverting dialectical language and gave an interpretative,
polemical tone to much of the writing about recent events.
Sometimes within a poem, and very often in implicit reaction to
another poem, a poet adopts a strategy which involves arguing one
possible position against its diametrical but also possible opposite.

The phrase 'diametrically opposite' occurs in the period[34] and 'blessed change', as a phrase, an idea and a poetic technique of inversion, appears often. To understand a poet's strategy it is necessary to consider his stance in relation to the polar opposites (rather than the concerted unanimity) which characterised the Restoration.

The conflict in the early part of the seventeenth century can be schematised in terms of basic antitheses: 'Obedience versus Conscience; the Divine Right of Kings versus the Balanced Constitution; the Beauty of Holiness versus Puritan Austerity; Court versus Country'.[35] These and related *axes* reappear in the Restoration, transmuted into rather more refined and sophistical forms. A central issue was whether or not the Restoration was the work of providence; whether the king had returned through his own merits or with God's help. Most panegyrists straddled the alternatives, but some attempted a resolution by making shaky distinctions. Martin Lluelyn distinguished between fortune and heavenly providence when he recollected Charles's valiant failure in the battle of Worcester (1651):

> Success crowns Rebel-fame, Yours higher flies,
> Nor are You Fortunes minion, but the skies...[36]

and Thomas Higgons, with more difficulty, saw Charles as dissociated from fortune but directed by both fate and heaven.[37] Many people had resigned themselves to Cromwell's government because success and efficiency seemed to validate it: providence appeared to have conspicuously neglected Charles. The king's return, then, could only be approved if it was the work of a higher power than had helped Cromwell — if it was regarded as a miracle. Both divine intervention and personal greatness were claimed as explanations of Charles's Restoration, and even the most hard-headed writers were able to find in the king a special quality which accounted for his return. 'Illustrious Qualities ... may serve his Flatterers for *Panegyricks*, but they will be of little benefit to his People; therefore it is necessary to evince his *Industry*.'[38] The disagreement about what powers and what qualities had determined Charles's return was in essence the old argument of divine right against proven power. The disagreement could be rephrased in terms of who had called the king back, whether the whole nation or the nation's 'natural' leaders,

knowing what was best. The uncertainty about precisely which
forces had brought back the king was reflected in the key
constitutional question of the period. If the king was God's agent,
his power must be large and his prerogative absolute. If the whole
population had voluntarily surrendered power to him, along the
lines of *Leviathan*, then his power must also be absolute. But if the
ancient constitution had been preserved and if Charles had been
invited back by parliament, then it was arguable that the king's
power should be limited. Panegyrists dallied with this question.
Henry Beeston managed daringly to compass the claim of
parliament within an extreme vision of absolute kingship:

> *You* are *Your Self* a *Senate*, Diet, *One*,
> A *single Council*, Parliament alone.[39]

On the other hand the author of *Englands Joy* (1660) hoped that
both sides could 'change their War for Unity', achieving a perfect
(impossible) balance between the king's claims and parliament's:

> The King shall his Prerogatives enjoy,
> The State their Privilege shall have,
> He will not Theirs, nor will they His anoy....[40]

These lines create an illusion of resolution by casting something
essentially dynamic (the relationship of king and parliament) into
a poised, ideally static mould. The subtleties of the debate were
reflected elsewhere in the way power was transferred by a finesse.
David Lloyd derived Charles's prerogative from Monck's
unwillingness 'to fetch home a fettered Majesty, and to restore a
captive Soveraignty'.[41] But these tables were turned when Charles
granted parliament the power to execute the troublesome areas of
the Restoration settlement, a concession more apparent than real
because it meant that parliament, not the king, had to make the
trickiest, most unpopular decisions.[42]

Another perspective on this debate is given by the opposition
between politic and ideal versions of the Restoration. Political
pragmatism was not new at the Restoration.[43] The quarrelling
between the various contenders for power in 1659 had been largely
a matter of politics and not principles, so naturally, when it came
to building the Restoration out of the confused circumstances of
early 1660, the same political considerations continued to be

paramount. But it proved relatively easy to disguise political
moves beneath the wave of loyalism and to weld politics to ideals
by rewards and social readjustments — if men were willing to take
on the politically right ideals. Ailesbury remembered bitterly
Clarendon's policy that 'his Majesty must reward his enemies to
sweeten them, for that his friends were so by a settled principle,
and that their loyalty could not be shaken'.[44] Thus the undeserving
advanced to preferments and preserved in the new regime a
severance between ineffectual ideals and effective politics.
Religion, which had been used as a political tool to proclaim
Charles and was one of the most intense sources of nostalgia for the
pre-war world, had undermined itself. Pepys visited Westminster
Abbey on 2 October 1660, not six months after the Restoration,
and commented:

> I find but a thin congregacion allready. So that I see religion, be
> it what it will, is but a humour, and so the esteem of it passeth as
> other things do.

The very vocabulary of idealism was undermined. The old puritan
opposition between liberty and licence (expressed in Milton's
grand twelfth sonnet) was reworked in the service of the
Restoration : liberty had come to signify enslavement to a
repressive, militaristic regime. 'False *Protectors*... obtrude/For
verbal freedom, real servitude', wrote one poet.[45] Thus the return
to the old laws could be seen as liberating rather than regressive
and restrictive : Charles had given 'free current to the good old
Laws', punningly taking revenge on the 'good old cause'.[46] Such
word-play brought about verbal restorations and emasculated the
language of sedition: 'if this King' wrote David Lloyd of Charles I,
'was a Tyrant, a Tyrant will become an innocent word again'.[47]

The opposing ideas which sat uneasily together at the Restoration
were part of its double nature as a moment which preserved an old
order and inaugurated a new. Historians have not generally been
disposed to appreciate the uncertainty at the heart of the
Restoration. Commonly one aspect of the period has been singled
out to take its place in a larger scheme, looking back to the civil
wars or forward to the Glorious Revolution. Contemporary
writers certainly also adopted such an approach. Milton, in *The
Readie and Easie Way*, identified England too closely with Israel,

and by the loftiness of his approach made the immediate confusion of 1659-60 seem unutterably trivial and thus came to overlook any possible arguments *for* the Restoration.[48] Clarendon's historiography was limited in the opposite direction, 'a history of the Puritan Revolution from which puritanism [was] left out'.[49] Later Hume followed suit. Macaulay on the other hand cited the beginning of his progressive modern age in 1688 : for him the Restoration was almost pre-history, the first buttressing of civilisation against barbarism when 'our ancestors... forgot old injuries...and stood together'.[50] Masson was so committed to puritan values that he was deaf to the values of the Restoration : he considered the exclusive concern of its literature to be the ridiculing of all things 'abstract, ideal, earnest, spiritual'.[51] More recent historians have tended to see the Restoration as woefully lacking the virtues of the Elizabethan age or the commonwealth. Tawney located the breakdown of natural affective bonds at the Restoration, when 'commercial classes, whose temper was a ruthless materialism' came to power, and the government was in the hands of 'rapacious' 'syndicates of goldsmiths'.[52] Christopher Hill described the 'compromise of 1660' as the occasion on which 'the idealists on both sides were sacrificed'.[53]

Historians have approached the Restoration in a variety of conflicting ways. At the time an interpretation of contemporary history was needed which in its dimensions and its persuasiveness would give the Restoration authenticity. But there was no single, convincing, commonly accepted version of what had happened, so writers of history and panegyric had a degree of leeway. A writer could construct his account with a chosen purpose in mind, with a deliberate intention or as an overt response to someone else's account. He had to work within the range of possible approaches, sharing rules and conventions and commonly available ideas. The historical moment was characterised by the whole range of possibilities, but the individual was obliged to make specific choices. These basic decisions — the adoption of one stance, one mode rather than another — circulated through the writer's language and coloured his usage of keywords like 'liberty', 'providence', 'success', 'innocence', 'truth', 'judgement', 'mercy', and, above all, the word 'restore' itself. The chapters which follow explore the various ideas of 'restoration' which were current in the wake of Charles's return.

3 Ideas of Restoration I : The Panegyric Task

Looking back after a half-century, Thomas, Earl of Ailesbury, could write of the Restoration that 'the king enjoyed a peaceful number of years, and his subjects most happy under his benign government'. He lamented Charles's passing 'not only for the public good of our then happy country, we living then in a golden age, but likewise for myself in particular'.[1] Ailesbury, who was five-years-old when the king returned, naturally added nostalgia for his own youth to his glowing account of the 1660s and 1670s. Nonetheless his reminiscence shows that the Restoration could be seen as a golden time to someone who had grown up in it. Ailesbury is one (among many) for whom the Restoration lived in memory as those who had promoted it would have wished. His recollection suggests something of the lasting success of those who, in their praises and in print, had built up such a positive impression of the new regime. It was impossible, however, to separate the regime and the ensuing period from the event which set it all in train. Charles's Restoration was so momentous that it contributed largely to defining the political issues, the social attitudes and even the art of what is still loosely called 'the Restoration', for a quarter of a century or more. Coming to terms with the king's return in 1660 was a central feature of any concern with contemporary society and for writers in the early 1660s giving voice to this focal event was an important task. In the same breath writers had to justify a political movement they supported and validate in imaginative celebration a world they longed to see 'restored'. The writer's task was to proclaim that with the king's return the nation had improved immeasurably, in peace, freedom and righteousness, in economy and the arts. This idea of restoration, running through all royalist responses, was of the widest possible application yet was based on an idea which had the willed truth of propaganda and of necessity, the imperative that

31

the Restoration settlement should endure. In the difficult twelve months before the king's return, one pamphleteer had written:

> some body or other must be trusted still, there being no living in the World without mutual confidence; and whoever is invested with power, may do injuriously, in despight of any foresight.... [2]

Marchamont Nedham had replied to this:

> A Great part of the Nation may be said to be *Neuters*; that is to say, persons not addicted to any one Party, but would fain have Peace, and no Taxes, and are possessed with a phantasie, that there is no way to procure the one, or be rid of the other, but by letting in *Charls Stuart*.... [3]

Both pamphleteers were addressing the problem of England's true 'interest' and together, though on opposing sides, they suggest that it was 'interest' — Restoration self-interest — which underpinned the settlement, and hence the panegyrics in its praise. Grandiose poetic versions of the Restoration were required to set the event in a context larger and nobler than interest, but the pressure of necessity could not be removed from the writers' outlooks. The new regime was precarious, and this affected literature. The severity of the press censorship meant that a free discussion of the issues uppermost in many minds was impossible. [4] The immediate past of the nation exerted the greatest fascination, yet it could be considered freely only by writers with a thoroughly monarchist, Stuart bias. 'All Positions Terminating in This Treasonous Conclusion, that, His Majesty may be Arraign'd, Judg'd, and Executed, by his People' must be suppressed, was the proposal of Roger L'Estrange, who became 'Surveyor of the imprimery' in 1663. [5] Doubt about the settlement could only appear obliquely. On the other hand the privileged nature of royalist poems lent them a degree of instability. The delirious praises of Rachel Jevon in her *Exultationis Carmen*, for example, look hysterical until her position is seen as an extreme reaction against other, now silenced, equally extreme positions. In general the business of writing a panegyric in the 1660s was problematical and the negative vein of scepticism ran very deep. Panegyric traditionally casts the object of its praise into a timeless scheme, predicating virtues and glories that would survive forever. At the Restoration there was special concern to vindicate the timelessly right order of Charles's kingship against the changes of the rebellion. But the very memory of all those changes so near at hand made it paradoxical and ahistorical to claim that the government of the country could be in no hands but the king's. Panegyrists had to resort to abstract, often awkward rhetoric, which readily invited scepticism. As the theme of restoration was reworked the very word 'restoration' itself became controversial, depending on the perspective adopted. David Lloyd in his usage was aware that the dialectical warp and woof of language crossed in such a charged word. In the third book of his *Eikon Basilike* (1660), entitled *The Restauration of His Sacred Majesty Charles the II.* — there the usage is strictly historical and royalist — he also spoke more abstractly of 'the restauration of pure Religion' (p.4). Thus he connected religious renewal with the king's return. But some pages later he spoke of the republicans after Oliver's death in the same terms, ironically:

> there is no mask that becomes innovation better than Religion; they ordered one day for thanksgiving for their restauration, (the poor Nation must not only feel the misery of slavery, but they must be thankful for it, they must make much of their oppression, and court their bondage)....(p.19)

With considerable virtuosity he has upended the saints' sense of a restoration of religion by applying to Richard's accession, parodically, precisely the hostile republican description of Charles's Restoration. Lloyd's 'court their bondage' is a phrase of the same kind as Milton's 'put our necks again under kingship',[6] but is applied to an opposite event. Lloyd has managed to transfer negative contemporary interpretations of the concept 'restoration' to the statecraft of the enemy.

The main problem the panegyrists had to face was the problem of change. People who had lived through the civil wars, the Interregnum and the Restoration had experienced massive and radical change, occurring so rapidly at times as to have seemed almost random. The changeability of the period was, in fact, often described in terms of bad weather. So Sir Robert Howard depicted factionalism:

> In Storms, ruine on ruine still depends,

Till want of giddy waves the quarrell ends...[7]

and William Chamberlayne wrote:

Tost in a storm of dark afflictions we
Floated at random....[8]

Elsewhere we find droughts, ice-ages, a 'long and black Eclipse'
and, with political overtones, the general notion of chaos.[9] Sir
Philip Warwick wrote that 'all changes are very hopefull, but
usually... deceitfull...; for upon a moveable thing (as faction is) an
immoveable (as peace should be) cannot be well sett'.[10] In the face
of such disturbing changeability something reliable and stable was
needed; and there was a need to base Charles's sovereignty on
something other than mere succession, which experience had
shown to be the most brittle, short-lived claim of all. But if change
was an enemy from the past, by virtue of the present it was
inexpressibly welcome, divinely ordained, and miraculous: 'our
blessed change' (*Astraea Redux*, 129).[11] Yet this blessed change too
became a *fait accompli* as soon as it had happened and the future
once again held the possibility of another problematic variety of
change. Would Charles's rule maintain its glorious stature? It was
the future that had to resist random change and be subject to a
higher ordering. Waller's poem *To the King* (1660) contrasted the
unknown future with the welcome change that had already
occurred:

The next experience of your mighty mind
Is how you combat fortune, now she's kind.   )

The poet took the opportunity to suggest that Charles should
ensure his safety by means of 'equal government', 'with power
unbounded, and a will confined', giving the people their
constitutional rights.

Change was most inimical when it appeared to be merely
brought about by fate or change. Fortune was often seen as
Charles's rival, unsuccessful in the end: 'nor could Fortune
e're/Eclipse his minde' wrote Richard Flecknoe.[12] The nation had
in the past been made a maygame.[13]   Now in the present mere
random change, the formless linear succession of events, had been
overcome by the intervention of a higher agent, providence, to the

king's aid. On the evidence of the Restoration Davenant
concluded that:

> Those who did hold Success the Cast of Change,
> And *Providence* the Dream of Ignorance,
> Might in these Miracles Design discern,
> And from wild *Fortune's* looks Religion learn.
> (*Poem to the Kings most Sacred Majesty*)

The commonwealth had been justified by an appeal to providence
on the grounds that its existence and survival demonstrated God's
favour. The royalist appeal to providence at the Restoration was
much greater. The royalists did not regard providence as running
in parallel with history, with what simply happened. During the
rebellion things had taken a wrong turn. The direct intervention of
God's higher agency was needed to set it right. So Sir Philip
Warwick argued:

> from the bottom of my heart I think, that it is a sacriledge to rob
> Gods providence of any part of it [bringing back the king];...If
> he had not in this work made his own arme bare, and his
> interposition visible, mans wisdom or policy had never brought
> it about.... [14]

The Restoration was seen as a uniquely favoured event. God was
acting beneficently to annul the rebellion. 'That some
Compensations might be made for the loss of the Royal Father,
which was irreparable, God gave the Crown to his eldest son.'[15] It
was the *unique* nature of providence's intervention that enabled
ideas of restoration to be put forward without restraint, for a
qualitatively different order was being initiated. The cry
'Welcome Plato's year' suggests the pristine and elect nature of the
time. The time took on an inspiring quality because it
accompanied the king's return:

> Who would not write in such a time as this
> The King's as well our Subject, as we his.[16]

The privileged nature of the Restoration moment made it
plausible and desirable to hold time still. Accordingly Charles's
regime could justify taking measures to prevent change. Ludlow

analysed Charles's disbanding of the army in 1660 in such terms,
the king 'being persuaded that they who had already made so
many changes in England, were able to bring about another, and
to turn him out again with as little consideration as they had
brought him in....'[17] Generally the political theory and
'mythology' used to support Charles inhibited change.[18]

Monumental language illustrated the desire to prevent change.
Sir Philip Warwick spoke of the Restoration as setting
'immoveable' peace on an old 'foundation'. Cowley spoke of
Charles's destiny 'his *ruin'd Country* to rebuild' (*Restoration Ode*,
297). In the early 1660s the impulse to monumentalise had a
counterpart in actual civic rebuilding. The king earned his
subjects' praise by undertaking public works. Even before the Fire,
developments in London gave poets a natural theme. Cowley
wrote 'On the Queens Repairing *Somerset* House' and Waller *On
St. James's Park*. The age was all too ready to contemplate itself in
terms of grand unchanging monuments, and political issues were
quickly linked with artworks — the religious settlement with the
rebuilding of St Paul's, for example.[19] As early as 1660 Richard
Flecknoe had published his *Heroick Portraits*, to depict and
commend Charles's physical and moral traits for the benefit of
those who had not yet seen him. David Lloyd adopted a similar
form to tell the story of the rebellion in *Eikon Basilike or, The True
Pourtraicture of this Sacred Majesty Charles the II*, at the end of which
twin statues of Charles and his father are erected in the Exchange
and our hero is seen to be immortalised. Ironically by the end of
the decade such rhetoric turned back on itself. When the
administration came under attack, reconstruction of a different
kind was demanded. At the time of Clarendon's impeachment his
splendid mansion in St James was a sign of corruption.[20]

The use of art to aggrandise the present and preserve it from
change took a particular impetus from the feeling that the
Restoration was a moment so blessed as to be virtually outside
history. The new society seemed to have arrived like a grand
completed edifice, for all time. Classical comparisons — London
as Rome — enhanced this self-image. Indeed it was felt that the
Restoration might re-enact and even surpass the glorious
achievements of the classical past. The whole of Antiquity, as a
single eminent entity, might be simply appropriated to the
Restoration present.[21] In such a vein David Lloyd contemplated
Charles's oak at Worcester and, joining the two moments in time,

declared it 'now reverend for *Antiquity*'. Such ideas sound far-fetched when stated baldly, but timelessness and immobility were pressing concerns in the 1660s, whether the immemorial, immobile ideal was sought in a balanced 'ancient' constitution or in a divinely ordained, patriarchal, absolutist monarchy. Attempts to confront the problem of change produced equally problematic, unstable notions of the immutable.

Some of these tensions are caught up in an interesting poem by Sir John Denham, 'The Prologue to His Majesty At the first Play presented at the Cock-pit in Whitehall', delivered to Charles on 19 November 1660 and subsequently published as a broadside.[22] The king is welcomed to 'this place/which *Majesty* so oft was wont to grace' before the troubles. The abstract *'Majesty'* extends the reference from Charles to all those monarchs who had patronised the theatre, and the vagueness of 'this place' reaches to all places that had undergone the mysterious transformation into a stage. From the beginning the poem looks beyond the present. The theatre and the monarchy have enjoyed an intimate relationship of curiously mutual dependence, the continuity of one promoting the continuity of the other:

> This truth we can to our advantage say,
> They that would have no KING, would have no Play:
> The Laurel and the Crown together went,
> Had the same Foes, and the same Banishment:
> The Ghosts of their great Ancestors they fear'd,
> Who by the art of conjuring Poets rear'd,
> Our HARRIES and our EDWARDS long since dead
> Still on the Stage a march of Glory tread:
> Those Monuments of Fame (they thought) would stain
> And teach the People to despise their Reign.

There is almost an analogy between the perpetual life art confers on past kings and the perpetually instituted existence of the monarchy, embodied in successive kings.[23] The tradition of the theatre reveals eternal truths and exposes the rebels' falsehoods: hence the rebels closed the theatres. Paradoxically, while the actors were off fighting for the king, the rebels substituted for the real theatre their own showy, dissembling spectacle of statecraft: 'Ours were the *Moral Lectures*, theirs the *Farse*'. Only by wielding the full oppressive power of a dictatorship were they taken seriously. Then with the Restoration everything changed. Yet here Denham hesitates:

> If feigned Vertue could such Wonders do,
> What may we not expect from this that's true!
> But this Great Theme must serve another Age,
> To fill our Story, and adorne our Stage.

His poem has argued in terms of a complex theatrical metaphor that great events only acquire full significance and glory as they are legitimated by the continuing tradition of art. The unknown future will become heroic only as it becomes material for the stage. The unchanging order of art will vindicate and preserve the 'blessed change' of the Restoration present against the unlawful changes of the past.

An abstract and static concept of kingship lies behind Denham's poem. The unworldly face of sovereignty was revealed for better or worse at the Restoration when perpetual continuity was proclaimed for a line which had in fact been discontinued for twelve years. Sovereignty was more mysterious than ever; as David Lloyd argued, it

> shifts Persons as neatly as *Pythagorean* souls s[h]ift bodies: That day that saw *Majesty* and life taken from one sacred Person against law, is given to another by the law: out of the first *phoenix* ashes springs up a second.[24]

The phoenix was a common image for Charles's return and generally the appeal to mystery was a convenient way of glossing over difficulties in interpreting the Restoration.[25] Mystification was a well-worn technique of royal statesmanship and Charles's poets effusively cloaked him in mystery.[26]

> With what Amazement our lost Phansies burn,
> At this Your aenigmatical Return,
> Mysterious Prime!

exclaimed Martin Lluelyn.[27] Such abnormal excesses of marvelling suggested that a special cosmic magnanimity had been given to Englishmen, and the signs confirmed this. Charles returned to London on the same day as his birth, which had been marked by the daytime appearance of an unnaturally bright star, a latterday star of Bethlehem. [28] The new king apparently inspired in poets the power of ecstatic visionary ascent. The most ecstatic of all was Rachel Jevon whose remarkable *Exultationis Carmen* (1660) can still evoke 'admiration', a cardinal poetic virtue in her time.

> Great CHARLS, Terrestrial God, Off-spring of Heaven,
> You we adore, to us poor mortals given,
> That You (*Our Life*) may quicken us again....

In the space of fifty lines Charles is Phoebus, David, Noah's dove, the Royal Hunter, the Lion and the Royal Oak. Finally Charles is crowned not once but five times, with cumulative incantatory effect. Each crown corresponds to a different claim to the throne. In amassing them so wondrously the poet obliterates any dispute between these various supposed rights:

> The first [crown] of glory which shall ever last,
> In Heaven of Heavens, when all the rest are past;
> The Second shines with Virtues richly wrought
> Upon Your Soul, with Graces wholy fraught.
> The Third resplendent with your peoples Loves,
> Their Hearts of joy being knit like Turtle-Doves.
> The Fourth's compleat by Your high Charity,
> Which hath subdu'd and pardon'd th'enemy.
> The Fifth shall shine with Gold and Jewels bright,
> Upon Your Head *O Monarch*! our Delight....

Many poets followed Jevon's ploy, bundling Charles's claims together to justify him in all possible ways. 'Who'd be absolute in everything ... should be a King', wrote Richard Flecknoe. [29] 'Take him as a King, as a Gentleman, as a pious prudent Person and Father of his Country, or a Couragious Person and yet highly Clement' wrote Carew Reynel in his poem *The Fortunate Change*. [30] Other poets were more fastidious. Robert Howard singled out the king's goodness: 'So much 'tis easier to be Great then Good'. [31] Martin Lluelyn stressed Charles's calling back by the English people: instead of the subjects' sovereign, 'Thou their Choice'. [32] David Lloyd, in his prose portrait, attempted to derive Charles's right from Henry VIII's and 'the antient *Brittish* right to the Crown imperiall'. [33] He did this in the face of the historical counterclaim that 'the pretended Title of this young man [Charles]... will be found upon search, like all the rest of the Titles founded upon usurpation, one after another, since *the Conquest*'.[34] History was deemed necessary to combat the radicals' recurrent claim that under an unwanted king Englishmen 'remain under the *Norman* yoke of an *unlawfull Power*'.[35] It took an independent mind like Hobbes's to disqualify arguments from history on the grounds that they proved facts, but not matters of right.[36]

On top of the rights put forward by theoreticians some of the poets, in their desire for elevation and mystery, claimed for Charles a right in terms of poetic justice, a penitential, almost sacramental right. So Martin Lluelyn added: 'our *Numerous* Prince,/ By Birth, and Virtues first, by Sufferings since...'; and William Chamberlayne said that the king restored liberty (that is, himself) 'by suffering in a righteous cause'.[37] Charles was an intermediary with providence, a priest-figure who caused 'regeneration' in the nation, and in a sacramental act 'Saviour like, turne[d] Water into Wine'.[38] The nation was 'cleansed' by '*Tears* due to CHARLES his *Crown* recovered'.[39] In a benign universe it was proper for the breach to be healed and so Charles ascended the throne for 'dayes as long as those to which nature designed his blessed Father'.[40] In other words he was Charles I risen from the dead. The sacrificial scheme of Christ's death and resurrection was projected on to Charles's life as a poetic argument for his right to the throne.

> The truth of Resurrection is by *You*
> Confirm'd to all, and made apparent too...

so Davenant addressed Charles in his *Poem to the Kings most Sacred Majesty*. Poets concerned with Charles's right to the throne were concerned with the relationship between king and people. In a sense the theme of any address to Charles was the address itself, the controversial interdependence of monarch and subject. So Waller's poem *To the King* was basically a plea for forgiveness: 'Offenders now ... begin/To strive for grace....' The king was at once the poets' 'sacred judge, their guard, and argument' (line 120), and had the power to inspire virtue, in Davenant's words:

> Thus shewing what *you are*, how quickly we

Infer what all your *Subjects* soon *will be!*
For from the *Monarchs* vertue *Subjects* take
Th' ingredient which does *publick-vertue* make.
(*Poem upon His Sacred Majestie's most happy Return to His Dominions*)[41]

The poem 'To His Sacred Majesty' by the young Rochester argued an even more specific relationship between poet and king. Rochester's father had served the king, so the son, too young to serve in arms, honoured his father's memory in poetic service of Charles, thus establishing himself as the rightful heir:

Whose one ambition 'tis for to be known,
By daring loyalty, your Wilmot's son.

Rochester's relationship with the king was almost as filial as with his own father.

Perhaps Charles was regarded in such abstract terms because little of the man was known. He was held to be clement and fears of harsh retribution led writers to stress his merciful nature, comparing Charles with Christ, the Holy Spirit and the dove of peace: 'Dove-like Galless Soul' cried Rachel Jevon, 'mild and gaulless *Dove*' echoed Cowley.[42] The king was also known to be young, handsome and manly: 'young, airy and liberal' according to Richard Bulstrode.[43] Charles's virility gave his patriarchal status an extra charge. The nation was 'the rebell son', suing for pardon from 'the common *Father of his People*'.[44] Charles's fatherliness was depicted by Cowley, in a patriarchalist spirit, in the royal family's hierarchical quasi-angelic procession at the end of the *Restoration Ode*. Charles was a father in an additional sense too, the reincarnation of his own father, Charles I. Such images of the king led to visions of securely familial posterity. Charles was also regarded as the nation's husband, a relationship which was seen as intimate, sexual and fertile, and in which the people submitted voluntarily. In Dryden's *Astraea Redux* the nation had wedded Charles in 'Virgin Love' and now awaited his bed. In Jevon's *Exultationis Carmen* the 'courteous' Thames spread her arms, 'proud to receive [Charles] to her watry Bed'. 'The Espousals of our King' to Albion were to be celebrated. Earlier Robert Wild had seen the country as a love-lorn creature, crying:

Oh, give me that for which I long and cry —

Some thing that's sovereign, or else I die![45]

Charles's very mildness was ravishing, subduing the nation's hearts 'by Love', making English nymphs rejoice to lay 'their faint Limbs... Under the shadow of th' Illustrious *Oak*'.[46] Flirtatious delight fills Katherine Philips's Restoration poem, 'Arion on a Dolphin', in which Charles 'swift as Desire' and 'with a sweet resistless art/Disarms the hand, and wins the heart'. From the country's erotic relationship with its king would flow domestic harmony, generation and mercantile fecundity:

> Ships by Trade each other still improve
> More fruitfully then Sexes do by love...

was Davenant's argument in his *Poem to the Kings most Sacred Majesty*.

An important element in the 1660s' vision of restoration was the desire for stability, a dream of security and protectedness. This is reflected in the dreamily deliquescent language of Dryden's restoration poems, suggesting a mood of careless bliss. 'Melting strains', 'Bees in their own sweetness drown'd', 'sacred Oyl', 'Incense', 'soft western winds', 'wanton with rich Odours', 'the fraischeur of the purer air', 'tears', 'thaw', 'swarmes', 'Extasies', 'well ripened fruit' and 'Coelestial dew': all are to be found. Even 'Times whiter Series' shall run 'smoothly' through 'soft' centuries (*Astraea Redux*, 292–3). The new age must have felt like heaven to Dryden (at least as he was to caricature heaven in *The State of Innocence* in the 1670s, where 'seraph and cherub...all dissolved in hallelujahs lie', I, i). Charles's return was ravishingly potent, bringing the nation ecstasy, fertility, and also a degree of oblivion. At its extreme this political version of sexual bliss resembled an almost mystical state, leading to the extinction of self-consciousness. The longed-for respite from insoluble political worries gave a note of helpless surrender to much early Restoration panegyric. Perhaps it also heightened the concern with another kind of oblivious bliss in the later literature of the period, the sex-comedy of Etherege and Wycherly and the lyrics of Rochester. At any rate as early at 1661, in *To His Sacred Majesty*, Dryden found Charles's 'perfection' in his capacity for 'oblivion'. When over a decade later he wrote sadly to Rochester, 'you may thinke...as little as you please; (for in my opinion), thinking it selfe, is a kind of paine to a witty man', he sounds a note which seems characteristic of Charles II's quarter-century reign.[47] From the first panegyrical reactions to Charles's return there was a tendency towards escapism and towards abdication from critical thought or responsibility. But this tendency should in turn be understood to derive from anxiety about the precariousness of the present and about what the future would bring. The desire to control or at least make sense of change is a fundamental and ancient impulse. The anthropologist Mircea Eliade has argued that in response to the 'terror of history' man has evolved myths and ideas to enable him to tolerate history's irreversible, often destructive, apparently meaningless course. In pre-modern societies men defended themselves against history,

> either by periodically abolishing it through repetition of the cosmogony and a periodic regeneration of time or by giving historical events a metahistorical meaning, a meaning that was not only consoling but was above all coherent, that is, capable of being fitted into a well-consolidated system in which the cosmos and man's existence had each its *raison d'être*. ...This traditional conception of a defense against history, this way of tolerating historical events, continued to prevail in the world down to a time very close to our own.[48]

History was seen to participate in a transcendent order, working according to an eternally ordained pattern which Eliade calls generally 'the myth of the eternal return'. Increasingly in the modern period such an attitude towards history came into conflict with secular and historical ways of thinking. The tension was acutely felt in the early Restoration where notions of eternal return, whether to a golden age or to a providentially determined end, were repeatedly invoked in the face of the painfully growing awareness that men, as groups or as individuals, made their own history.

4 Ideas of Restoration II: Looking Back and Looking Forward

One solution to problematic immediacies was to look away from the present to large-scale historical schemes, a perspective which could work backwards or forwards. Looking back the closest object of nostalgia was the pre-war world of Charles I, and administrative measures were taken to revert the nation to that former state of things. Charles II was sometimes regarded as a glorious reduplication of his father: '*Charls* from *Charls* must be the greatest of that name', argued John Collop.[1] The first Charles in turn derived his right from Elizabeth's donation and the Restoration was also eager to preserve its bonds with her most illustrious reign. The serious dramatists in particular, as Denham's prologue suggests, were intent on revivifying and refining the great and pertinent political histories of the Elizabethan stage. In general, ancient national greatness was to be restored, as Edwards and Henrys stepped out on to the stage, as Charles became '*Alfred-like*' and as Drayton's *Poly-olbion* was recited in Ogilby's version of the coronation triumphs. 'Welcome our ancient Form', cried one panegyrist, greeting the survival of the immemorial constitution.[2] Nor was the finding of past precedents restricted to the British Isles. It reached crucially to the great figures of imperial Christianity:

> You are a second Constantine to stay
> Our *Holy Church* from falling to decay.
> Haile *Charls* the second; second unto none...
> Greater then *Charls* the first, sirnam'd the great...
> Heav'n, and brave *Monck*, conspire to make thy raign
> Transcend the Diadem of *Charlemain*.[3]

Finally ancient Rome, notably during the rule of Augustus, was

44

arrived at as the Restoration's main historical analogue. So Dryden heralded the new Augustan age:

> Oh Happy Age! Oh times like those alone
> By Fate reserv'd for Great *Augustus* Throne!
> When the joint growth of Arms and Arts foreshew
> The World a Monarch, and that Monarch *You.*
> (*Astraea Redux*, 320-3)[4]

The finest achievements of civilisation would be inspired in England by Charles. As the young John Locke put it in his poem on the Restoration:

> Wit too must be your Donative, 'tis You
> Who gave AUGUSTUS, must give MARO's too.[5]

Very soon, by the highest classical standards, the moderns were reckoned to be surpassing the ancients. Davenant, for example, wrote in 1663 that 'the *Dramatick* Plots of *Greece,* and *Rome,*/Compar'd to ours, do from their height decline '(*Poem to the Kings Most Sacred Majesty*); and the theme became recurrent, even obsessive.[6]

A central text in this process of self-aggrandisement was Virgil's 'Messianic' fourth eclogue and Dryden cites its key line as the epigraph to his Restoration poem: *iam redit et virgo, redeunt saturnia regna.* The verb 'redire', occuring twice there, could be translated 'to be restored'.[7] Dryden has assimilated Charles's Restoration to one of Europe's most resonant myths. By sleight of mind the imperial splendours of Virgil's *Aeneid,* the Augustan classic, could be appropriated to the new world of the 1660s, not just as a literary dream, but to be actualised in fact.[8] By a further mental synecdoche, the eclogue's classic formulation of the myth of the golden age could be claimed as an even more compelling model. The golden age anticipated in Virgil's poem was the golden age of *pax romana.* This set in train a whole host of pleasing correspondences for newly Stuart England in the 1660s: 'A Golden Age in *Charls* is sure foretold'.[9] In John Ogilby's translation, published first in the year of Charles I's death, then again with illustrations in 1654, the Stuart meaning of the eclogue had been unmistakeable. The poem's occult passages were said to foretell 'the restauration of the golden Age under the happy government

'the restauration of the golden Age under the happy government
of *Augustus*' and the 'future greatness' of princes; the illustrations
showed a lion under an oak (Charles's personal emblem after he
had hidden in one during the battle of Worcester) and a lion being
crowned; the Latin *sandyx* (scarlet) had become 'Princely
purple'.[10] Even without Virgil, of course, the idea of a golden age
was powerful and had long since been appropriated by the Stuarts,
whose first panegyrists had made use of its traditional links with
ideas of restoration. Ben Jonson's masque in 1615, for example,
had been called *The Golden Age Restored* and had featured the
descent of Astraea, the fair and just virgin. Astraea, who had once
upon a time been identified with Elizabeth, descended again with
Charles II: 'with You to earth *Astraea* fair is come', cried Rachel
Jevon to the king in 1660.[11] 'You do their Golden Times Revive',
said Fame to Charles in *London's Glory* (1660) and both in poems
and actually in the streets fountains ran with wine, a feature of
golden ages.[12] Impressed, Cowley wrote in his *Restoration Ode*:

> With *Wine* all *Rooms*, with *Wine* the *Conduits* flow;
> And *We*, the priests of a *Poetick* rage,
> Wonder that in this *Golden Age*
>   The *Rivers* too should not do so.

The rhetorical coin is well-worn and devalued: the wonder is that
it can be used at all, as Cowley's slightly worried stress on 'this'
modern golden age suggests.

The return of the golden age signified peace, prosperity and the
flourishing of the arts: *iam regnat Apollo*. It was a pastoral vision but
not an indolent one, as Virgil makes clear:

> *pauca tamen suberunt priscae vestigia fraudis,*
> *quae temptare Thetim ratibus, quae cingere muris*
> *oppida, quae iubeant telluri infindere sulcos.*
>   (31-3)
> Yet, of old Fraud some footsteps shall remain,
> The Merchant still shall plough the deep for gain:
> Great Cities shall with walls be compass'd round;
> And sharpen'd Shares shall vex the fruitful ground.
>   (Dryden's translation)

In fact, by virtue of its Augustan associations, the well-being of
the golden age could be seen in imperial terms — power, wealth

and metropolitan growth — and it was largely on this basis that the myth was applicable in the 1660s. Thomas Higgons, for example, concluded his comparison of Charles and Aeneas straightforwardly.

> This is the time has been foretold so long,
> That England all her Neighbours shall command.... [13]

Not surprisingly, the 'fam'd Emporium' to rise on Thames's banks in Dryden's *Annus Mirabilis* was called Augusta, 'the old name of *London*' designated as it were from eternity (1177). The golden age betokened a vision of world-empire, which was also an argument for loyalty towards a rightful ruler. The association of the golden age with the Roman empire under Augustus had been passed down to the Restoration through a long tradition of justifying the imperial rulers of church and state. [14] It was in this spirit that Charles could be compared to Constantine and Charlemagne, his predecessors as universal Christian monarchs, fulfilling the messianic prophecies admitted by Virgil's eclogue. [15] Charles was born, or restored, as a redeemer. Such was the language and vision of imperial panegyric, elaborate, metaphorical and metaphysical. It was quite traditional, had flourished under Elizabeth and was carried across to the early Stuarts. [16] At the Restoration writers were nostalgically willing to recollect the imperial dreams of those by-gone days, and historically their impulse was not complete nonsense. The monarch's imperial prestige, reclaimed so vehemently at the Restoration, was the swansong of the all-encompassing iconographic grandeur Elizabeth had embraced, to the detriment of her less charismatic successors. [17] The myth of the golden age expressed complex historical aspirations in which idyllic prelapsarian longings could be reconciled with the active, aggressive tendencies of imperial dominion. The desired end was found to exist changelessly in the past. So the golden age was recommended, always perfect, always the same, yet requiring genuine restoration and return.

It was in civilised achievements, especially in the arts, that the return of the golden age would be most clearly demonstrated. Progress, refinement and the peculiar beatitude of the new age would all help the Restoration to match and overtake the triumphs of classical antiquity. The moderns would strive for the highest standards of classical art — and for 'nature', the highest standard of all — and surpass the ancients on their own terms.[18] In short the Restoration adopted an attitude of renaissance, and wished to see itself as a high point on Panofsky's 'undulating curve of alternate estrangements and *rapprochements* with respect to the classical model', a curve describing the development of western art and reaching its height with the (Italian) Renaissance.[19] But the Restoration was unable to establish direct contact with the inspiration of antiquity. The version of the antique available was mediated by the substantial achievements of the recent modern Renaissance. The quality which particularly distinguished Renaissance classicism from the secular, civic Augustanism to come was its fusion of Christianity with Platonic idealism. The Restoration inherited such idealism as the essence of its classical model. This is borne out in many works: Cowley's otherworldly Horatian poems and pindarics, Dryden's religiose panegyrics, and the Platonised drama of the 1660s. There were other complications too in the Restoration's impulse to 'classicise' and 'naturalise' itself. The achievements of the near past cast a shadow over the new age and sometimes writers displayed a sense of troubled insecurity or uneasily dismissive braggadocio before the greatness of their predecessors. The Sheldonian Theatre in Oxford had been conceived by Wren 'with a View to the ancient *Roman* Grandeur discernible in the Theatre of *Marcellus* at *Rome*'.[20] The ceiling was painted by Robert Streater to depict the triumph of truth and scientific enlightenment, and Robert Whitehall in a panegyrical poem related truth's triumph to the defeat of rapine and civil strife, that monster seen 'in 48' which 'Magistracy hates'. The painting was a tribute to Charles's Restoration: 'the day's *our own!*' Whitehall considered the painting 'so sublime':

> That future ages must confess they owe
> To STREETER more than *MICHAEL ANGELO*.[21]

The artistic merits of Streater's mediocre painting were dissolved in its high ideological merit to make credible its claims to have risen above the Renaissance's own high-water mark.[22] The artistic relationship suggested here with Michelangelo was paralleled among the dramatists. Dryden concluded his *Essay on the Dramatic Poetry of the Last Age* (1672 ?) in a confident mood:

> To conclude all, let us render to our [immediate] predecessors

what is their due, without confining ourselves to a servile imitation of all they writ: and, without assuming to ourselves the title of better poets, let us ascribe to the gallantry and civility of our age the advantage which we have above them, and to our knowledge of the customs and manners of it the happiness we have to please beyond them.[23]

The argument against the ancients stretched to Shakespeare, Jonson and Fletcher. The modern age succeeded by virtue of greater knowledge and greater refinement. A decade after the Restoration, Dryden could claim securely that his age had triumphed, that the promise of renovation inherent in Charles's return had been fulfilled and the battle for true cultural restoration won. He explicitly viewed the age's refinement in a political context. The nation was 'lost as much in barbarism as in rebellion', he wrote, when Charles returned with his spirit cultivated by 'the most polished courts of Europe'. It is a variation of the penitential idea of restoration. The triumph of the arts was a direct result of Charles's return: 'if any ask me whence it is that our conversation is so much refined, I must freely, and without flattery, ascribe it to the Court; and, in it, particularly to the King, whose example gives a law to it'.[24] The arts had to flourish above and beyond preceding ages to fulfil the sibylline prophecy of the eclogue and the claims of panegyrists in 1659-60 — hence an element of self-conscious striving for greatness. 'Our Selves we'll conquer' declared the bold prologue to the *Reviv'd Alchemist* (probably 1660), somewhat nervously in the face of the task's magnitude: 'Since all Tradition, and like Helps are lost'. But self-doubt must be overcome and the show must go on: 'howsoe're we'll venture; have at All'.[25] Writers struggled to achieve satisfactory grandeur, seeking effects in mannered, insecure, overdecorative styles. It was as if, to adopt John Shearman's description of mannerism, they felt obliged to continue 'a refining process begun in the High Renaissance, and they had little incentive to notice that the swing had gone beyond the mean'.[26] Such was the parasitic attitude of the Restoration towards the past.[27] Ironically the work which most vindicated the age's 'Renaissance' claim was quite out of sympathy with it — *Paradise Lost*. It was some years before the appearance of those great achievements which we now regard as truly expressive of the new 'spirit of the age': Wren's Great Model for St Paul's in 1673,

Dryden's *Absalom and Achitophel* in 1681, Purcell's *Dido and Aeneas* in 1689, and also in the 1680s the work of Newton and Locke. But that is another story. In terms of the models writers and artists looked to in the 1660s it was already too late, or still too early. In effect the first years of the Restoration fall into a penumbra before the first glimmerings of a new kind of light, the zenith of which, we might say in shorthand, came with the Enlightenment. And if such an account of the early Restoration's place in cultural evolution seems itself chronically bald and sweeping, that to an extent reflects the overliteral, barefaced confidence of the time. Blandly facile, knottily difficult, with conflicting frames of reference and vying centres of interest, displaced, compromised, uncertain, the run-of-the-mill topical writing of the early 1660s exhibits such confidence — and betrays it.

A good example of backward looking is given by Edward Waller's smoothly refined, newly 'Augustan' poems on Charles's return. Waller was among the oldest Cavaliers, born in 1606, before Milton or Clarendon, so it is perhaps to be expected that his poem *To the King* (1660) is dominated by the idea of return, calmly assured that things have turned out for the best. Charles is like the sun, long obscured but now bursting out from behind the clouds to dazzle. The surprise is real, although the sun, like the monarchy, has always been there invisibly. All the blame for the rebellion is laid on the people who tried to encroach on the king's power, as vainly as the republican Dutch try to encroach on the sea. Now in a natural process of restoration Charles, compared to the sea in a conventional image of magnaminity, reasserts himself and in doing so rebalances the old constitution. It is a movement back to a pastoral and Virgilian golden world, which will also see the revival of trade and 'increase' (after the depression of 1659):

> Faith, law, and piety, (that banished train!)
> Justice and truth, with you return again.
> The city's trade, and country's easy life,
> Once more shall flourish without fraud or strife.
> Your reign no less assures the ploughman's peace,
> Than the warm sun advances his increase;
> And does the shepherds as securely keep
> From all their fears, as they preserve their sheep.
>   But, above all, the Muse-inspired train
> Triumph, and raise their drooping heads again![28]

A quotation from Horace was added in 1664 which tacitly aligns Waller with Horace and Virgil (Ep.II.i. 248-50). It is a prosperous imperial peace the poet imagines entering from the wings.

The following year Waller wrote *On St. James's Park, As Lately Improved by His Majesty*. It begins with a timeless pastoral idyll, wondrously happening 'here' and 'now' in the park. The scene is curious, at once immutably preserved and fleetingly evanescent. 'A flock of new-sprung fowl', for example, is said to '[hang]in the air'. The poet's picturesque way of fixing the occasion causes its casual gracefulness to harden:

> The ladies, angling in the crystal lake,
> Feast on the waters with the prey they take....

Waller is worried about preservation, as he is worried about the fate of his own 'lines that shall this paradise relate'. Concern with time disturbs the golden scene, and leads the poet to hope that Charles at least may 'live long enough' to see the newly planted trees grow. The poetry, however, is painterly and static. Birds become 'a feathered cloud', there are 'silver fishes' and 'a thousand Cupids on the billows'. Incongruous biblical decoration also serves, with animals coming from 'Noah's ark, / Or Peter's sheet'. Even decay is subsumed to the overall aesthetic purpose:

> All that can, living, feed the greedy eye,
> Or dead, the palate, here you may descry....

Even ice can be kept in underground caves and preserved in the middle of hot July, 'like crystal firm, and never lost'. And meanwhile Charles plays pall-mall, the picture of youthful vigour and loveliness. The poem seeks to restore an impossible vision. Then towards the end Charles becomes more serious and moves into prominence, looking across to Whitehall, 'the structure' ordained to embody an unchanging, perennial institution, like 'that antique pile' (Westminster Abbey) 'where royal heads receive the sacred gold'. It is such ideal institutions which make rulers 'like gods', 'suns of empire', and preserve 'the circle of their reign'. Charles with this special awareness becomes 'the people's pastor' and thinks on 'ancient prudence', suavely considering:

> How peaceful olive may his temples shade,

For mending laws, and for restoring trade;
Or, how his brows may be with laurel charged,
For nations conquered, and our bounds enlarged.

He compares himself to Augustus, so even here at its most
messianic the poem remains classical. Charles is to be a secular
world-emperor: 'A prince'

Born the divided world to reconcile!...
Reform these nations, and improve them more,
Than this fair park, from what it was before.

But such rhetoric seems cheap, coming alongside the senselessly
self-indulgent scene we were shown initially:

The gallants dancing by the river's side;
They bathe in summer, and in winter slide.

Waller's attempt to graft rhetoric of the order of Virgil's fourth
eclogue on to his urbane pastoral is sadly self-defeating. The highly
ornate centrelessness of the poem attenuates the relationship
between the eternal king and the fleeting modernity of the park,
until it is beyond the reader's grasp. The huge classical claim
collapses into a much more precarious idyll and Waller's world-
weary sense of the ephemeral leaves his idea of restoration in the
background.

Johan Huizinga has characterised the movement towards
Renaissance as 'always a longing to go backward in time: *renovatio,
restitutio, restauratio*': 'the symbol of the world pining for renewal
and liberation was for Dante and for Petrarch lamenting Rome....'
But despite its predominance of nostalgia, Huizinga was concerned to place the movement within 'a much broader hope of
revival', relating the backward-looking ideas to forward-looking
ones. He wrote:

The origin of the whole chain of ideas lies in the New Testament
notion of being born again, which itself was rooted in concepts
of renewal in the Psalms and the Prophets. The gospels and the
epistles had acquainted the mind with ideas of renewal, rebirth,
regeneration, some of them related to the effect of the

sacraments, especially baptism and communion, some of them to the expectation of ultimate salvation, and some to the conversion of the living man to a state of grace. The Vulgate used the terms *renasci, regeneratio, nova vita, renovari, renovatio, reformari.*

This sacramental, eschatological, and ethical concept of a spiritual renewal was given another content when, late in the twelfth century, Joachim of Floris transferred it to an expectation of a really impending transformation of the Christian world.... A new leader would arise, a universal pope of the new Jerusalem who would renew Christian religion.[29]

This idea of renewal meant infusing worldly political and historical processes with religiosity. The religiosity was not primarily doctrinal or theological, nor always Christian orthodoxy; rather it was an irrational, emotional, visionary mode of perceiving contemporary events. To say that religion was secularised in the process is only a half-truth because any distinction between earth and heaven was obscured. In its extreme form this tendency led to millenarianism, a flourishing heresy in seventeenth-century England and one of the dominant myths of the revolution.[30] Millenarian motifs and rhetoric also occurred in panegyrics to Charles, signalling one kind of religious restoration associated with his return.[31] 'The World will end so soon, that we/ Terrene joyes longer shall not live to see...', wrote one panegyrist, 'for what can seem strange,/ After this great and unexpected change'.[32] Charles was seen as the great Christian leader heralding peace after terror and chaos. So the royalists could throw apocalyptic language back at the saints, who had spoken 'the Language of the Beast' and had 'the Devil' as 'their good Lord'.[33] The holy father-and-son team of Charles I and II had now overcome the anti-Christian Cromwells. The identification of Charles with Christ and other biblical heroes was intense and appears almost blasphemous unless understood as part of the traditional cluster of antecedents and prefigurings gathered around the imperial Christian ruler:

Kings are God's Christs: *Charls* Christ-like doth appear
For Reformation in His Thirtieth Year.[34]

He was also Moses, David and Solomon, the *reparator orbis* of the prophecies: 'the worlds reformer by a Prophecie,' proclaimed John Collop, 'the most Christian King'.[35] Accordingly the murderers of the first Charles became 'insatiate' monsters, the 'Jews [who] with unheard-of Pride,/Arraign their Lord and Master....'[36] These are all traditional elements of millenarian feeling and it is salutary to be reminded that the ancient primitivism resurrected in seventeenth-century radical literature found a sophisticated reflection in royalist propaganda. In this respect, millenarianism is only the most extreme case. From early in the century radical (and not-so-radical) literature had expressed, in varying forms and intensity, a yearning belief in the coming renewal and reformation of the world. The belief had wide intellectual ramifications, as well as startling specific manifestations (as in the proposals of the Levellers or Winstanley's Diggers).[37] It is ironical that the Restoration's vision of world-reformation should have had such rich and strange antecedents. What is even stranger, one should note sardonically, is that the manifold disappointments of the mid-century, for every side, did little to diminish the royalists' keenness to try it all on again in their version. Or perhaps their sincerity was dimmed.

Such outlandish claims were made for Charles with a political purpose, building up a personality cult. Only a vague and selective view of the king's personality was available, but what was known served. Charles was reported to be merciful and peace-loving, but also vigorous and sporting. Sacramentally he made the nation an ideal partner, patriarchal husband and father, regaining the innocent abundance of paradise. It was a kind of Adam-cult, underwritten by the derivation of Charles's patriarchal sovereignty from Adam. Henry Beeston saw that Charles's stock was 'sunk in Adam's Entrails'. Dryden compared Charles to Adam in *Astraea Redux* and Cowley praised him for restoring the '*Felicity* and *Innocence*' of paradise (*Restoration Ode*).[38] Charles was a living god capable of restoring the first blessedness, not by reverting to a golden age, but by radically transforming the world, perfecting the creation. If the form was traditional and the motive propagandist, however, the impulse for such beliefs came from deeper anxieties. Millenarian longings grow among those whose customary way of life has collapsed, as much the displaced gentry in late Interregnum England as the common people and the 'masterless men'.[39] The regicide was a catastrophic event, the psychologically disturbing effect of which increased as years of social disorder and economic depression followed. Even those who prospered feared 'ruine... and the bringing in of endless confusion'.[40] For many writers, men like Waller, Dryden, Wild and Cowley, the future was uncertain and they wrote wishfully. Of all panegyrics the most messianic was written by Rachel Jevon who declared herself to be 'the Unworthiest of His Majesties Handmaids' and yearned feverishly to see 'Coelestial CHARLES' trampling down all those 'Tyrants' who dared deny 'His Univeral Right'.

There were some practical consequences from the belief that under Charles things would improve immeasurably. The renovation of London and its buildings, although at times tactlessly managed, was impressive and effectively countered the destructive cry of enthusiasts in 1659 that it was 'a time of breaking, and pulling down all worldly Constitutions'.[41] As Christopher Wren realised, 'architecture has its political use, publick buildings being the ornament of a country; it establishes a nation, draws people and commerce; makes the people love their native country'.[42] Much of the rebuilding harked back to earlier designs but in spirit the commitment to reconstruction was distinctly millenarian.[43] Thomas Sprat in his *History of the Royal Society* saw an Adamic vantage-point in the new London: 'A *New City* is to be built, as the most advantageous Seat of all *Europe*, for Trade, and command', which will provide a 'universal, constant and impartial survey of the whole *Creation*'.[44] Waller saw the Queen Mother's rebuilding of Somerset House as repairing 'the first creation' and for Cowley it was the restoring of 'Heaven's Likeness'. A few years later in *Annus Mirabilis* Dryden was to compare London to the New Jerusalem. Improvements to the city also reflected the economic growth which had been a prerequisite of Restoration ambitions from the first, when in February 1660 Monck had declared to the readmitted members of the Rump that London would become 'the Metropolis and Bank of Trade for all Christendom'.[45] As usual, though, the official version is un-trustworthy — trade did not really pick up for another decade.[46] In 1663 one lone voice complained:

And that's the *Times*: for never were they worse,
As by Experience knows my empty Purse.
Trading is dead, is every mans complaint....[47]

The growth of trade was closely dependent on sea power and the development of the navy was Charles's special claim, 'the Royal work' as Dryden was to call it in *Astraea Redux*. From the moment of his coming in by sea Charles's restoring power was seen to centre in the nautical arts, extending outwards from there to other areas:

> The Muses, long disorder'd by their fears,
> And had no moisture left them but their tears,
> From your best influence shall numbers raise
> T'outlast the Cedar, and reserve the Bayes:
> The Seamans Art, and his great end, Commerce
> Through all the corners of the Universe,
> Are not alone the subject of Your care,
> But Your delight, and You their Polar-star:
> And even Mechanick Arts do find from you
> Both entertainment and improvement too....[48]

Yet once again, despite the intimate and enduring associations between the later Stuarts and the ocean, the Restoration naval administration was not notably better than under Cromwell.[49] Pepys commented mordantly in 1660: 'The want of money puts all things, and above all things the Navy, out of order; and yet I do not see that the King takes care to bring in any money, but thinks of new designs to lay out money'.[50]

Sprat's *History of the Royal Society*, written between 1663 and 1667, is the most sustained attempt to argue that Charles was fostering incomparable advancements in knowledge, the 'Mechanick Arts' and hence prosperity. Sprat advances a vision of London as a 'perpetual habitation' for 'the Universal Philosophy' (p.86). In a historical résumé he explains that, partly because of 'the *Noble*, and Inquisitive Genius of our *Merchants*', London surpasses 'all the former, or present Seats of Empire' (p.88). Not only is the nation 'to attain the perfection of its former Civility and Learning' but also 'the improvement of arts, as *Great* and as *Beneficial* ... as any the wittiest or the happiest Age has ever invented' (p.3), including the 'last perfection' of the English language (p.41) and 'an infallible course to make *England* the glory of the Western world' (p.79). Sprat is explicit in attributing these eternal felicities to the agency of Charles: 'Your *Majesty* will certainly obtain *Immortal Fame*, for having establish'd a perpetual Succession of *Inventors*' he writes in the Epistle Dedicatory (sig.

A4[b]). The whole mission derives its urgency from the need to repair the damage of the civil wars, and Charles's return symbolised this healing: 'a work as necessary to be done, in raising a new *Philosophy* as we see it is in building a *new London*' (p.323). After 'those dreadful revolutions' the *'blessed issue* of the Work' was a clear-headed search for 'the true Remedy' and 'the *King's* Return' and Sprat is thankful 'that Philosophy had its share, in the benefits of that glorious Action: For the *Royal Society* had its beginning in the wonderful pacifick year, 1660' (p.58). Philosophy is now endeavouring to combat the *'eternal instability'* of things by building on a sure foundation (p.106) and the language of building, literal and metaphorical, abounds, along with other characteristics of restoration, such as the epic sense (*'Invention* is an *Heroic* thing', p.392), the notion of 'the Stage of the World' (p.28) on which history, true and false, is fought out, and the intention of straining to the 'admirable' limits of nature (pp.214-15). Most importantly, there is an excited sense of millennial anticipation. Sprat slights the golden age as a poet's vanity (p.400), but through philosophy he is happy to have exposed to him the more pious *'Garden'* at Creation's centre (p.327) and in his peroration the heavenly direction is openly revealed:

> the State of *Christendom* will soon obtain a new face; while this Halcyon Knowledge is breeding, all *Tempests* will cease: the oppositions and contentious wranglings of *Science* falsly so call'd, will soon vanish away: the peaceable calmness of mens *Judgments*, will have admirable influence on their *Manners*; the sincerity of their *Understandings* will appear in their *Actions*; their *Opinions* will be less violent and dogmatical, but more certain; they will only be *Gods* one to another, and not Wolves....
> (pp. 437-8)

One of Dryden's Restoration poems makes brisk work of a similar theme. 'To my Honour'd Friend, *Dr. Charleton*, on his learned and useful Works; and more particularly this of STONE-HENG, by him Restored to the true Founders' (1663) praises Charleton for rescuing truth from tyrannous superstition. Charleton had proved that Stonehenge was really a royal palace, and not a temple as formerly believed. The scientist's work of restoration is authenticated by Charles's Restoration in a special sense, because Charles had once hidden in Stonehenge; thus, when Charles is recognised as the true king, Stonehenge becomes retroactively a seat of kings: 'but, *He* Restor'd, 'tis now become a *Throne*' (58). The false tyrannies of Aristotle and Cromwell are overthrown simultaneously.[51]

Such visions of the advancement of knowledge represent the abstraction of ideas of improvement to the point where they become assimilable to a notion of millennial total transformation. With the Restoration a 'blessed change' had occurred and it followed that any benefits ensuing from it would come with similarly sweeping, momentous suddenness, making a radical alteration. Something quite extraordinary was imagined: Henry Bold, for example, said that Charles's line would make 'all *Christendom* a *Paradise!*' and Thomas Edwards saw the Restoration as a '*Vision Beatifical*' in which Charles gained England, 'this *Promis'd*, which *You* make the *Holy Land*', centred in 'the *Paradise* of *Your* blest *Court*'.[52] The rhetoric was uneasy but not yet satirical. The rebellion was a catastrophe, an image of apocalypse, which worked as a penance ending in beatitude. So Sir Robert Howard addressed Charles:

> As in the low declining of the day,
> Mens shaddows more enlarged shew, than they;
> So in the worlds great, last, adversity,
> When every Element their power must try;
> To dissolution they must all retire,
> And leave but one pure Element of fire.
> All that was grosse, which from weak nature flows,
> In your great trialls, so expiring shows.
> And all unto your Nobler Soul resign'd,
> Nothing seems left in you, but what's refin'd.
> No longer, now, subject to what is frail,
> But have from Nature, cut off the entail.
> (*Poems on Several Occasions*, pp. 5-6)

The alchemical language here confirms that the transformation was both material and spiritual, and would endure. Samuel Pordage in the panegyric saw the king 'purifi'd' from 'afflictions Furnace', 'brighter then try'd gold... and lustrous *Sol*', with a magical redemptive power of *Love*... to raise the slain'.[53] The notion of such a transformation is also expressed in the imagery of halcyon calm after storm and of Charles as a sun-king bringing in spring, in Dryden's words, 'not King of us alone but of the year'.[54] Jevon called him '*Our Breath*' (p.5). Imagery of healing is another version of the same attitude: to William Chamberlayne Charles was a cure-all, a 'Panpharmacon'.[55]

The fervent and religiose tone with which many writers regarded the Restoration must be understood against the highly charged atmosphere of the early 1660s. For many people, most notably some of the radicals, the battle against anti-Christ was still being waged and millenarian (and related) rhetoric could still serve a subversive purpose. 'Great talk among people how some of the fanatiques do say that the end of the world is at hand and that next Tuesday is to be the day — against which, whenever it shall be, good God fit us all': Pepys is dry but not entirely dismissive.[56] Even apart from the alarm caused by the small body of Fifth Monarchists, apocalyptic talk was current. Some curious instances are found in the 'Prophetical Almanacks' *Montelion*, 1661 and *Montelion*, 1662, half-nonsensical popular annual compendiums of predictions and odd information.[57] Their would-be lunatic prophecies parody and subvert the imperial and millenarian rhetoric so seriously offered to Charles. In June, for example:

Magog shall rise up and tread out the Moon with his foot, and put out the Sun with an Extinguisher; Then shall the whore of *Babylon* grope in the dark.... In Heaven shall be such a confusion as was never known before, nor never shall be again. For the great Bear shall break loose and tumble old *Cepheus* out of his chair, which causes the Dog to bark, the *Lion* to roar, and the *Crab* to crawl out of the Zodiack. Hercules goes to ravish the virgin *Astrea* [sic]....

Under the cover of the anarchic self-defeating nonsense a degree of unease about the new regime could be voiced. In July a man would come out of the east to preach 'that *Knipperdoling* is as much in heaven as *Hercules*, and proving that no Bears can live in the sky for want of honey'. (Knipperdollinck was the Münster millennarian leader; the Bear was otherwise known as Charles's Wain, an equivocal pun). February prophesied that 'the Eagle... shall destroy the Minister of Iniquitie and bruise the Bear'. In September the prophesy went as far as saying 'that if ever *Oliver* be Protector of *England* again t'will infallibly fall out to be the 4th day of this very Month'. Cromwell had died on 3 September 1658, the date also of his great military victories in 1650 and 1651. November and December would hold ill-omens and '*all manner of plots, Villanies....*' For June of the next year, *Montelion* predicted 'wars encreasing, factions encrease' and the possibility of 'a general Rebellion'.[58] Such rhetoric was slippery but resilient. Even the most frenzied sixteenth- and seventeenth-century millennial thinking lingered on into the Restoration. Its flexibility made it available to royalists who could add, no doubt insultingly, their own smooth elegance, as when Dryden declares 'And now times whiter Series is begun' (in *To His Sacred Majesty*).

History, whitened and purified, was coming to an end. David Lloyd wrote in 1660 that 'a compleat History of our late twenty years would be an History for the World'.[59] And Charles was the emperor of the last days who would have no successor. Pepys recalled praying in 1660 'for the long life and happiness of our King and dread Soveraigne, that may last as long as the sun and Moone endureth'.[60] 'Let Charles Live Lov'd Unto Eternity', cried Rachel Jevon.[61] Panegyrics commonly ended with perpetuity, drifting off into visionary timelessness in which Charles or his sons would rule 'till time shall be no more'.[62] It was a grand fiction, a 'whole History', an 'incomparable Piece' which concluded with the Restoration: 'And thus the good Angel of God brought him honourably and peaceably home'; 'in order to which all things go on as well as heart can wish'.[63]

Providence is seen to be dramatically and wondrously at work, through Dryden's eyes, in *Astraea Redux*.[64] The poem reveals the transformation and renewal signified by the Restoration. Charles's landing at Dover is its focal moment. The poem's long first section deals with the events up to the king's return, the first verse paragraph covering the rebellion and exile, the second concluding with Charles's sailing in. The poem's second section depicts the merciful king being welcomed at Dover, and then looks from that day to a vision of national happiness in perpetuity. At its largest level the poem moves chronologically, and also from a state of division to a state where not just the nation but the world is united for a new age with its rightful monarch. The poem has no central passage, as such; its occasion is the landing at Dover (250-91), which is flanked by the process of 'our blessed change' (105-249) and the visionary coda (292-323).

The poem opens with 'a general Peace' from which England is

divided, having instead her own tense, false peace: 'An horrid Stillness'. Heaven has resolved the other countries' divisions, in Sweden 'Ruine' converted to 'Peace' and for France and Spain 'mortal Quarrels' composed. By contrast England is divided against herself, unnaturally. Youth envies age. The image of 'cross Stars' is reflected in the intersections of the line: 'Madness the Pulpit, Faction seiz'd the Throne'. The natural leaders, the nobles, have been overthrown by designing power-seekers and the gullible vulgar. Dryden then insets five decorative similes: like aroused elephants, like Typhoeus, like wild winds, like blind Cyclops, like ignoble savages. In the middle of the second he recesses a further, strictly unnecessary intensifier, which para-doxically states the moral at its baldest and most compelling:

(What King, what Crown from Treasons reach is free,
If *Jove* and *Heaven* can violated be?)

The identification of Charles with God is smuggled in, its very peripheral nature drawing attention to itself.

The second phase of the verse-paragraph shifts from the rebellious nation to the absent king and emphasises the fund-amental severance at the nation's centre. 'How Great were then Our *Charles* his Woes': Charles, bound by history to bear his father's burden, has had his youth's sweetness converted to 'a Pilgrimage'. Such bifurcations mirror the disparity between a king's two bodies when the earthly status is not acknowledged. Charles has inherited his father's sorrows without his kingdom, but this otherwordly role enables him to 'live above his Banish-ment'. The real sun is in the sky while onlookers only see the reflection in the water. A higher force than mere favourable wind directs Charles. (Dryden is at pains to dissociate Charles from Roman fatalism, hence the old dissimilitude with the suicide Otho (67- 70).) He is Heaven-directed. His double role is reflected when he puts his romance position of unacknowledged king to good use by becoming a 'Royal Factor'. He maintains his patriotic spirit even while exiled and unrecognised, because in the realm of ideals he is still king. Generally he reinforces his right to the throne by the advantage he takes of his peregrinations. It is the intervention of the spiritual realm into the fortune-tossed material realm that promotes these advantageous transforma-tions:

Since struck with rays of prosp'rous fortune blind
We light alone in dark afflictions find.

The next verse-paragraph begins with a disapproving yet wistful recollection of an age of 'supine felicity' (to be demolished later by the true golden age Charles restores). But by contrast, now, the present age seems painful, 'too too active'. It is a strain to be in the spotlight of history, runs the implication. But at last Charles's 'shipwrack'd Vessel' has been cast ashore and now comes the full account of the 'blessed change', which heaven gave to the nation gradually, imperceptibly, like a master-painter's colour-gradations, like a mild thaw, like 'a gift unhop'd'. Providential intervention works in harmony with nature's 'kindly heat'.

After looking at the abstract process of change, the poet turns to Monck, the agent of providence who alone could understand and manage the subtle work (159-62). His was a priest-like task, dispensing the holy monarchical spirit through the nation as an agent of 'Mans Architect'. But his mystery was also mastery, 'like a patient Angler', like a wise doctor, like a canny politician; and organic, too, producing 'well ripened fruit'. The confrontation between Monck and the conscienceless rebels who turned 'Religions name against it self' has resulted in the blessed change, the king's return and the nation's reform. Commemorative and majestic now, the narrative moves to the events at Scheveling in Holland, first the swarms arriving and waiting, then the readiness broken by the cannon sign — 'in sudden *Extasies*', the extra rhyme-word bursting out of the poem's only triplet (225-9) — and finally the embarkation of the royal family, transforming the ships as the ships' names have themselves been changed. The union is emphasised by the sexual image: 'the *Naseby*... lost in Charles (Like some unequal Bride in nobler sheets)/Receives her Lord'. On the peaceful, providentially guided voyage to England, the ocean itself submits too.

The poem might almost end here. It has completed a static, balanced shape and makes a monumental tribute to the king's return, but so far without much regard for the future. It depicts a change from one side of an antithesis to the other, and in that sense an impasse. Now in the third and final verse-paragraph, separated physically on the page, Dryden looks to futurity and shows not just the geographical reunion of king and country (one of the dislocations earlier), but also the union of the eternal and the temporal order, a far larger claim. The historical third person changes at once to the direct second person address: 'And welcome now (*Great Monarch*)'. It is as if the verse changes gear. 'Now' had been used three times in the first 50 lines of the poem, to depict the divided world, and then not again until Charles boarded the *Naseby*, *now* named *Charles*. Here 'now' returns with the importance of an eternal present: 'now times whiter Series is begun'. The land returns in the white of 'penitence and sorrow' to a king who represents the new covenant, making the 'rigid letter' of the law (the Mosaic tablet) 'softer': 'Your Goodness only is above the Laws'. The passage is decorated with a tempestuous wind mollified by perfumes and with a wine refined by its troublesome lees — ever so graceful sacramental glances. Here the sacrament is absolution: 'tears of joy ... expiate our former guilt'. Immediately Charles has demonstrated his 'Heav'nly Parentage' by forgiveness, the 'triumphant Day' can be joyously described. Charles has 'renew'd the expiring Pomp of *May*' and the daytime star of his nativity has renewed 'its potent fires'. The event is a second coming, to restore the world.

The peroration takes up this theme:

And now times whiter Series is begun
Which in soft Centuries shall smoothly run.

Dryden alludes to the fourth eclogue in its messianic interpretation. His vision of the 'Happy Age!' is anything but parochial. It is imperial and boundless in the largest sense. The image for the new empire is the sea, 'in boundless Circles' with 'no Limits'. England, as the ocean, will swallow up all seas, as time swallows its offspring. Under Charles the world will be as if timeless. The merchants will no longer be mere adventurers, subject to hap. Even, Dryden adds wittily, 'factious souls' will be wearied into the peace of a golden age. The Augustan age foreshadowed Charles's age, but Charles is to be greater than Augustus. He is the prophesied messiah 'whom Heav'n hath taught the way' and whose 'Life and Blest Example' wins most. Dryden only uses the parallel with Augustus to dissolve it, as throughout he has denigrated the Roman powers of fate and fortune in the service of his vision of providential history. The last verse-paragraph recasts the poem, drawing out the concern with maturation and organic processes, which now culminates in a grand accumulation of couplets envisioning a perfect future, all clouds dispelled (292-323). The balance is thrown from a static, completed picture to an imminent vision, so the parenthetical Christian allusions throughout (39-40, 79-82, 262-5) are highlighted and take an other than decorative place in the poem. Charles as a spy in foreign courts was compared to David: 'Thus banish'd *David....*' The simple simile appeared to be a suggestion too extraneous to be blasphemous: the triumph of Dryden's craft is that this light, early touch, irrelevant to the classical panegyric, becomes of profound importance to the prophetic vision superimposed.

Religiosity informs Dryden's virtuosity in *Astraea Redux*. The poem is obsessed with art. Superficially the 'blessed change' is compared to the 'turning Scene' of a masque, watched from Heaven. Painterly images abound: 'black clouds' draw down the skies while 'winged Thunder flyes'. The poem is self-confessedly a monumental painting and Dryden piles up figurative, ornamental details to create wonder and admiration. Sometimes an array of different similes (34-42), sometimes a 'difficult' passage (the physiological analogy for Monck, 163-8), sometimes a strained *chiaroscuro*, conferring 'on Night the honour'd name of *Counsellor*'. But the art Dryden values is not on the surface, but rather a mastery which perceives the inner significance (however oblique) beneath the surface. Monck's statecraft is such a matured art, the agent of the heavenly architect. Sometimes an actor, Monck has the subtle power of the pencil, whose 'one slight touch' can effect a total change (157-8, 179). Similarly Charles in exile ripens his knowledge into 'Method':

> As they who first Proportion understand
> With easie Practice reach a Masters hand.

These are the true 'Empires Arts' which can secure future felicity above and beyond any primitive happiness. They are the 'Arts of Peace' which restless Cromwell disdained, the classical *and* natural values most desired by artists. Ultimately they derive from God who instituted the blessed change exactly as a master artist or statesman:

> Yet as wise Artists mix their colours so
> That by degrees they from each other go...

So on us stole our blessed change....

Dryden in *Astraea Redux* is an anxious, straining artist. Beneath a highly wrought and would-be classical surface (proclaimed by the title), he subtly works out another form which derives its strength from being forward-moving and end-directed. All the mannerist adornments, insets and local symmetries find a resolution in the end's glorious vision of the transfigured world.

In Dryden's second Restoration poem, *To His Sacred Majesty, A Panegyrick on the Coronation* (1661), a similar theme is developed more gracefully, but with a degree of indeterminacy still hanging over the future. The poem celebrates the mysterious union of king and country, symbolised by the coronation, displayed in the king's role of forgiving father and to be paralleled by Charles's own marriage to his queen. But Charles has yet to choose between the Spanish and Portuguese candidates for consort. The choice is of the utmost importance because only by legitimate and productive union will Charles translate the beatific vision of the coronation into historical perpetuity. Then Charles's paternal and gallant style will unite with the natural renewing powers of the poem's opening, restoring time and religion and allowing his subjects to 'possesse/with their own peace their Childrens happinesse' securely and lastingly. In *To My Lord Chancellor* (1662) Dryden continues his concern with a world transformed into a safely immutable state. Clarendon here is the great statesman, the earthly aspect of the divine monarch, bound to him in intimate but decorous relationship. He is the opposite of a Cromwell who unnaturally attempted to roll statesman and monarch into one. The 'mighty swiftnesse' of Clarendon's mind turns the earth so its motion seems like rest, whereas Cromwell in Marvell's *First Anniversary* had run 'the stages of succeeding Suns', trying overambitiously to contract 'scatter'd Time'. Clarendon uses his activity, his 'restlesse motions', for 'the Arts of Peace'; in Marvell's *Horation Ode* 'restless *Cromwel*' was unable to 'cease/In the inglorious Arts of Peace'. Clarendon's virtue is above hostile change and personal advancement. He represents the immortal resurrection of the old order and 'th' impression wears/ of Love and Friendship writ in former years'. The poem is an anniversary of the new year and as new years are ceaseless, so will be the course of the new administration: 'it must... immortal prove,/Because the Centre of it is above'. In praising the minister, Dryden is praising the king too, chiefly in terms of his eternal status. Kings'

> ...Heav'nly bodies do our time beget.
> And measure Change, but share no part of it.

Dryden's panegyrics of 1660-62 rework common and conventional motifs into an expressive and interpretative form. His idea of restoration involves taking the notion of a regression to classical order and recasting it in the mould of providential history, where a millennium at once spiritual and secular is shadowed forth. Dryden's aim, not always quite realised, is to render topical occasions and personages timeless and he confronts the difficulty of mediating smoothly between the ideal significance of the king's return and the disparate elements of the contemporary situation. The unifying force of Dryden's vision seems to lie beneath the surface as, like Clarendon, the poet passes the royal virtue through his hands to the contemporary world in which it shall be immanent, gathering 'more,/As streams through Mines bear tincture of their Ore' (*To My Lord Chancellor*, 65-6). Dryden's idea of restoration rests on his belief in god-like monarchy, which in turn grows out of his need to look away from the individual and transient to larger patterns of order and significance.

5 Ideal Restoration and the Case of Cowley

From early times 'restoration' had been a theological term. Before his ascension the apostles had asked Christ: 'Lord, wilt thou at this time restore again the kingdom to Israel?' (Acts 1:6). He replied that the time was not for them to know. The debate which ensued, continuing into the seventeenth century, about the date and nature of this restoration was long and complicated. Would it be heavenly or terrestrial? Would it involve the return of all things bad as well as good to a blessed state? Could it be anticipated or experienced inwardly in this world? Peter had spoken of 'the times of restitution of all things', promised by God, 'the times of refreshing' for repentant souls (Acts 3:19-21). 'Restoration' and 'restitution' came to be virtually synonymous. The strong sense of a wholesale return to a pristine state was crucial to the meaning. This element of eschatology had been modified by the Christian Platonists of Alexandria, notably Origen. Origen was denounced by St Augustine, and throughout the Middle Ages was considered heretical in many details of his thought. It was not till Erasmus defended him that he recovered respectability and by the middle seventeenth century his interpretations of scripture were favourably received by many, including Gerard Winstanley and the Cambridge Platonists Henry More and Ralph Cudworth.[1] These seventeenth-century thinkers found several aspects of Origen's thought sympathetic. Origen consistently allegorised Biblical history, especially eschatological discourse, having a greater interest in the philosophical significance of the events. He considered it necessary to allegorise the notion of the millennial kingdom while maintaining the full sense of urgency before a real, although spiritualised, event.[2] The spiritual apocalypse was still 'the last act of the most real of all dramas'.[3] The kingdom to be restored after the great restitution would resemble in most respects the present creation, except that righteousness would fill it thoroughly. Henry More expressed it thus:

The Renovation of the state of things will be, as S. *Peter* speaks, into new Heavens and new Earth wherein *Righteousness shall dwell*; wherein *real Sanctity* and *universal Peacefulness* shall bear sway; ... And truly the *Millennium* being in such a sense as this is stated, it is both probable and very desirable....[4]

The renewed kingdom would be qualitatively different because it would achieve spirituality by a gradual refining away of earthly impurity. In this Christian Platonic scheme of things there was no absolute distinction between this world and the next, rather an uninterrupted development from one to the other.[5] Elsewhere More made it clear that the soul's existence after death would in every way resemble the life before, down to the very operation of the five senses, except freed from its material tenement.[6] Furthermore, More affirmed that the restored kingdom would properly speaking be a kingdom, preserving political order under the sovereignty of Christ: 'Now if there be *Angels*, and if the *Souls* of men *subsist* and *act* out of their Bodies, they must also ... needs fall into *Political* order and government, and therefore must have some *Head* over them'.[7] The divine restoration was conceived as the restoration of a sublunar state: More extended the similarity in his eagerness to counter naive forms of millenarianism, which he considered subversive to the political order of both divine and temporal realms.[8]

The original Greek for the 'restitution' of which Peter spoke is *apocatastasis*. In addition to interpreting this in an allegorical sense, Origen took it to mean that God, who was unalterably One and whose Love was boundless, would in the end restore *every* created being to its original state. Devils would become angels, evil would be removed from the universe, and by a gradual punitive process the damned would be restored to heavenly bliss.[9] Sir Thomas Browne admitted to this heresy, believing 'that God would not persist in his vengeance for ever, but after a definite time of his wrath hee would release the damned soules from torture'.[10] This was the final stage of the creation, when all would be restored to its pristine innocence. Ralph Cudworth was tempted by the tradition. He mentioned, speculatively, 'the *Apocatastasis* of the World', when 'the *Supreme God*' will restore things 'from their *Degeneracy*', destroying the world by fire or water '*to restore it to its ancient form again*'.[11] Henry More favourably mentioned 'the happy *apocatastasis*'*: when the damned have been wearied 'into an utter recess from all Matter' Nature will become 'youthful again' and the souls of all living creatures 'will awaken orderly in their proper places'.[12] The vision of apocatastasis was doubly ideal, requiring not just a kingdom of righteousness, but one from which nothing was excluded. As an ideal it represented the extreme reward at the end of an ordeal of punitive suffering and atonement. Not surprisingly it was popular at a time when the future was utterly uncertain, a time regarded by many royalists as an interminable durance. The prevalent Platonised theology of the 1650s was abstract, idealised and rhetorical and characteristically overshot difficult details of religious and political practice. For this very reason it promoted compromise and quietism. The imperfect actual world could be reconciled with an ideal frame of reference by suitably abstruse and religiose theologising. And when Charles returned, the notion of ideal restoration which had grown up could be applied to, but could also bypass, the actual Restoration, which was small and disappointing compared to the unflawed superhuman ideal.

By the late 1650s a significant section of the community, including many intellectuals, was faced with adapting to a new regime which seemed permanent. It was necessary to reintegrate apparently irreconcilable attitudes and perspectives. Many men attempted to repair allegiances divided between royalism and parliamentarianism. anglicanism and puritanism. If Marvell's pivotal *Horation Ode* fully and realistically heralds the complexities of the period, subsequent writers struggled to manage a more precarious or less convincing poise. A common tactic was to couple ideal, abstract, internalised, allegorical thought with what was happening in the world. Here Platonised theology was especially in tune with contemporary impulses. Indeed Benjamin Whichcote, the Cambridge Platonist, was Vice-Chancellor of the University from 1650 until his ejection as a puritan appointment in 1660 and advised Cromwell on the toleration of the Jews.[13]

Whichcote gave a special and important sense to the idea of 'restitution' or '*apocatastasis*', deriving again from Origen who tended to interpret eschatology, even when allegorised, in terms of the individual Christian's religious experience in this world. In accordance with his idea of a progressive refining away of corporeality, he taught that an individual soul can here and now in spiritual contemplation approximate to restored beatitude.[14] Ralph Cudworth agreed that it was possible in this world to experience some similitude of bliss: 'Again, there are sundry places of Scripture which affirm that the *Regenerate* and *Renewed* have here in this Life, a certain *Earnest* of the Future *Inheritance*'. The soul would then, after death, have a further 'dwelling from God' prior to its final restoration.[15] Benjamin Whichcote was even more certain that restoration, in the full theological sense, could be achieved by the human intellect. Indeed the motion of 'Self-Restauration' was an essential part of religion, amounting to 'the Reason of the Mind'. 'In the Intellectual World of Souls and Spirits, there is also a Principle of Restoration and Recovery...' he wrote.[16] It was the business of 'Religion' to effect 'a mighty Change', making new creatures 'not by Transubstantiating our Natures, but by Transforming our Minds....' Without this restoration to innocence no man could be happy.[17]

The idea of restoration is radically metamorphosed here. It is now entirely internal and present, yet still preserves its imperial vestiges and crucially requires God. In this way, Whichcote affirms, the virtuous man can inhabit the ideal state:

> *Those that live in, who Drudge in a degenerate State, in the midst of the Corruptions of the World; yet they carry themselves, as if they lived in* Plato's *Common-wealth.*[18]

The kind of restoration of the individual soul envisaged here is close to the common usage of the word to describe a spiritual regeneration without eschatological implications. This meaning readily flows into the medical sense of the word, preserved in the noun 'restorative', where it refers to physical healing. George Herbert in 'The Size' (1633) combined the simple religious and medical senses when he said that 'a bit' of spiritual joy did 'for the present health restore'. The dominant senses in the early seventeenth century were medical and legal-commercial, and Donne in one line managed to combine both with a spiritual sense of regeneration: 'Gold is restorative, restore it then' he commands his mistress in 'The Bracelet' (dated early in the 1590s by Helen Gardner).[19] Elsewhere he illustrates how the diffused religious sense could be used in a secular context to express wonder. In an epithalamium he says that 'Nature again restored is' by the union of the phoenix bride and groom.[20] Nevertheless the strict theological sense maintained its force. Shakespeare draws most movingly on its power in the last line of Sonnet XXX. After contemplating, amongst other things, his dead friends, he thinks on his living friend and 'All losses are restor'd and sorrows end'. The resurrection of the dead is hinted at. Although it cannot be quantified, it seems that the theological sense of restoration increased in the course of the seventeenth century. Marvell in 'Mourning' imagined weeping eyes 'to restore' their woe to heaven, enacting figuratively the remittance of pain and the return of an ungrieving, innocent state (dated early 1650s). Joseph Beaumont in *Psyche* (1648) used 'restoration' to refer to the world's redemption initiated at Mary's annunciation:

> All *Nature* heard the *sound*, which in her ear
> Spake life and joy and restauration.
> (Canto VII, stanza 106)

The metaphorical usage of the medicinal and legal senses made possible a transference to a vague spiritual meaning which took its force from both Christian eschatology and the Platonic sense of return to an ideal form. Its vagueness both contributed to and was a consequence of its extremely wide currency, in many forms, in mid-seventeenth-century England. Instauration, reformation, renovation and restoration are all, in the final reductive analysis, different aspects of a common cast of mind. My purpose here, however, is not to seek the peculiar theological concept of restoration underlying all the others, but simply to suggest that it was possible for men to move with the same terms and frames of reference from one distinct realm of thought and experience to another.

The spiritual idea of restoration, as expounded by the Cambridge Platonists, came to describe the attainment of one's rightful nature, through the grace of God. John Smith wrote that a body was made happy by 'a restoring of it from disturbing passion and pain, to its just and natural constitution' and a soul became a 'vigorous and puissant...thing, when it... was once restored to the possession of its own being'.[21] Indeed such a process of restoration, termed by Smith 'apocatastasis' in accordance with Whichcote's usage, was the essence of religious eschatology:

> Thus we see how true religion carries up the souls of good men above the black regions of hell and death. This, indeed, is the great *apocatastasis* of souls: it is religion itself, or a real

participation of God and His holiness, which is their true restitution and advancement.[22]

Such ideas verged on heresy because they disregarded the world of matter. The necessary grace could only operate in a mind that had elevated itself above the material to an ideal plane. Hobbes, in *Leviathan*, put forward a basically similar idea of restoration. The purpose of Christ's first coming, he wrote, 'was to restore unto God, by a new Covenant, the Kingdome, which being his by the Old Covenant, had been cut off by the rebellion of the Israelites in the election of Saul'. But Christ's time of preaching did not initiate that 'Kingdome'; it was rather 'the *Regeneration*', 'an earnest' for believers of what was to come. (He uses 'earnest' in the same way as Cudworth.) Hobbes elaborates: 'For which cause the Godly are said to bee already in the *Kingdome of Grace*, as naturalized in that heavenly Kingdome'.[23] Hobbes's use of the term 'regeneration' implies that to his mind the restoration has already occurred at a spiritual level. Like the Cambridge Platonists he suggests that the kingdom of grace can be entered, optionally, by an individual. Earlier in Part Three of *Leviathan* Hobbes had troubled to explain that 'the *Kingdome of God*', which divines also 'terme the kingdome of Grace', was a proper kingdom. Henry More, as we have seen, shared his opinion. It was not just 'Eternall Felicity' but 'a *Kingdome properly so named*, constituted by the Votes of the People of Israel in peculiar manner'.[24] Hobbes is not exactly saying here that the kingdom of God will come into existence in this world. That would be naive millenarianism. Rather he is saying that God's kingdom will resemble an earthly kingdom. It will be a replica of the perfect state. Later, more tentatively, he suggests that the place of eternal life might after all be on earth — not an earthly kingdom as such, but 'conformable to the Restauration of the Kingdom of God, instituted under Moses'.[25] The philosopher appears to say, rather cautiously, that the kingdom of God restored after Christ's second coming will resemble the kingdom of grace restored by Christ's first coming. The forms of the kingdom are equivalently ideal but exist at different stages of Christian history. Hobbes has managed to preserve a historical concept of Christian restoration alongside the philosophical, allegorical restoration. With more or less trouble Origen and his followers, down to Henry More, had endeavoured to do the same.

Complex, non-specific ideas of restoration and of the relationship between providence and history, such as I have been discussing, were worked out during the decade preceding Charles's return. Such ideas are of interest here because of what became of them when they were brought into conjunction with the actual Restoration of the king. The tendency towards high, intricate abstraction and towards mystical gesturing, the pressure of reconciling different realms, the attempt to straddle the earthly and the spiritual, the historical and the suprahistorical — such attitudes of mind, at least, were handy when it came to thinking about the monarch's return. A line of continuity can be found in the usage of the concept of restoration itself. What matters here is the intersection of a quality of rhetoric and a historical situation, as registered by an individual. It is difficult to grasp what the Restoration was like to those who experienced it, without thinking in terms of an interaction — almost a collision — between vertiginously ideal philosophies, tricky and uncertain political manoeuvres and adjustments, and troubled, fortune-tossed individual biographies. To get the best sense of such an intersection it is worth looking in some detail at a writer whose life and work were shaped by the forces of his time. The solvencies of the 1650s, and particularly the disembodied theorising of thinkers such as Henry More, opened up a set of evasive possibilities for a number of writers. In literary discourse an oblique but continuous interplay could be managed between political and religious, external and internal focuses. This way of writing was useful at the Restoration, and carried on afterwards, and it catches better than anything else the contradictions and difficulties of the time. The poet who made the most of these strained possibilities, and who best illustrates them, is Abraham Cowley. 'Who now reads Cowley?' asked Pope in 1736. Probably even less people read Cowley now. But although he is not a great poet, and no amount of context can make him so, an informed reading of his work can illuminate the pressures he faced and, by way of partial explanation, suggest something of the relationship between his crippling engagement with his world and his limited poetic achievement. Lack of fierce conviction left Cowley open to the full confusion of his period. In his poems he confronted the problems his friend Hobbes and his probable teachers, Whichcote and the other advanced Cambridge theologians, had explored in their prose.[26] In many ways Cowley's is the representative voice of the late Cromwellian period, as he weighs the possibilities and seeks accommodation and reconciliation. As far as the renovation of the world went, Cowley managed to gloss over the breach between what was imagined to exist already, ideally, and what was foreshadowed as a radical change for the future. Within or without, a transformation of the world was pending, which made the immediate world insignificant. When Charles's Restoration actually occurred, there was a body of thought already in existence which enabled men like Cowley to celebrate and explain the event sublimely and allegorically but without conspicuously praising Charles. The Restoration which really mattered was that which responded to the previous decade's spiritual yearnings for total transformation. Cowley was one bearer of these tangled attitudes. When he greeted Charles in 1660 with his elevated *Ode Upon His Majesties Restoration and Return* he was able to propound, covertly, a significant dichotomy between ideal restoration and the contemporary event.

The most significant decision Abraham Cowley made was to submit to the Protectorate in the middle 1650s. Having been a staunch royalist and having been in exile in the Louvre, a servant of Henrietta Maria, Cowley returned to England in 1654 and made his peace with Cromwell. His submission was motivated by his sense of the dissolution of the old world. The force of his belief in God's mysteriousness, together with his commitment to an inward and abstract restoration, helped him to accept contemporary history. But to slight the world of immediacy was a less than successful strategy for Cowley. His ideological sea-change has never been taken as anything more than an about-face, and the fine poems in which he works out his sense of the relationship between ideas, ideals and the material world have gone unappreciated.[27]

Cowley formally abandoned his royalism in the preface to the 1656 edition of his works. In a pacific tone he recognised that God's benign will operated over and above the political commitments of individuals:

> yet when the event of battel and the unaccountable *Will* of *God* has determined the controversie, and that we have submitted to the conditions of the *Conqueror*, we must lay down our *Pens* as well as *Arms*, we must *march* out of our *Cause* it self, and *dismantle* that, as well as our *Towns* and *Castles*, of all the *Works* and *Fortifications* of *Wit* and *Reason* by which we defended it.[28]

Cowley is doing more here than acknowledge the inevitable forward movement of history. The language he uses — *'dismantle'*, *'General Amnestie'*, 'the *Art* of *Oblivion*', 'extinguished' — and his readiness 'to burn the very copies' of his royalist writings suggest a radical change of state in anticipation of the highest peace. In acquiescing the poet behaves lawfully, because to do so is only to render Caesar what is Caesar's. In the same acquiescence he adumbrates his belief in a dissolution of worldly strife. He uses, figuratively, the term *'Redintegration'*, which carries with it the sense of an apocatastasis, a renovation to a state of harmonious perfection:[29]

> The *enmities* of *Fellow-Citizens* should be, like that of *Lovers*, the *Redintegration* of their *Amity*. The Names of *Party* and *Titles* of *Divison*, which are sometimes in effect the whole quarrel, should be extinguished and forbidden in peace under the notion of *Acts* of *Hostility*. And I would have it accounted no less unlawful to *rip up old wounds* then to *give new ones*; which has made me not onely abstain from printing any things of this kinde, but to burn the very copies, and inflict a severer punishment on them my self then perhaps the most rigid Officer of *State* would have thought that they deserved.[30]

Redintegration became Cowley's abiding theme.

The sincerity of this preface and of Cowley's submission to the Protectorate has been doubted by his biographers. His friend Sprat, whitewashing Cowley's life after the Restoration, considered the recantation 'rather... a Probleme of his Fancy and Invention than ... the real Image of his Judgment'.[31] But Sprat was arguing, as later biographers have done, that Cowley acted as an undercover royalist spy to the end of the 1650s.[32] A re-examination of the evidence, however, suggests otherwise: indeed the conventional evidence is inadmissible. There are three letters to the royalist activist Nicholas Armorer in the Clarendon State Papers, written in April-May 1656. One appears to be endorsed 'This is Mr. Cow. letter to me' and the editors conclude that the author is Cowley.[33] But a fresh appraisal of the handwriting makes it clear that they are not Cowley's.[34] Thus the only concrete evidence for Cowley's royalist activity after 1654 is removed. His submission must then be taken at its face value; and only in this light does it square with the consequences for Cowley. Hyde was angry and unforgiving,[35] and Cowley's reinstatement into the king's favour after the Restoration was tricky and only partially managed. Henry Jermyn, secretary and favourite of Henrietta Maria, interceded for Cowley with Ormonde early in 1660. Ormonde was beginning to doubt that Cowley 'thinkes not fitt' to make a complete recantation and Jermyn wrote that the poet:

> is farre from justifying the error of his words of his preface he onely justifies himself from the malice of them and he cannot doe otherwise without ofending God and ... his conscience for without doubt he had noe mallice....[36]

Jermyn's nice distinction between 'error' and 'mallice' disavows any propagandist intention against Charles in Cowley's utterances, even while allowing that the words were meant at the time. The 'error' was simply that of identifying the final outcome (the expression of God's will) with the Cromwellian rather than the Stuart ascendancy. As Cowley had written defensively to Ormonde in the first place, 'I am fully satisfyed in conscience of the uprightness of my own sence in those [two] or three Lines which have been received in one so contrary to it'.[37] But it was a case of subtle arguing and, if Cowley was officially forgiven by Charles, the advantages of loyalty did not accrue. His Restoration allegiances remained suspect. He differs here from Waller, whose essentially Caroline outlook was subjected to mere timeserving under Cromwell. Cowley's desertion of the king's cause was a more serious, irrevocable act of judgement, paralleled by the moves of other independent minds in the community, including Cowley's friends Dr Scarborough, Samuel Tuke the playwright-to-be, George Villiers, the second Duke of Buckingham and even, in a way, Cowley's admirer Dorothy Osborne.[38]

The compromise Cowley arrived at in the late 1650s is epitomised in a poem celebrating that marriage between Maria Fairfax and Buckingham which readers of Marvell's *Upon Appleton House* find so bizarre to foresee. The marriage on 15 September 1657, although it infuriated Cromwell, brought about the reconciliation of one of the most illustrious former royalists and one of the noblest moderate parliamentarians. It allowed Buckingham to repossess a good part of his vast estate and introduced a dashing continental tone into the unglamorous

Fairfax household.

> Beauty and strength, and witt, togather came
>   Even from the Birth with *Buckingham*....[39]

Maria's beauty, Fairfax's strength, and Buckingham's wit were united now as happily and as momentously as the general had formerly been victorious in the military arena.

> Thy Husband triumphs now no less than He [the father],
>   And it may justly question'd be,
>   Which was the happiest Conqueror of the two
>   One Conquerd England, the other Conquerd you....

(Later the text was revised and the last couplet was replaced by 'Which was the Happiest Conqueror of the Three' to erase the embarrassing reference to national conquest.) Love 'has repair'd/The Ruines which a luckless War did make'. Love has made the 'rougher Victorie' a 'milder one', graced 'with gentle Triumphs'. Opposing styles have been harmonised by a reconciling fate which is 'the noblest Poetry'. 'This match' concludes the troubled 'turnings of the play', which is described as Buckingham's 'Tragi-comedy': the union, both actual and symbolic, is the result of a mature choice made in the aftermath of bitter worldly experience.

In his twenties Cowley had left Cambridge to rally to the king's side. In 1642 he took up residence in Laud's own college, St John's, Oxford. There, urging an Anglican *via media*, in a vein of intense royalist polemic, he wrote *The Puritan and the Papist* and also three books of *The Civil War*, after Lucan's *Pharsalia*.[40] The 'epic' was fuelled by the heat of immediate passions, driven on by belief in the rectitude of the royalist cause, and ended abruptly with the disastrous separation of providence from the king's fate. Cowley wrote that his poem reached 'as far as the first *Battel* of *Newbury*, where the succeeding *misfortunes* of the *party* stopt the *work*'.[41] The poem in conclusion transforms itself into a moving elegy for Lucius Cary, Lord Falkland, 'the Guardian Angell of a Land', whose death seemed to dispel hopes for a victory of the nation's noble spirit.[42] Cowley was never again to write straightforward polemic: with the elegy for Falkland —an elegy for a court-centred vision of civilisation — Cowley relinquished that style of panegyric which enabled king and culture to be praised together in one utterance.

While in Oxford Cowley entered Henrietta Maria's service and went into exile with her. After 1649 a schism in the royalist party was accentuated by the proposed treaty between Charles and the Scottish Covenanters. Hyde and others wished to see a complete restoration and replication of the old order. The Queen Mother's party, including Hobbes and Buckingham, on the other hand, tended towards progressive rationalism and favoured a compromise. Supporting the treaty, Cowley must be numbered among the latter, and in his poems of the period, *To Sir William Davenant* and *On the Death of Mr. Crashaw* he countenances new, conciliatory solutions, straining between what is desired and what is possible:[43]

> So will our *God rebuild* mans perisht frame,
> And raise him up much *Better*, yet the *same*.
> So *God-like Poets* do past things reherse,
> Not *change*, but *Heighten* Nature by their Verse.
> (*To Sir William Davenant*)

Indeed in the elegy for Crashaw Cowley speculatively embraces a simulacrum of Catholicism, perhaps under pressure from Henrietta Maria in 1651, the lowest ebb of royalist fortunes.[44]

> And I my self a *Catholick* will be,
> So far at least, great *Saint*, to *Pray* to thee.

By 1654 Cowley had returned to London where he was imprisoned. He was released on bail in 1655, and in 1656 he renounced his royalist sympathies and published his works, including four books of his unfinished religious epic, the *Davideis* — put out as a new and by implication 'Cromwellian' poem.[45]

The *Davideis* relates how the Israelites, itching for a king, invited upon themselves the tyranny of Saul; how David came before Saul, arousing envy and hostility; how Saul persecuted David, who had received a divine vision revealing his status as forerunner of the redeemer of the world. The story admitted a conflicting range of contemporary interpretations and Cowley obliquely gives it a local habitation: the bloody battle for dominion over Israel in Book II takes place in 'a Kingdom, not half so big as *England*' (p.315).[46] There are some passing anti-Stuart thrusts, slighting

traditional ideas of kingship. The sage Samuel explains that
'though a *King*/Be the mild Name, a Tyrant is the Thing' (p.371)
and in the notes '*Augustus*' is deemed 'a God little superior' to Nero
and Domitian (p.266). Yet the poem is fiercely opposed to
internecine strife, depicted with vivid rhetorical horror (pp.298-
9), and finds the desire for change vengeful and inconsequential:
battle 'could not... the fatal strife decide; God *punisht one*, but *blest
not* th'other side' (p.298). Neither side has right and the sword cuts
both ways. It applies equally to the republicans in England who in
the 1640s rebelled against divinely ordained kingship and to
royalists who would recklessly attempt to overthrow the
Protectorate in the 1650s. The moral that applied to the tyrant
Saul applies to all rulers: 'The *two-edg'd Oath*, wounds deep,
perform'd or broke' (p.391). The only recourse in the search for a
permanent order is to an overpowering deity, above partisanship.
Such a God is 'resolv'd... T'outweary' men from '*Sins Variety*'
(p.373) and indeed the final submission is a weary one:

> Thus changes *Man*, but *God* is constant still
> To those eternal grounds, that mov'ed his *Will*.
> And though he yielded first to them, 'tis fit
> That stubborn Men at last to him submit.
>   (p.375)

Such a notion of providence is little more than fatalism imposed on
man because of his sinfulness. The poem's wearily submissive
attitude relieves the poet of the burden of commitment. Although
some incidental passages appear to criticise a tyrannical monarchy,
the overall detachment from worldly affairs undermines any
support of an alternative regime. The completeness of
the poet's uncertainty makes for an air of lassitude, and it
is not surprising to find the piecemeal epic unfinished. The only
intensely directed passage occurs when 'th '*Eternal Infant*' is
foretold to David, who will inaugurate the universally desired
mystic kingship, restoring earth to heaven:

> Ev'n now old *Time* is harnessing the years
> To go in order thus; hence empty fears;
> Thy Fate's all *white*; from thy blest seed shall spring
> The promis'd *Shilo*, the great *Mystick King*.
> Round the whole earth his dreaded name shall sound,

And reach to *Worlds*, that must not yet be *found*.
The *Southern Clime* him her sole *Lord* shall stile.
Him all the *North*, ev'en *Albions stubborn Isle*.
   (pp. 304-5)

Retrospectively these lines foreshadow Restoration panegyric, but
at the time of publication Cowley's vision of restoration must have
seemed hugely vague and generalised — sheer yearning, in the
face of an indifferently determined universe, for an unknown
transformation, for the last solace of a second coming. The formless
unspecified longing for restoration which informs the *Davideis*, as
the answering angel descends clothed in a skyey mantle with a
meteor for hair, 'wrought by heavenly loom', removes the poem
from historical epic to masque. History and the poet's vision of
heaven, far from being reconciled, push apart.

   Cowley's most original achievements of the decade were his
pindarics. His version of Pindar's manner suited him well, offering
classical authority, monumentality and distance, and also
allowing him to write changeably, fantastically, indirectly,
incorporating conflicting attitudes to the contemporary situation.
The pindaric style was useful to his intellectual concerns and to his
search for technical innovation and made possible three fine odes.
In *To Mr. Hobs*, *Destinie* and *Brutus* Cowley wrote poetry
commensurate with the new historical reality he had come to
recognise. The poems date from after 1654 and although the
elliptical and divided qualities have not gone, Cowley has now
managed to bring his metaphysical ideals down to earth. It is
poetry of personal meditation, not yet 'poetry of statement', and
the varying line length makes for a style of speech which is
intelligently, soberly conversational, flexible yet pithy. The
thought keeps moving, questioning and qualifying without self-
indulgence, aiming at those moments where the poet can speak
about the conditions of life directly and plainly; where his personal
musings achieve the power of a commonplace. *Destinie* presents a
chess-game:

   Here I the losing party blame
   For those false *Moves* that break the *Game*,
   That to their *Grave* the *Bag*, the conquered *Pieces* bring,
   And above all, th'*ill Conduct* of the *Mated King*.

It is an allegorical means of criticising the royalists for mismanaging their cause. But having made that clear, Cowley immediately draws back from the situation to notice that men were not in charge at all, but angels: 'An *Unseen Hand* makes all their *Moves...Desti'ny plays us all'*. But there is a way out, and it is here that a new note sounds. By construing the missing benefits of good fortune as worldly vanities or even evils, one can create for oneself a genuine happiness in the very face of fortune's adversity. This is not a 'dog-in-the-manger' attitude, but a profound and restorative spiritual exercise. The exertion involves keeping a firm grip on the actual nature of things, at the expense of resorting to Utopian dreams:

> No Matter, *Cowley*, let proud *Fortune* see,
> That *thou* canst *her* despise no less than *she* does Thee.
> > Let all her gifts the portion be
> > Of Folly, Lust, and Flattery,
> > Fraud, Extortion, Calumnie,
> > Murder, Infidelitie,
> > Rebellion and Hypocrisie.

Destiny is transcended through the rigours of individual conscience. Cowley's position is now compatible with liberal versions of puritanism. Retirement from worldly strife is viewed as a hope *in this world*, in a quietistic, almost Quaker manner. In the very act of submitting to the authority of the Protectorate, Cowley is enabled to disown the Cromwellian success. *To Mr. Hobs* demonstrates a comparable faith in new solutions in *this* world. Here the vista which has been revealed is of 'the *Golden Lands* of *new Philosophies*', made apparent by 'the *Natural Heat*' of Hobbes's intellect. The philosopher has overthrown Aristotle's '*universal Intellectual reign*' to make available a whole new arena '*planted, peopled, built*, and *civiliz'd*', and the innovation will prove permanent. Like its inspiration in Hobbes it will prove immortal and 'for ever must be *Young*'. Cowley's celebration of a new, unorthodox '*Idea*' (a total conception of the universe) marks his change in political posture.[47]

In *Brutus* Cowley wrote what was for the most part a panegyric of Cromwell.[48] Brutus is characterised as an ideally virtuous ruler capable of uniting the discordant elements of things into a free and naturally moving '*Whole*', the highest example of rational humanity: 'Virtue was thy *Lifes center*'. It is this excellence that led him to take arms against a tyrant, an act emanating from the 'supreme *Idea*' of Virtue itself and hence justifiable in the highest human terms:

> What *Mercy* could the *Tyrants Life* deserve,
> From him who kill'd *Himself* rather then *serve?*

These lines, in which virtue is aligned with political *virtù*, were taken by many as a defence of regicide and used against Cowley at the Restoration. There is no doubt that the poet supports Brutus's republican action, and the proof of Brutus's honour, that he refused Caesar's crown for himself, serves to increase the identification with Cromwell, who had declined the title of king in 1653. Yet as usual Cowley is not as straightforward as he might have been, for in the fourth stanza Brutus himself is seen as subject to 'Ill Fate'. He is confronted by a terror of the night 'in Philippi's field'. There is a submerged reminiscence here, working against the republican hero, of that other *fatal* battle when parliamentarian fortunes had been high and the royalist hero Falkland had fallen, dejected in spirit:

> Unhappy *Newberry*...
> ...In Horrors you *Philippi's* Field out-vy'd,
> Which twice the Civil Gore of *Romans* dy'd.[49]

In *Brutus* Cowley gives way to fatalistic pessimism, which overwhelms his faith in Brutus's cause:

> What joy can *humane things* to us afford,   ⸾
> When we see perish thus by odde events,
>   *Ill men*, and wretched *Accidents*,
> The best *Cause* and best *Man* that ever drew a *Sword?*

If the poem is about contemporary events, Cowley is imagining Cromwell's death and the subsequent destruction of his achievements, which in fact came to pass only a few years later. The historical Roman setting allows a modulation from panegyrical to philosophical poetry, but Cowley's intellect recoils from pursuing such depressing meditations: 'These mighty *Gulphs* are yet/ Too deep'. Human reason is inadequate, and the last stanza shifts the frame of reference entirely, moving from Rome to Jerusalem:

A few years more, so soon hadst thou not dy'ed,
Would have confounded *Humane Virtues* pride,
And shew'd thee a *God crucifi'ed.*

Cowley directs his attention away from the heroic, pagan, political state to anticipate the imminent incarnation of God who will redeem the world. No more will human nature have to manage unaided, for nature will be 'improv'ed by *Grace*'. As the poem's opening pointed out, this wondrous event has already happened, pre-empting praise from the earthbound virtue of Brutus and in the modern English context reminding people of the possibility of a second coming and the promised redemption of the world by Christ. Against this background the acknowledgement of Cromwell's skill as a ruler is of no significance and certainly no crime. Unlike most panegyrists of Cromwell, Cowley does not identify the Protector with God's messianic plan. Cowley's conception of restoration is far above politics, but here in its pietistic form it is positively reconcilable with praise of the republican hero. It also provides an unspecific surety for the future.

Cowley's only piece of political prose bridges the gap between the end of the Protectorate and Charles's return. *A Discourse by Way of Vision, Concerning the Government of Oliver Cromwell* purports to be written during Richard Cromwell's Protectorate, 1658-9, but was not published until 1661. The lack of explicit Stuart reference and the pervading anxiety of tone ('Ah, happy Isle, how art thou chang'd and curst', pp. 343[50]) suggests that some at least of the work was written directly after Oliver's funeral, although it indulges in the vilification of Cromwell that flourished at the time of its actual publication after the Restoration. The work begins in two minds about Cromwell: 'sometimes I was filled with horror and detestations of his actions, and sometimes I inclined a little to reverence and admiration of his courage, conduct and success' (p.343). This ambiguity of attitude is then developed by means of a dialectical discussion between the dreaming narrator and a Protector Angel, who represents the nation's guiding spirit in recent years and the Cromwellian ideal of history. The angel gives a panegyric character of Cromwell, praising his personal ability —'to leave a name behind him, not to be extinguisht, but with the whole World, which as it is now too little for his praises, so might have been too for his Conquests' (p.348) — and putting the *de facto* argument. Because it has happened, God must have wanted it: 'Neither is it ... unlawful for *Oliver* to succeed *Charles* in the Kingdom of *England*, when God so disposes of it' (p.354). The dreamer in turn responds, attacking the bare pragmatic values lying behind such a justification of Cromwell's rule, speaking 'not... out of any private animosity against the person of the last *Protector*', but because he wants to cut *all* tyrants out of history (p.351). He appeals to higher moral values and to a truly godly historiography to set against the history men have produced for themselves. He appeals to 'the laws of the New and Old Testament, and those which are the foundation of both even the Laws of Moral and Natural Honesty' (p.348). *Virtù* is countered by virtue; right is unchangeable. Indeed the dreamer argues that the troubles were 'only to be meant for a temporary chastisement of our sins, and not for a total abolishment of the old, and introduction of a new Government' (p.362). In any case Cromwell's new government was no sort of restoration to pristine virtue. It was 'no more like the Original ... than an artificial Plant ... is comparable to the true and natural one'. (pp.359-60). The narrator is on the defensive and when he reveals his concern not for monarchy but for the true commonwealth, which Cromwell is accused of slaying, he provokes the Protector Angel's scorn: 'But I see you are a Pedant, and Platonical Statesman, a Theoretical Common-wealths-man, an Utopian Dreamer. Was ever Riches gotten by your Golden Mediocrities? or the Supreme place attained to by Virtues that must not stir out of the middle?' (p.373). To the diabolical Angel, confident of his machiavellian rationality and adaptability, the narrator's heavenly values are nothing more than dull moderation. The debate has reached ideological deadlock when the Angel sneers at the dreamer's 'old obsolete rules of Virtue and Conscience', offering modernity in place of a view of history so providentially complacent that it can willingly incorporate even an Anti-Christian Cromwell (pp.372-3). But at this point the matter is resolved, in the manner of a masque, by the appearance of another angelic figure, both kingly and Christ-like, although not specifically either Christ or Charles Stuart:

> The comliest Youth of all th'Angelique Race;...
> His Beams of Locks fell part dishevel'd down,
> Part upwards curld, and form'd a nat'ral Crown,

Such as the *British* Monarchs us'd to wear....
   (p.375)

The tyrannical Protector-demon is chased away and the work is stopped. The unexpected heavenly intervention has brought about a sweeping transformation. In effect the earth has been restored by the removal of the recalcitrantly evil part of the creation. The *Discourse* concludes by asserting with deliberate generality the possibility of a miraculous deliverance, the dream of a happy ending belonging to art rather than politics.[51] Cowley's concept of restoration is tied to such formal considerations. At the end of the *Discourse* our attention is directed away from untractable worldly strife to the exalted, picturesque vision of a Christ-like guardian, summoned up as abruptly as the descent of grace itself. Similarly Cowley had dissolved the *Brutus* ode by looking away to the birth of Christ. In such poetic epiphanies his impossible hopes were invested.

Surveying Cowley's life and opinions before the Restoration it is evident that when Charles returned the poet's position must have been a peculiar one. In his *Ode* on the occasion, Cowley succeeded in performing the delicate task of sincerely welcoming the king while incorporating the range of doubts and complexities inherent in his thinking by 1660. By comparison with other panegyrics, Cowley's subtly deflects interest away from Charles, withdrawing into an Olympian overview of the nature of beneficial suffering as part of spiritual evolution. The stars have conjoined happily, but not accidentally, because a higher pattern is at work, inaugurated by the appearance of that bright latter-day star of Bethlehem at Charles's birth. The pattern reveals the intricate, difficult relationship of suffering and final joy (matched by the syntactical design):

> For loe! thy *Charls* again is *Born*.
> He then was *Born with and to pain*:
> *With*, and *to Joy* he's *born* again.
>   (23-5)

Through such a process the first perfection can be recovered; Cowley's language at once looks backwards and forwards:

> Then when we were to entertain

Felicity and *Innocence* again.

But as yet it is a question of potential felicity only. *Will* Adam and Eve return? asks the poet. *Will* peace return securely? *Will* the spirit descend?

> Will ever fair *Religion* appear
> In these deformed Ruins?....
>> Will *Justice* hazard to be seen...?
>> (48-9, 51)

The juxtaposition of '*Justice*' and 'hazard' illustrates the tension involved. The answer can only be conditional, located evasively in an indefinite time:

> Then may *White-hall* for *Charles* his *Seat* be fit.
> If *Justice* shall endure at *Westminster* to sit.
>> (56-7)

The poem moves in a ruminative, at times even circular fashion, as the poet contemplates the Restoration, keeping one eye over his shoulder at the past, yet reaching beyond the present event for larger, more ideal significances and possibilities. Justice and religion concern him more than the monarchy, 'Return, return, ye *Sacred Four*', he pleads, and while it has been suggested that the four are Charles's brothers and sisters,[52] the force of the pleading actually derives from the underlying reference to the cardinal virtues:

> For *God* does *Him*, that *He* might *You* restore,
>> Nor shall the world him only call,
> *Defender* of the Faith, but of *ye All*.
>> (76-8)

After heralding the advent of angelic personifications of virtue in the first five stanzas of his poem, Cowley then considers the miseries of the recent past, where men feared

>> That the three dreadful *Angels* we
> Of *Famine*, *Sword* and *Plague* should here establisht see;
> (*God's* great *Triumvirate* of Desolation).... (103-5)

To illustrate the way in which the regicide and troubles played a necessary part in a grand regenerative scheme, Cowley compares the curse on England with the curse on Jerusalem after the crucifixion of Christ (114-23). But at the same time Christ's passion is specifically distinguished from Charles I's. Christ is the man of '*greater Blood*' who instructs men in the apolitical, sacramental nature of redemption. Any redemption offered by Charles I's 'resurrected' son can be, by comparison, only political, historical or symbolic. The otherwise blasphemous equation of Christ and the Stuarts throughout Cowley's poem only serves to measure the mortal (and find him wanting) against the ideal and universal restorer. The credit for the Restoration lies with God. It is an act like the Creation, larger than the individuals concerned, unfolding a '*beauteous work* of *Order*' never before known:

> Already was the *shaken Nation*
> Into a wild and deform'd *Chaos* brought
>   And it was hasting on (we thought)
> Even to the last of *Ills, Annihilation,*
> When in the midst of this confused Night,
> Loe, the blest *Spirit* mov'd, and *there was Light.*
> For in the glorious *General's* previous Ray,
>   We saw a new created *Day.*
> We by it saw, though yet in *Mists* it shone,
> The *beauteous Work* of *Order* moving on.
>   (124-33)

Inspired, we are supposed to believe, by God and Charles, Cowley's own work unfolds similarly, gathering component details up into a recreation of the happy process. The key to the mystery is Charles I's martyrdom, described in a brief stanza highly wrought with rhymes and half-rhymes, almost an alchemical act by which blood is transformed into a force for life:

> The *Royal Blood* which dying Charles did sow
> Becomes no less the *seed* of *Royalty.*
>   (176-7)

Charles II has partaken of this mystery and by doing so has bound himself to the truth of ultimate reality. Political power and stability are only possible when they rest on the absolute power and stability of God. By recognising the dichotomy between the two, Cowley enforces the need for them to become one:

> The *King* and *Truth* has greatest *strength*,
> When they their sacred force unite,
>   And twine into one *Right*....
>   (191-3)

It is this restorative motion towards union which Charles's return begins:

> Such are the *years* (great *Charles*) which now we see
>   Begin their *glorious March* with *Thee*:
> Long may their *March* to *Heaven*, and still *Triumphant* be.

But this is only the beginning. Charles like a coin is a sign of God's covenant with man, imprinted on one side with the image of '*suffering Humanity*', on the other with the '*glorious Image* of ... *Power Divine*' (272-4).

Stanza sixteen gives a picturesque reimagination of the royal family's sufferings, in which they glide incorruptibly '*like Heavenly Saints*' through 'their *Purgatory*'. The ideal, insubstantial pageant inspires the poet to pray — 'Come, mighty *Charls*' — and as if in response it happens. An explosion of rejoicing occurs, images pile up and the people become 'the *Priests* of a *Poetick* rage', responding to the mystery with 'one *wild fit* of *chearful folly*'. It is an overwhelming exaltation of the mind, for which the increasingly visionary and spiritually abstract tendency of the poem has prepared the way. We see now that the king's return shadows forth a momentous revelation, as at the last day, when what has been obscured reverts to its pristine truth.

The poem concludes with a triumphal procession, imagined and not reflective of the actual events. It opens with 'the *Royal Mother*'. She did not in fact return to England until October 1660, but it is symbolically appropriate that the ecstatic apprehension of a world restored, as at Christ's coming again, should be accompanied by Henrietta Maria, 'the *Happiest Queen,* and a type of her namesake, the Virgin. She is an icon, 'a *bright Example*', containing within herself the mystery of suffering at the poem's centre. Like Mary with her five joys and five sorrows, Henrietta has been chosen to embody and reconcile (as the word-order does) 'the wide *Extreams/* Of great *Affliction,* great *Felicity*' (388-9). Redemptive suffering, under God's grace, works by a process of tempering until a conversion occurs from one state to its radical opposite. So Henrietta Maria '*Wife* of *Martyrdom*' has become '*Daughter* of *Triumphs*'. Cowley's devotional tribute to her, appropriate to her Catholic beliefs, implies her beatification. Next in the procession comes 'that *Heroick Person*', Monck. He is praised as the effective cause of the Restoration, and for choosing 'the *solid Great* above the Vain', in other words for not taking the crown himself: 'more 'tis to *Restore*, than to *Usurp* a *Crown* (411). Cowley's lengthy praise of Monck effectively endorses the General's sense of the immediate public good in this world. Monck is not an ideal image of anything, but a real hero, a practical statesman who makes Cowley's verse 'ill-proportion'd'. Monck as lynch-pin in the balance between king and people (at this stage) is an example of how ideals can be actualised. He is a figure of John the Baptist, who 'leads it on', where 'it' refers vaguely to a general '*Felicity*' yet to come. The stress on the constitution then concludes the poem. The final stanza introduces the Houses of Parliament and ends with an upbeat directing our future attention to 'the *Long,* the *Endless Parliament*'. In the last moment a linguistic restoration is achieved. 'Long Parliament' loses its frightening connotations and becomes a worthy ideal. Indeed the suggestion is made that 'Marble-*Statues*' of the present members should be erected to be 'th' *Example...* of *Truth, Religion, Reason, Loyalty*' so that as government reverts to its rightful agents their right is seen to derive from the higher ideals they represent. Although dealing with political organisation, Cowley still allows a gap between the actual and what might be imagined, where the latter, like the statues, serves both to inspire and to safeguard the actual. Henrietta Maria, Monck, parliament — each embodies an attitude to monarchy substantially removed from Charles's and the poem's monumental scope is increased by this massy array of independent focuses. While strictly speaking it is denoted by the king's return, in its totality the Restoration comprehends much more. It is a large and mysterious act of God's will working in time through the sufferings of his people. The parallels with Christ's birth, passion and second coming indicate that potentially Charles's return represents the regeneration of man at the end of history, while the distinction between Christ and Charles makes such large-scale restitution only possible spiritually. The restoration of truth, justice and religion is adumbrated optimistically, but depends on each entity in the nation warranting and achieving its own individual restoration. Cowley's poem intercedes between the local situation and a perfect sovereignty, the Kingdom of God held up in the distance.

The poet's precarious optimism did not last long, however, and in the early 1660s he turned to pastoral, a more straightforward mode than public verse. Freed from having to adopt a polemical stand on matters of state, Cowley could regard the world from a distance, his natural way of criticising it. By translating and imitating classical poems of retirement, he was able to express his disillusionment with life in the new City and under the new court. Although never criticising Charles personally, Cowley does attack many characteristics of the society resulting from the Restoration settlement. Life in town is driven by lust for gold, the tyrannous root of evil, while also the agent of the new regime's imperial claims:

> the great art of Peace, the Engine 'tis of War;
>   And Fleets and Armies follow it afar,
> The Ensign 'tis at land, and 'tis the Seamans Star.
>   (*Essays*, p.441)

Cowley is dismissive of all that

> the Tumult of vain greatness brings
> To Kings, or to the favourites of Kings.
>   (p.417)

Only in the country, where an inner retirement is possible, can the psychological tyranny which beset the Restoration world be escaped:

> Much will always wanting be,
>   To him who much desires.
>   (p.442)

The language of Cowley's private restoration is plain and down to earth, less loftily idealising. Indeed he takes a puritan attitude, proud of the self-denial which makes for spiritual abundance: 'poverty itself in plenty flowes'. (p.461). He is quite out of step with the age's longing for expansion and excess, and perhaps recognising his suffering in the public arena, there is a degree of self-mortification about his poetry of retirement. 'Cover me Gods, with *Tempe's* thickest shade', he begs.

His divorcement from the court is most strongly conveyed in *The Complaint*, written in 1663 after his failure to procure the Mastership of the Savoy. At Clarendon's instigation the post went to Gilbert Sheldon instead of to Cowley as promised.[53] In the poem the Muse takes the poet to task for abandoning her in favour of political ambitions in 'Courts and Cities'. As a result Cowley's poetry has suffered, but neither has he managed to procure himself any compensating secular honours. His failure contrasts lamentably with the prosperity of other loyalists at the Restoration. While his 'fellow Voyagers... possess the promis'd Land', Cowley is left 'upon the Barren Sand'. The Muse taunts him with the miracle of the Restoration by which all the ground was 'quickned', all the plants crowned with 'pearly dew', but the Muse's fleece left unrestored. Heaven was bountiful to the unjust but 'a Heaven of Brass' to the godly. The image hints at the brazen falsity of the Restoration paradise. The Muse warns Cowley that it is really 'a hard and Barren season' and that if he flings himself 'into the Courts deceitful Lottery' again he will suffer:

> Thou, to whose share so little bread did fall,
> In the miraculous year, when *Manna* rain'd on all.

The miracle is now regarded bitterly and sarcastically.

But 'the Melancholy Cowley' retorts. It is the pursuit of ideal forms, 'Golden Indies in the Air', that has disabled him from readily thriving in a thoroughly unideal political environment, and that habit was inculcated by the Muse. His mistake was being 'a demy-votary', like Ananias, not fully committing himself to either the poetic or the political reality; but, as we have seen, his life's poetry was a struggle to reconcile the two independent spheres. When the Muse slights the Restoration, the poet-speaker carefully takes the blame on to himself, shifting it from the king in a pose of martyr-like loyalty. The tactical hope is that Charles will vindicate Cowley's humble goodwill by extending his bountiful arms in the poet's direction. But the lines are undermined by a violent irony as we realise that one man's abundance is another's deprivation:

Teach me not then, O thou fallacious Muse,
  The Court, and better King t'accuse;
The Heaven under which I live is fair;
The fertile soil will a full Harvest bear ....

All are not under the same heaven.

Cowley's disillusionment stems from his failure to bring reality into alignment with his ideal version of things. Its quality can be appreciated by noting in passing how it differs from the reductive cynicism of Cowley's friend, Samuel Butler. Butler had begun his notorious poem *Hudibras* probably in 1658, and when the First Part was published in 1662 and the Second Part in 1663, Butler enjoyed a resounding success.[54] The poem was popular with men who had found the religious and political conflicts of the previous decades absurd and tedious. More thoughtful, pious men, like Samuel Pepys, found its belligerent burlesque less satisfying.[55] But in these years it was Butler's voice, not his contemporary Cowley's, that found its audience, although Cowley reflected the divided undercurrent in the nation more sensitively. *Hudibras* is characterised by its refusal to take any kind of abstract debate seriously. The language debases and reduces to a low physical level everything it touches, just as the endlessly hammering rhythms induce a feeling of impatience and exhaustion at the interminable pedantic discourse of the poem's characters. Samuel Butler is exceptional among writers of the period for having no genuine conception of restoration at all. To him the whole principal of regeneration, reformation and renovation, whether political or religious, is so much cant:

Call Fire and Sword and Desolation,
A *godly-thorough-Reformation....*
  (I, i, 199-200)

For Butler controversy, commitment and public professions of faith are all motivated by self-interest: 'when Disputes are wearyed out/'Tis *interest* still resolves the doubt' (II, i, 481-2). In the second canto of Part Three (not published until 1677) Butler gives his pithy verdict on the proliferation of sects and the fragmentation of the nation leading to the impasse of 1659 and subsequently the Restoration. A Presbyterian *'States-Monger'* is speaking:

For who e're heard of *Restoration,*

Until your *thorough Reformation*,
That is the Kings, and Churches Lands
Were Sequestred int'other hands?
For only then, and not before,
Your eyes were opened to restore.
And when the work was carrying on,
Who crost it, but your selves alone?
    (III, ii, 1227-34)

Butler's contempt for the motives behind political and religious change is too extreme, too severe, to amount to much more than pathological misanthropy. In his *Characters* he remarks that he cannot remember one good thing done by the people in any government.[56] Not so much anti-democratic as opposed to whatever his fellows attempted, Butler's disillusionment with the world was endemic to his nature, whereas Cowley's was a response to a particular and uncongenial historical situation.

In his retirement Cowley continued to be engaged with the philosophical questions which had occupied him publicly earlier. There is some evidence of renewed Catholic sympathy. In *On the Queens Repairing Somerset House* (1664) he praised the Catholic Henrietta Maria for her 'God-like' power of promoting *concordia discors*.[57] Typically Cowley's praise is pluralistic: 'the Active and the Quiet Mind/By different wayes equal content may find'. It may seem strange that a man who had recently espoused puritan beliefs should now be sympathetic towards popery, but in the years after the restrictive Act of Uniformity nonconformists of various kinds were forced into limited allegiances and in general the situation was one in which very complicated and mixed religious dispositions could be tentatively worked out.[58] In his last years Cowley seems to have been working towards an all-embracing kind of proto-Deism. In the *Hymn. To Light* he identifies Light with 'th' Empyraean Heaven' as the source of all things. Sprat in his *Life* of Cowley was anxious to claim that the poet's final faith was orthodox Anglicanism, but the tone is defensive and Sprat himself had Deistic leanings. An unusual *religio medici* is what one would expect from Dr Cowley, a faith to transcend those 'many controverseries... introduced by zeal or ignorance and continued by Faction'.[59]

In the *Essays* of his last years the detachment from and disbelief in the values of the Restoration world continues:

I never then proposed to my self any other advantage from His
Majesties Happy Restoration, but the getting into some
moderately convenient Retreat in the Country, which I thought
in that case I might easily have compassed, as well as some
others, with no greater probabilities or pretences have arrived
to extraordinary fortunes....
    (*Essays*, pp. 458-9)

Indeed in relation to his own obscure retirement he develops an
idea which stands as a justification of his own uncommitted and
sceptical dealings with the world. The good and happy man is he
who *deceives* the world, who lives an obscure life, unnoticed by
public events and having no effect in the ultimately delusory
theatre of the world:

This Innocent Deceiver of the world, as *Horace* calls him, this
Muta persona, I take to have been more happy in his Part, then
the greatest Actors that fill the Stage with show and noise, nay,
even then *Augustus* himself, who askt with his last breath,
Whether he had not played his *Farce* very well.
    (p.399)

Cowley's abiding interest was in ideal forms and the struggle to
reintegrate them with the actual world. His poetry was divided
and uninvolved in the world for its own sake. In the end, with his
private idea of restoration, he deceived the cause of royalist
propaganda. The price was his separation from the culture and
patronage of the court, but his poetry of the period gained its
distinctive, speculative, internally divided quality. Cowley's stress
on the need to purify the mind made him unable to accept happily
the superficial trappings of the state and it made him sceptical of
old-fashioned intellectual modes which he saw as so many
'Pageants of the Brain'. He preferred to turn to the truths he
considered basic. His ode *To the Royal Society* (probably the last
thing he wrote, in 1666-7) depicted the new philosophy
overthrowing the usurping tyrant of (Aristotelian) authority:

But 'twas Rebellion call'd to fight
For such a long-oppressed Right.

Bacon had first broken 'that Scar-crow Deitie' and now the Royal

Society was to follow that Moses and restore 'Deposed Truth'. The language of rebellion here reminds us that it was largely a reforming puritan interest in God's book of nature that fostered empirical science in the seventeenth century, an interest channelled into Whiggish notions of social improvement partly by members of the Royal Society.[60] Cowley, praising Hobbes in the 1650s and writing his own *Proposition for the Advancement of Experimental Philosophy*, had always been ready to countenance new ideas. The ode *To the Royal Society* is especially successful in integrating Cowley's belief in scientific advancement with his religious concept of a general restoration. Bacon has once more opened the orchard where the tree of life grows and man has now only to bow down before external nature, using his senses not his preconceptions, and he will be in Eden. The expulsion of the false god allows the rehabilitation of the true God, which here is equivalent to Nature. The gathering of factual observations leads miraculously to 'a Nourishment Divine', and the submission to 'the Natural and Living Face' of things is tantamount to a revelation achieved through devotion. Through the scientific search for truth, Cowley claims in a variation of his accustomed theme, earth will become the simulacrum of heaven:

> Io! Sound too the Trumpets here!
> Already your victorious Lights appear;
> New Scenes of Heaven already we espy,
> And Crowds of golden Worlds on high....

Yet the task is man's. Despite the sovereignty of nature the individual consciousness must be correctly attuned. In this scheme Sprat is the hero, the saviour '*Hercules*' who acts as God's agent in pouring the celestial spirit of truth into men. Cowley parodies the Restoration of the monarch in his last poem, but characteristically the parallel with the secular power only provides an ironic gloss on the true restoration which works spiritually and intellectually. In Natural Philosophy, itself a hybrid of the abstract and concrete, the poet has found the perfect mediator between his two realms.

By the late 1670s Cowley had erroneously acquired a posthumous reputation as an old-fashioned royalist. Yet at his death he was regarded as a monarch in his own right, 'the King of Wit'. His intellectual kingdom was set over against the political state by an anonymous memorialist, making the point that Cowley is greater than anyone else below *or* above ground in Westminster Abbey:

> for it was fit
> Amongst our Kings to lay the King of Wit:
> By which the Structure more renown'd will prove
> For that part Bury'd, than for all above.[61]

Thomas Higgon's elegy goes further, to imply that Cowley's official neglect is an indictment of Charles, by comparison with the ideal monarch of the past:

> If he had flourish'd when *Augustus* sway'd,
>   Whose peacefull Scepter the whole world obey'd,
>   Account of him *Mecoenas* would have made...
> It is not now as 'twas in former days....

The Stuart comparison with Augustus had turned sour in the year of the disastrous Dutch War, and Higgons swears that Cowley will live as long as Petrarch because he has not only won 'Victories', but victories 'in which blind undiscerning fortune had no part'.[62] The contemporary verdict on Cowley, then, was that his political vacillation, his retirement, and his verse, at once topical and aloof, represented a genuinely noble response to a world which in the end was as contemptible as it was contemptuous of the ideal intellect. He was read dutifully in the half-century after his death and admired, in Pope's words, for 'the language of his Heart'. Beneath the smooth, almost lapidary surface of Cowley's verse the poet was engaged in a deep and carefully articulated struggle to bind together the disparities of his experience in forms, however strained or static, of reconciliation. Saying what he had to say, but would often rather not have been saying, was an exceptionally taxing and at times constricting business for Cowley. Yet in the end he managed.

6 The Poetry of the Second Dutch War

The atmosphere of 1660-61 had been fertile for panegyric, but once its initial outburst in those years was over public poetry of praise dwindled. Poets had to find less obvious objects for their rhetoric of restoration: so Dryden addressed the New Year 1662, while Waller wrote about urban improvements and Cowley about the Royal Society. After its narrow political service in 1660-61, the idea of restoration was beginning to establish an independent status as a general literary theme. Then after the middle of the decade the second Dutch War once more caused the restoration theme to be applied to explicitly Stuart issues. The war marked a new phase of political unrest as well as providing a fresh topic of controversy and launching a new wave of public poetry. The central arguments of the mid-century, about the nature of power, authority and government in England, were revived, transmuted now into debate about the management of the war. Parliament was able to call the king's ministers to account for their conduct, thus achieving a temporary supremacy over the monarch and severely curtailing the royal prerogative.[1] Clarendon was dismissed and exiled and this meant, effectively, the defeat of the Chancellor's out-moded vision of a balanced government mediated by privy council. By the end of the war the nation was in a disastrous state economically and in terms of trade, defence and foreign policy. With considerable justice, blame fell on the wartime administration — a group dominated by Clarendonians, old Cavaliers and aspiring new courtiers. In short those attacked for their conduct of the war were those responsible for the Restoration. The key agents in 1660 — Charles, James, Monck (now Albermarle) and Clarendon — were the figures singled out for praise or blame. The war provided an opportunity for the constitutional problems and political discontents, apparently smoothed over at the Restoration, to be brought to the surface again and indeed, for controversial purposes, the war amounted to little more than those few pivotal incidents which raised questions about the administration's competence and authority.

Popular and mercantile enthusiasm, on top of naive eagerness for national glory, favoured a war against the Dutch, who were thought to have encroached on English trade. Charles and Clarendon were pressured by mercantile interests at court, by old commonwealthsmen wanting to return to action, and by young Cavaliers keen to prove themselves. But they procrastinated because the war could be ill-afforded and, although advantaging some sectors, might not be generally beneficial to national trade. The pro-war lobby was in the main hostile to Clarendon. Finally Charles realised that the war would help to unite the nation in patriotism and loyalty, and would also give him a certain means of extracting money from parliament. After initial skirmishes, war was declared in February 1665. Fortune favoured the English at first, but mismanagement, amateurish diplomacy, and the Plague in mid-1665, led to a series of debilitating engagements in the second year of the war. The Dutch had the upper hand and, after the Great Fire in London in September 1666, feeling in England ran high against the war and its cost. Peace negotiations began, and naval retrenchments were made which precipitated the ultimate disaster when in June 1667 the Dutch invaded the Medway and attacked the naval depot. Much of the fleet was destroyed. The invasion revealed 'a state of mismanagement and disorganisation unparalleled in our history' and the war ended in humiliation, compromise and a spate of parliamentary recriminations.[2] But paradoxically, after scapegoats like Clarendon were found, power devolved to those very men who had promoted the war in the beginning, administered it and then successfully shifted the blame elsewhere: men such as Coventry and Arlington, and other future members of the Cabal. In his *The Last Instructions to a Painter* the 'country' gentleman and member of parliament Andrew Marvell had warned Charles — in vain — against turning from the devil he knew to such 'new men', the devils he didn't know.[3]

The concern with questions of internal policy made it inevitable that poetry dealing with the war should continue the vein of political poetry which had flourished in the early 1660s. In Book Six of his Latin *Plantarum* Cowley quite explicitly treated the battle of Lowestoft, the first engagement of the war, as but the latest stage in the long history of the Stuarts, growing out of the civil wars and Charles's exile and return.[4] Robert Wild, who had praised Monck in 1660, wrote a rollicking, jubilant piece about the war, repeating a motif from his earlier poem in which all the sea's 'scaly regiments' pay tribute to Charles.[5] But it was Edmund Waller who initiated the major strain of war poetry. Much earlier Waller had written in praise of Cromwell's navy. There was, in fact, a considerable body of Cromwellian anti-Dutch and anti-Spanish naval panegyric. As with most of it (for example, Marvell's), the mood of Waller's 'Of a War with Spain, and a Fight at Sea' was straightforwardly jingoistic and trumpet-blowing. His *Instructions to a Painter*, published in 1666, had larger aspirations. Through an idealised and heroic account of the battle of Lowestoft Waller elaborated the royalist themes of his Restoration panegyrics. Like that of *To the King* (1660), the peroration of *Instructions to a Painter* anticipates the nexus of peace, security, trade and increase under the guidance of Charles the prime mover. Waller was the first English poet to exploit the *ut pictura poesis* device in the service of contemporary history, although Dryden had used explicitly 'painterly' language to heighten historical incident in *Astraea Redux* and the verbal 'portrait' was a common form of praising Charles II and his predecessors. In 1658 Sir Thomas Higgons, later also to write a Restoration panegyric, published his translation of Busenello's Italian poem retitled *A Prospective of the Naval Triumph of the Venetians over the Turk* and this introduced the painter device into English poetry.[6] Higgons's rough, picturesque version of the conflict between Christians and infidels attempts to create an eternally commemorative monument:

> Let these my lines in marble written be,
> And give this history eternity....[7]

Waller takes up Higgons's approach and, using the *ut pictura poesis* convention in an heroic form, concentrates on the power of historical images, purely as images, to create a representation of the events which is simplified, beautified and exalted. The method does not allow analysis of cause and effect, nor any great psychological complexity, nor vividly observed detail. But it suits Waller's polemical purpose. The symbolical power of the king and his brother can be celebrated and the symbolical nature of the battle for dominion of the ocean can be revealed.

> Then draw the parliament, the nobles met,

And our great monarch high above them set....
  (299-300)
For a less prize, with less concern and rage,
The Roman fleets at Actium did engage;
They, for the empire of the world they knew,
These, for the Old contend, and for the New.
  (113-16)

Waller is especially concerned to glorify James, the commander of
the fleet, Mars to Charles's Jove, and he does so simply by asserting
the force of James's mere presence. 'The trembling Dutch the
approaching Prince behold' (273) and at once 'allow our title to
command the deep' (284). It is York's 'extraction, and his glorious
mind' that fills the fleet's sails (19, 124):

What wonders may not English valour work,
Led by the example of victorious York?
  (277-8)

Only by virtue of the decorum of public painting can such
excessive claims for an heroic image have any force. Waller does
not inquire further. His war is a Caroline idyll in which the
classical panoply and the beauty of the protagonists, such as James
and his Duchess Anne Hyde, Clarendon's daughter, contribute
more to the total effect than the events themselves. The sea shines
'with gallantry'. The idea of Charles's empire as a languorous
golden world holds sway. As a result, necessarily, the reasons for
the war are blurred. James is fighting for 'his brother's glory, and
his country's cause' (14), to establish Charles's 'eternal title to the
main' (308). Waller straightforwardly identifies the forces at play
in the war with the iconic values of Stuart individuals and excludes
the pertinent question of the relationship between Charles's
personal cause and his country's.[8] So the poem becomes sweepingly
ahistorical and merely polemical, establishing a subsequently
unfortunate imagistic connection between the court and the
administration of the war.

Waller's orderly vision of the war, constructed out of
grandiloquence and mythological generalisation, was reduced to
chaos by the lampoons which followed. The *Second Advice to a
Painter* (author unknown) was in circulation late in 1666, reusing
the painter device to undermine the superficiality of Waller's

approach.[9] Painting is seen as the means by which the wealthy and powerful buy self-glorification. So if Coventry is shown as 'cerulean' or 'ultramarine' it is because those most expensive colours indicate his venality; Anne Hyde requires 'pencils of ermine' (25, 30, 54). The *Second Advice* adopts a stance of hard-headed realism which is to be read as honesty. The poem is vehemently determined to expose the truth, depicting the battles as 'terribler... than the Last Judgment was of Angelo' (112-3), presenting in detail the viciousness of contemporary politicians like Clarendon. But the poem's 'honesty' is little more than wildly energetic, reductive scepticism. Along with Waller's impotent panegyric, all other attempts to understand the war are demolished:

> Thus having fought we know not why, as yet,
> We've done we know not what nor what we get....
> (317-18)

In their turn lampoons of the received version of the war produced responses. Christopher Wase's *Divination* (written in 1666) was concerned to make the real issue clear: no subject should take the liberty of speaking against the government — to do so was treason:[10]

> Him that great James's courage dares deny;
> The same may question his loyalty,
> Then follow the Dutch justice with applause
> And in the end revive the Good Old Cause.
> (157-60)

Fear of renewed rebellion was strong, and unrest had to be stopped at all costs, even to the extent of covering up corruption and maladministration. Wase scorned the satirist who:

> What every faithful subject ought to hide
> (His country's shame) makes his delight and pride.
> (191-2)

Patriotism was invoked in order to quell internal dissent.[11] On the other hand the *Third Advice to a Painter* (of unknown authorship and also appearing in 1666) turned such patriotism to opposite effect. [12] The poem focuses on Albermarle who was to some extent a popular hero for his part in restoring the monarchy and signified the people's ultimate right to choose their king. Now, however, he has been corrupted by his new title and his association with the court: 'How far the gentleman outcuts the lord' (42). His difficulties against the Dutch are contrasted with his victory over the Rump in 1660. The comparison hints that things are now as bad as in 1659-60, warranting a further restoration and the removal of the degenerate and incompetent court party, which has renewed 'the causes of [its] first exile' (234). The poem typically concludes with a plea to the king to free himself from his unreliable counsellors. The restoration required is moral and internal: 'only let vice be damn'd and justice flow' (444). Let England only learn Troy's lesson in time, so that virtuous Philomel may be 'restored to voice' and freed from 'tragedies of court' (454-5).

The pastoral idea of restoration is introduced here with new force. Now the hope is for a restoration of good government. Such restoration — a kind of reform — can only come about with the removal from power of the present court party, the very party that had so ruthlessly restored itself in 1660. Underlying the obsession with administrative competence in these poems is the sense that if the government is wanting the people have the right to demand an administrative restoration. Here we see, as yet dimly and incoherently grasped, the kind of position Locke was to express some fifteen years later in his *Second Treatise of Government*. Locke argued that when the abuses and mismanagement of government were such as tended towards arbitrary power, then the people had the right to 'rouze themselves, and endeavour to put the rule into such hands, which may secure to them the ends for which Government was at first erected'. [13] Locke made quite clear that this return to true, traditional forms of government was not to be considered as a rebellion, but was rather '*the best fence against Rebellion*'. It may more accurately be considered as a restoration of the state to itself. Here the language of restoration is beginning to be reworked in a way which was to prove politically constructive, and stubbornly subversive of the Stuart cause. When in the heyday of the Glorious Revolution Locke published his *Second Treatise* he confidently reclaimed Charles's old title and heralded William of Orange as '*our Great Restorer*'. His title confirmed by '*the Consent of the People*', William had '*saved the Nation when it was on the very brink of Slavery and Ruine*'. [14] In 1666-67 it was very important to arrive at a true account of the state of affairs in the nation, so that the administration could be accurately judged. Whereas early in the decade huge propaganda claims were eagerly believed, now generalised scepticism was the prevailing mode of political discourse and retribution was invited on all purveyors of false, official attitudes:

> Now joyful fires and the exalted bell
> And court-gazettes our empty triumph tell.
> Alas, the time draws near when overturn'd
> The lying bells shall through the tongue be burn'd;
> Paper shall want to print that lie of state,
> And our false fires true fires shall expiate.
>   (*Third Advice* 163-8)

It was against a background of sharpened scrutiny and scurrilous but sometimes realistic criticism of topical events that Dryden wrote *Annus Mirabilis*. His aim was to offer a monumental record of contemporary history which was also an argument for Stuart rule, but in the circumstances his task was harder than Waller's. His tactic was to appeal to a vision of history and heroism that made a concern with the realities of the present look short-sighted and trivial. But it was a risky approach because his poem also had to be journalistically accurate enough to be convincing. Dryden took Virgil as his 'Master in this poem'[15] and found there his answer. By persistently loading the incidents he recounts with a freight of similes, allusions and painterly decoration, from a wide array of contexts, Dryden delights us, impresses us, and draws our attention away from the subject immediately at hand.[16] Bizarrely, for example, the cannonade against the spice ships is described as causing death by 'shatter'd Porc'lain' and 'Aromatick splinters' (115-16). As we pause to admire the curious conceit and elegant patterning of the stanza we are diverted from the narrative sequence, the thrust and parry of the war, to other things. Dryden exhibits all his linguistic richness here and the poem's imagistic glamour and artifice work to shadow forth the riches of civilisation which victory will bring. The war, as in Waller's poems, is already a courtly and romantic reminiscence in which English 'Lovers' fight rival Dutch 'Husbands' with 'frantick passion', in which the sea provides a 'glittering silver' backdrop with 'smiling Eddies dimpled', and in which sailors dream happily while breezes rest in the 'high beds' of their ships' sails. 'Realms are households which the Great must guide' (552) and the war is a country-house affair in which enemy ships stand about like 'servants' or like those disconsolate neighbours with their 'wasted Patrimonies' and 'thin scatt'ring Trees' (378, 501-4). The figurative dress is so profuse and variable that in the end we suspect the war of being little more than an emblematic masque for which heaven has provided the lights (63-4). But by dividing and squandering our interest Dryden removes the focus from practical administrative incompetence to the disparate dreams behind the war and the even vaguer 'nature of things'.

Nonetheless it is possible to identify the poem's design and its polemical strategy. In the first part Dryden gives a complicated, apparently blow-by-blow impression of the war from mid-1665 to August 1666 (taking considerable historical liberties with the disposition of his material).[17] He engages with each of the war's controversial incidents in an attempt to show that, contrary to appearances, honour rather than dispraise is due to the Stuart leaders. So Albermarle's narrowly averted disaster when the fleet divided is seen as heroic survival:

> Where not to be o'rcome was to do more
>   Then all the Conquests former Kings did gain.
>   (319-20)

Then a transition is made to the God-like king whose providential mission provides the ultimate justification of the war:

> So looks our Monarch on this early fight,
>   Th'essay, and rudiments of great success,
> Which all-maturing time must bring to light,
>   While he, like Heav'n, does each days labour bless.
>   (557-60)

It is Charles who restores the fleet and inspires the continuation of the war. This leads into a digression on the development of shipping, made possible by the co-operation of king and people, which ultimately will establish England's world supremacy. 'The Universe' shall become 'one City' centred in London over which Charles shall have imperial sway. But the war's progress is interrupted by the Fire. The second part of the poem, then, the last third, describes London's deliverance from the Fire, brought about by Charles's mediation between God and Londoners. A covenant is enacted between God, the king and the metropolis and this sets the seal on the nation's Stuart destiny — and at the same time definitely validates the war. Dryden's concern in *Annus Mirabilis* is to reveal the balanced, but hierarchical harmony between king and people, in which the king confers divine meaning on otherwise mundane and distressing events. Constitutionally he gestures towards 'balance of government', but in practical terms at the time of publication *Annus Mirabilis* was an argument for the preservation or redressing of the king's prerogative in the face of increasing parliamentary encroachments.[18] Even Charles's much-attacked reluctance to fight fits into Dryden's vision of the monarch's role:

> But peaceful Kings o'r martial people set,
>   Each others poize and counter-ballance are.[19]
>   (47-8)

Different kinds of balance are kept in play as the poem progresses. On the one hand there is the symmetry and harmony of the poet's visionary perception, often reflected syntactically; for example:

> But, when approach'd, in strict embraces bound,
>   *Rupert* and *Albermarl* together grow:
> He joys to have his friend in safety found,
>   Which he to none but to that friend would owe.
>   (465-8)

On the other hand there is the balance of war's vicissitudes, as fortune favours first one side then the other. Dryden does not disguise the confused ebb-and-flow of the war and in flamboyant *sententiae* proclaims that fate is man's enemy universally:

> Such are the proud designs of human kind,
>   And so we suffer Shipwrack every where!
> Alas, what Port can such a Pilot find,
>   Who in the night of Fate must blindly steer!
>   (137-40)

But in practice the fatalistic moral only applies to the Dutch, because the greater power of providence favours England and the very vicissitudes and reversals of the war work to advance the English cause. So balance becomes part of an overarching order. In his preface Dryden determined to describe 'the beginning, progress and successes of a most just and necessary War'.[20] The war is necessary, economically and historically, to translate England's destiny into fact — and *ipso facto* just. Dryden's stance is designed to pacify the growing ominous fatalism which gathered around the number and year 1666.[21] Dryden speaks confidently and knowingly of the 'successes' of the war. Variants of the word 'success' occur seventeen times in the prefatory material and the poem, and the double meaning of the idea of 'success' precisely illustrates Dryden's two-sided understanding of history. Events can be seen either as succeeding one another merely sequentially ('amidst these foils succeeds the balmy night', 389) or as unfolding in their succession a pattern which expresses the divine will. History can bear meaning such that each event carries within it the ultimate victor's success. Hence Albermarle muses on 'the succeeding day' which in the long perspective contains 'the rudiments of great success' (396, 558). By means of a word-play Dryden transforms a journalistic sense of history into a visionary one. And what underlies the word-play is Dryden's staunch belief in the Succession, and the Restoration of England's Stuart line.

The Great Fire proves the vanity of merely casual contingent success: 'how unsincere are all our joys!' (833). The negative power of fate persistently threatens to decimate man's heroic aims. The indifferent fortune of the war is here elevated into a diabolic demi-urge capable of thwarting England's national destiny, aided by hubristic Englishmen who after their 'late successes on the Foe' now urge 'an unseen Fate to lay them low' (837-9). Rebellion is a part of this anarchic force and Dryden brilliantly compares the fire to a monstrous political usurper, a Cromwell:

> As when some dire Usurper Heav'n provides,
>   To scourge his Country with a lawless sway:
> His birth, perhaps, some petty' Village hides,
>   And sets his Cradle out of Fortune's way ....
>
> In this deep quiet, from what source unknown,
>   Those seeds of fire their fatal birth disclose ....
>   (849-52; 865-6)

While traitors and fanatics rejoice at the Fire, and Dutch winds fan it, for true Englishmen it becomes a trial of loyalty, an ordeal of suffering which will prove the worth of their Stuart king. Charles takes on the role of penitential and pious hero, at once holy and fatherly:

> More then his Guards his sorrows made him known,
>   And pious tears which down his cheeks did show'r:
> The wretched in his grief forgot their own:
>   (So much the pity of a King has pow'r).
>   (957-60)

(In fact contemporaries praised his active efficiency in preventing the Fire's spread.[22]) Dryden's account has a daemonic, hallucinatory quality, catching the infernal chaos which menaces the city. His intense, immediate apprehension of the scene is heightened by weird, picturesque figures: the flames 'first lay tender bridges of their fume,/ And o'r the breach in unctuous vapours flie' (983-4). Such ornate, even theatrical comparisons also remind us that the poem is a work of art written after the event, a triumph of the culture which has revived from the Fire. In such a spirit, witty, self-delighting and serious at once, Dryden presents the fire as an image of apocalypse, 'a dismal picture of the gen'ral doom' (1014). From this starting point he can go on to depict the drama of London's recovery as an image of the world's restoration to eternal glory after the Last Judgement, through the mediation of God's anointed son. London's fate will be:

> Great as the worlds, which at the death of time
>   Must fall, and rise a nobler frame by fire.
>   (847-8)

To this end Charles asks God the 'Patron' to lay judgement on his own head only, and final purification by eschatological fire is anticipated (echoing Isaiah 34:4):

> We all have sinn'd, and thou hast laid us low,
>   As humble Earth from whence at first we came:
> Like flying shades before the clowds we show,
>   And shrink like Parchment in consuming flame.
>   (1061-4)

Charles prays that God's sentence may not be 'unconditional', in other words that mankind should have the possibility of transcending mortal fate through grace. The Almighty's answer is the extinction of the Fire by a 'more than natural change' and, as in earlier panegyrics, images of restoration follow. Charles, like the spring, dispenses bounty, his divine status endorsed: 'Thus God's Annointed God's own place suppli'd' (1142). Now the covenant is sealed the poet can confidently envisage London as the New Jerusalem:

> Me-thinks already, from this Chymick flame,
>   I see a City of more precious mold...
> ...Renew'd her Charters date,
> Which Heav'n will to the death of time allow.
>   (1169-70, 1175-6)[23]

Simultaneously the transformation is imperial. London is now 'more *August*', which is to say, more Augustan (1177). But the metropolitan millennium can only be secured in reality by trade, and that depends on the successful outcome of the Dutch wars. In a final turn the vision becomes propaganda, demanding that the people support the king's military cause:

> They have not lost their Loyalty by fire;
>   Nor is their courage or their wealth so low,
> That from his Wars they poorly would retire....
>   (1153-5)

The inconclusive action of the first section of *Annus Mirabilis* is completed by the significance of London's deliverance from the fire. The last section enacts symbolically the ideally pious relationship of king and country, and relates London's trials to her great imperial destiny. The same relationship appeared in the first part, incomplete in its impure historical unfolding, in terms of the actual steps taken by the regime to achieve its mercantile aim. The fire section is direct and coherent, with its eschatological metaphorical pattern properly integrated into the narrative. It offers the ideal of restoration that will be possible if the desired constitution is preserved. The way Charles is depicted at the end reinforces Dryden's conception of the balance of government. Poetically Dryden makes Charles an heroic image and invests him with the symbolic, iconic power of bringing order to the discordant, often contingent events of his poem. Analogously, Charles is invested with spiritual power by the Londoners: they accept him as their intermediary with God. Both the poetic and the spiritual roles of Charles reflect the supreme ordering power that Dryden would like the English people to invest in their king. But if the king's image ultimately contributes order to the events of the war, so the war is actually the mundane way of bringing about the glorious destiny promised symbolically at the end. Dryden's tactic is to reverse the relationship, so that the war derives its validity from the covenant with providence, rather than the covenant being made true by the political and mercantile exertions of self-determining Englishmen. The poem strains to unite the disparate realities of symbolic sacramentalism and poetic journalism.

Dryden's idea of the restoration of London is, as it were, a second-generation idea of restoration, depending first on Charles's restored kingship and second on the people's readiness to support Charles in order that their metropolis may be restored. What must be restored is no longer the king, nor the nation, but a particular relationship between king and people. The mere presence of the restored king is not enough, and Dryden is forced to admit a discrepancy between the monarch's Restoration and the general, metaphorical ideas of restoration to which he was also committed: trade, power, peace, science and art. The optative nature of Dryden's remarks dedicating his poem to the metropolis has become transparent by the end:

> Never had Prince or People more mutual reason to love each other, if suffering for each other can indear affection ... You [London] are now a *Phoenix* in her ashes, and, as far as Humanity can approach, a great Emblem of the suffering Deity.... I am therefore to conclude, that your sufferings are at an end; and that one part of my Poem has not been more of an History of your destruction, then the other a Prophecy of your restoration.[24]

Annus Mirabilis is a heroic but wishful apology for the sorry year in which Englishmen found themselves.

A new ferocity comes to painter poems with Marvell. *The Last Instructions to a Painter* was written in 1667 to expose the administrative corruption that had led to the burning of the English fleet in the Medway. But the intensity and compendiousness of Marvell's vision make his poem a small epic, a proto-*Dunciad* vehemently indicting the foolish and vicious degeneracy of the times. Art — painting — is raised to the role of scourge by the artist's moral anger, and paradoxically its desperate, uncontrolled wildness leads to a thorough depiction of truth that would have been impossible if regular, urbane aesthetic standards were regarded:

> [The Painter's] Anger reacht that rage which past his Art;
> Chance finisht that which Art could but begin...
> So may'st thou perfect, by a lucky blow,
> What all thy softest touches cannot do.
>   (23-4; 27-8)[25]

The poet's pressing aim is to see England's historical situation clearly and realistically. In the manner of a parliamentary inquiry, he is concerned to scrutinise the characters and events of the immediate past in order to wake the nation and the king to the dire situation. To strip away the illusions fostered by poems like *Annus Mirabilis* and to arouse people to a sense of the self-blinding insulation of the nation's leaders, it was necessary to adopt a violent disruptive poetic technique. The crowding, the fluctuations of tone, the abrupt transitions, the excesses of *The Last Instructions* are crucial to Marvell's attempt to reveal an unpalatable, unthinkably depraved state of affairs. Critics have found the poem unpleasantly difficult — obscured by topicality and overinflated in style. But the vision which Marvell would show his contemporaries *is* unpleasant.[26] The seeing is painful and for this very reason the regime has remained immured against it, protected by illusions. For example, 'our feather'd *Gallants*', who had originally in a naive spirit of adventure urged the war, come to Gravesend to watch the Dutch engage the English in England's most inglorious hour: they come 'to be Spectators safe of the *new Play*' and leave 'when first they hear the Gun' (596-600). These young Cavaliers quite fail to appreciate the full measure of the disaster. Indeed those in power are committed to preserving illusion and mystification because they fear the consequences of harsh, truth-seeking scrutiny. Clarendon abhors operating in the full sunlight of open parliament, like a sinister plant that 'shrinks

from the Mornings Eye;/But blooms all Night....' He is a comet
that, in the absence of the sun (the king), all 'Earth and Heaven
burns' (343-8). The courtiers, counsellors and administrators are
obliged to operate under the cover of obscurity because of their
corruption. All are in each other's shadows because all are bound
together in a web of self-interest, privilege and debt. The court
party in parliament is entirely motivated by such considerations
and all are subservient to the diabolic figure of Clarendon, who is a
parasite on the king and the nation for his own glory. The poem's
most grotesque image parodies the idea of freely circulating money
and presents a monstrous servile nexus:

> Horse-leeches circulating at the Hem'roid Vein;
> [Clarendon] sucks the King, they him, he them again.
> The Kingdoms Farm he lets to them bid least:
> Greater the Bribe, and that's at Interest.
> Here Men induc'd by Safety, Gain, and Ease,
> Their Money lodge; confiscate when he please.
> .   (497-502)

Those financially bound cannot be free to resist the pressure of
administrative corruption. In parliament those who represent the
country against the court are able to oppose the imposition of a
crippling Excise simply because they have 'clear *Estates*': they are
not indebted, and their consciences, too, are free, 'clear' and in the
light. The light of historical actuality is hateful to the
Clarendonian administration because it reveals that England's
disgrace at the hands of the Dutch is not only the inevitable but
also, bitterly, the just consequence of governmental misconduct.
When de Ruyter sails up the Thames in triumph, he is on the crest
of an historical wave, caused by the corruption of the English
regime. Naturally he appears in broad daylight and finds 'the Sun
much brighter, and the Skies more clear ...' (529). Marvell, as a
patriot, is the first to admit that such light is odious, but
nevertheless grants that the retribution is just. He curses the
morally black day which brought England's inevitable,
unfortunate fate:

> Thou, and thy Fellows, held'st the odious Light.
> Sad change...

since Neptune resigned his immortal empire to the union of the

Thames and the Medway (746-50). And it is certainly a sad
change since Cromwell achieved for England a qualitatively
improved kind of time and light: Cromwell shone

> ...the Jewel of the yearly Ring.
> 'Tis he the force of scatter'd Time contracts,
> And in one Year the work of Ages acts....
> (*The First Anniversary of the Government under O.C.*, 12-14)

Now even the traditional sun, Charles, has been obscured with
'Spots' which 'seem his Courtiers, are but his disease' (950-2).

A bad government is an agent of darkness, because it restricts a
clear apprehension of its own and the country's situation, and
because it is prevented from acting with acuity and therefore with
any chance of success. The English government appears in
Marvell's poem in its full inefficiency and inaction, bizarrely
catalogued in fragmentary factions, almost taxonomically: 'the
Troop of *Clarendon* Haters of Fowl', 'the Miter Troop', 'the
Troop of Priviledge', 'the Projectors', 'the Eaters Beef', 'the
Drinkers', 'the *French* Standard' (151-218). The members of
parliament are caricatured, reduced to the lowest common
denominator of comic grossness, and conglomerated in a list which
obscures their individuality and with it their moral probity.
Clumped together to support the rapacious Bill, these members
become unregenerate matter, unenlightened by spirit or civic
responsibility. 'Gross Bodies, grosser Minds, and grossest Cheats;'
they form appropriate raw material for the speaker, a 'Master-
Cook' who:

> Well was ... skill'd to season any question
> And make a sawce fit for *Whitehall's* digestion....
> (871-4)

The wilful blindness of these men is exaggerated by Marvell into
insentience, and their uselessness is underlined, to comic effect, by
the way they crowd together and crowd the poem. During the
inquiry into the disaster they all bray together, reducing sense to
mere noise: '*Pett...Pett...Pett*'. *The Last Instructions* is a packed, dense
poem, because such constrictive superfluity of matter reflects the
degenerate stage the Restoration has reached. The sheer
numerousness of the corrupt blocks out the light. In a similar way

the crowded narrative of political manoeuvring proliferates in ineffectual activity, which prevents any conclusive action being taken. The Chancellor, like a comic butt, is repeatedly thwarted and repeatedly has to change his tactics. While the war was still in progress, although he already felt assured of an imminent peace, Clarendon tried, by means of the Excise Bill, to procure a large sum of money from parliament. But when the Bill was rejected, he found himself having to avoid the peace he had desired long enough for a new Land Tax Bill to be introduced, in another attempt to get money from parliament. Then, when these funds had been procured and immediately used up, the expected peace turned out to be a delusion. While ineffectual protests were made to Louis, in terms of scriptural and chivalric authority, no more forceful than a schoolboy's tittle-tattle ('the *Hollanders* ... are naughty Boys', 429-30), and while frantic attempts were made to raise funds and an army from nowhere, the Dutch effortlessly invaded the Thames. In the aftermath, however, a scapegoat for everything was found, ludicrously, in Pett; and safe for the time being and oblivious to the state of the nation, Clarendon was able to prorogue the hated parliament in full stammering comic *afflatus*:

> Trembling with joy and fear, *Hyde* then Prorogues,
> And had almost mistook and call'd them Rogues....
>   (861-2)

Such is Marvell's plot. The lineaments of this saga of desperate incompetence are comic, but its meaning for England was tragic indeed.

'With what small Arts the publick game they play' comments the poet about the administration (118). By comparison his own art, although angry and debased by dealing with 'this race of Drunkards, Pimps, and Fools' (12), is a skilful, competent and active mode of true insight: 'Say Muse, for nothing can escape thy sight' (147). Marvell's scrutinising and reforming art suggests the values of good government which can be opposed to the decadent regime. Fittingly, at the end of the poem, the king himself is exhorted to perform the task of purging his counsel and revealing his own light, true, clear and free. In doing so, he must perform the artist's role and depict the truth, which will then be glorious:

> And henceforth *Charles* only to *Charles* shall sit.
> His Master-hand the Ancients shall out-do

Himself the *Poet* and the *Painter* too.
　　(946-8)

Marvell sees the degeneracy of his times in terms of the
degradation of an ancient ideal. Even English ships are now 'sick'
and 'molting', a sad falling off from

　　...Those Oaken Gyants of the ancient Race,
　　That rul'd all Seas, and did our Channel grace.
　　　　(578-9)

The ships are like the stag, 'once the forests dread' but now helpless
and frightened (579-80). And blame for this debased state of affairs
must be apportioned. The ancient ideals of peace, liberty and
government by king in parliament have been prostituted and
desecrated by the current regime. 'Our *Lady State*' has been
violated and perverted (1). Marvell reaches for imagery of rape to
convey as intimately and shockingly as possible what has occurred.
Remembering Spenser's account of the marriage of the Thames
and Medway, which betokened harmony, Marvell now describes
the Dutch invasion:

　　When aged *Thames* was bound with Fetters base,
　　And *Medway* chast ravish'd before his Face,
　　And their dear Off-spring murder'd in their sight....
　　　　(743-5)

The imperial dreams and pastoral ideals of *The Faerie Queene* (IV,
xi) are painfully distant. De Ruyter's sailing up the Thames
represents the rape of that golden world (523-50). Against the
buzzing ineffectuality of Clarendon's defensive measures '*Ruyter*
the while' enters the river unopposed, calmly and forcefully. The
smooth rhetoric befits his easy triumph as with 'fresh Blood, fresh
Delight' he

　　Sail'd now among our Rivers undisturb'd:
　　Survey'd their Crystal Streams, and Banks so green,
　　And Beauties e're this never naked seen.
　　　　(524-6)

The helpless victims react with astonishment and distaste at de

Ruyter's masculine display, as

> Like am'rous Victors he begins to shave,
> And his new Face looks in the English Wave.
>   (533-4)

His civilised suavity is itself a corruption of innocence. The golden world hovers in the background of Marvell's poem and its value is associated with the fair, just and popular government now so patently lacking. Another echo of Spenser occurs when Clarendon's proroguing of parliament lets one John Mordaunt escape charges of having prostituted a young woman. Marvell's lines notice the parallel with Spenser's Mordaunt, a pitiful knight whose luxurious intemperance caused his true love's misery and death:

> Now *Mordant*, may, within his Castle Tow'r,
> Imprison Parents, and the Child deflowre.
>   (349-50)

Conversely those who defend the ancient liberty are chivalric heroes, if rather too naive: 'Such once *Orlando*, famous in *Romance*' (275). Incorporated into Marvell's sense of ancient virtue are popular traditions as well, the Skimmington Ride as a means to justice and the romance motif of a king who learns from a humble subject:

> Prudent Antiquity, that knew by Shame,
> Better than Law, Domestick Crimes to tame....
>   (387-8)
> Kings in the Country oft have gone astray,
> Nor of a Peasant scorn'd to learn the way.
>   (959-60)

Rather than restoring the golden world the Restoration regime has so degraded the ideal that antique or Elizabethan dreams can now be no more than far-off fairy-tales, recollected in distorted fragments to admonish the present. The world has grown so decrepit that any politician who seriously attempts to apply golden age rhetoric to the current situation must be regarded as suspect and dangerous. Henry Jermyn is one such: comfortable in

France and all too ready to swallow Louis's avowals of peace and protection, he

> ....thought the Golden Age was now restor'd,
> When Men and Women took each others Word.
>   (47-8)

But Louis is a modern: 'Nor Word, nor near Relation did revere' (441).

Marvell dwells on the perverse sexual appetites of the leading figures in the regime because this most strikingly conveys their debasement and their readiness to prostitute the pure noble spirit of the nation. The poem opens with a caricature of Jermyn the 'Stallion' of the court, bestial in his indulgence of 'Nature' (29-48); then the jealous, ambitious, falsely chaste Anne Hyde, who 'assay'd,/How after Childbirth to renew a Maid' (49-78); then Lady Castlemaine, who 'discern'd Love's Cause' through 'her Lacquies Drawers' and burlesques the true penitence of Mary Magdalen in a mock-mortification:

> Nor scorns to rub him down with those fair Hands;
> And washing (lest the scent her Crime disclose)
> His sweaty Hooves, tickles him 'twixt the Toes.
>   (81-2, 94-6)

Perversions of nature abound: Excise is a monster, begotten 'of a female Harpy' and abused in the most unnatural manner by her very begetter (131-46); promiscuity, venereal disease, lechery, impotence run through the poem obsessively, cumulatively violating the reader himself. The poem — and this Restoration world — is unified by a depravity which infects everything. The society as a whole is being physically corrupted, and from our intense desire to reject this world comes the acquiescence we give to any attempt, however extreme, to preserve one's inviolateness. For this reason the tragic episode of Douglas the loyal Scot forms the powerfully exalted climax of the poem. Douglas is a figure of primal purity, young, 'modest', temperate, and with only 'early Down' on his face almost pre-sexual, so that 'envious Virgins hope he is a Male' (652). Chastely he has fled 'Love Fires' but now in battle must face 'that horrid Day'. Rough, intemperate, deleterious, fate advances on Douglas's smoothness and purity of

form, his 'harden'd and cool'd ...Limbs'. Douglas anticipates his
fate from the start fearing only 'lest Heav'n fall, e're thither he
ascend'. The youth wants to avoid the circle of mortal
corruptibility by advancing directly from the pristine to the
regenerate state. Accordingly, inspired by 'the Honours of his
ancient Race' (673), he submits himself to immolation, sacrificing
himself in order to preserve his own immaculate form against
corruption and the shame of cowardice. His idea of love, entirely
contrary to the prostitution of the court-party, involves embracing
his own death — a purifying heroic destiny:

> Like a glad Lover, the fierce Flames he meets
> And tries his first embraces in their Sheets.
>   (677-8)

By this act of effective suicide, he divorces himself from the fallen
world. His mortal body melts away and leaves him restored to a
divine, spiritual state. He becomes an image of Apollo, now his
true radiance is revealed:

> His shape exact, which the bright flames infold,
> Like the Sun's Statue stands of burnish'd Gold...
> And, as on Angels Heads their Glories shine,
> His burning Locks adorn his Face Divine.
>   (679-80, 683-4)

He is also like the bee (in Martial, iv, 32), dying as it wished, shut
up in its own sweetness as if in amber. Marvell stresses the
wishfulness of Douglas's death, but locates the way to restoration
in that self-destructive impulse. The only way to avoid the
contamination of life in the fallen world is to close oneself off from
the world at the beginning. So debased has the world become that
there remains no hope of attaining ideal values in actuality: they
are only to be found out of existence. Douglas consummates his
lovely nature by dying. Similarly nature must attain its
consummation, its perfect end, through a 'short-circuiting' process
which involves its extinction at the moment of its inception. So
Marvell, through the glorification of Douglas, puts forward a
radical metaphysical critique of an unregenerate creation.

This overarching motive of *The Last Instructions* (the very title
conveys a sense of extremity) threatens to jeopardise Marvell's

reforming intentions. The English regime, in its desperation, has taken the self-destructive impulse too literally and facilitated its own ruin. Ships symbolic of substantial entities in the state are burnt or captured, the '*Loyal-London*', 'the true *Royal-Oak*', the '*Royal-James*' and at last the '*Charles*'. Some ships teach themselves to dive into the river, while other merchant ships are burnt by the administration in their 'officious fear' (709). Unfortunately, however, no mysterious regeneration occurs for these secular bodies: all the riches of the Indies merely 'take a short voyage underneath the *Thames*' (720). The consequences of corruption cannot, in practice, be evaded, any more than the administration can erase its guilt by blaming the disaster all on Pett, crying facilely:

Had [Pett] not built, none of these faults had bin;
If no Creation, there had been no Sin.
      (787-8)[27]

At the end Marvell reverts to reformatory admonition. Although the only impulse of restoration left may be the apocalyptic one of destruction and transcendence, Marvell hesitates to follow this extreme vision to its true end. In conclusion he turns his spectral images towards the king who by virtue of his symbolic power is deemed to be capable of altering the course of the nation's corrupt destiny — if only he can act as the true 'Sun of our World'.[28] We see Charles visited by night-visions. First there is a helpless, blindfolded virgin, representing '*England* or the Peace', whom Charles only just avoids raping (906). Then there are images of Louis, seizing Charles's sovereignty, and of Charles's executed father and assassinated grandfather. Oppression and death are the consequences of improperly used power. As a result of these visions a frightened Charles decides to get rid of his Chancellor Clarendon, but then comes the most nightmarish moment of all. He realises that among the possible replacements there are no honourable men. Unless virtuous men are found to advise and govern the king, the nation's purity — peace and independence — will never be secured. The poem ends ambiguously with a plea that the king should seek out good men. But the validity of the poet's vision of an irremediably corrupted world is preserved by our fears that there will be no such good men.

The Last Instructions is not in any strict sense a polemic. It is an *Anniversary* of the Government under the restored Charles which diminishes into fantasy and impossibility the dominant ideology of restoration and triumph. The government is shown to have failed utterly to live up to its historical claims. Elsewhere Marvell subverted the rhetoric of restoration more simply, to indicate the political corruption of the times. In *Clarendon's House-Warming* (written in 1667) he exposed the chancellor's overweening ambitions by casting his newly built house in the mould of a grandly symbolic public monument: 'his Palace Mosaick', 'this Temple, of War and of Peace' where the 'Idol of State' can sit contemplating 'Scepter and Crown'. In the *Further Advice to a Painter* a few years later he compared London to Rome, not on the basis of mutual glory but rather because both cities were equivalently degenerate. Increasingly, finally, it was obvious that an irreparable disjunction existed between the idealistic longing for restoration and any practical possibility of bringing about improvement by political means. But having despaired of a radical change in the nature of the state, Marvell, the experienced man of politics, accepted that it was only through inadequate polemical methods that even the most minor amelioration could be brought about. On the anniversary of the Restoration in 1672 a statue of Charles was erected at Stocks Market. Once again Marvell used the occasion to attack the regime's corruption.[29] But on this anniversary of restoration, he also gives the idea its baldest most unsymbolical, most utilitarian turn yet:

> But with all his faults restore us our King,
> As ever you hope in December for Spring,
> For though the whole world cannot shew such another,
> Yet we'd better by far have him than his brother.
> (57-60)

Marvell's grudging acquiescence in the idea of restoration deprives it of all its mystery and all its nostalgic colouring. The poet is doing more than just slight James. In putting forward the most cynical, most bluntly pragmatic argument for Charles's claim to the throne, he deftly overturns all Charles's pretensions to unique, divinely-favoured virtue and strips away a key tenet of Stuart panegyric.

7 Theatrical Restoration

Every schoolboy once knew that the Restoration of the king meant the restoration of the theatre and it was often claimed that that very connection meant the degeneration of drama. Such simplified views point the way to a more complicated truth. From the first, Restoration drama, as we shall see, was essentially political drama, drawing on the circumstances and attitudes that had led to the theatre's reopening for its peculiar matter and flavour. It was new and effective but like much political drama rather limited. Although it derived from earlier drama, its distinctive affiliation was with contemporary panegyric, political pamphleteering and propagandist display. From the beginning Charles's return had called forth theatrical show on the grandest scale. The numerous official occasions provided an opportunity for lavish, ingratiating spectacles, presented before the king, mostly organised by the City of London and performed in the streets or important civic buildings. John Tatham's *The Royal Oak* for the Lord Mayor's Day 1660 had 'twice as many Pageants and Speeches as have been formerly showen', and the coronation triumphs in 1661 were reckoned greater than anything seen before in England or Rome.[1] The tradition of street pageantry was an old one and incorporated emblematic imagery, verbal and visual, with a long ancestry of political service. At the Restoration, public displays shared the desire of printed panegyric to praise the event while also determining what form the renewed nation should take. Like the writers, the organisers of pageantry sought to inspire in their audiences an exalted sensation of wonder.[2]

That entrepreneurial classicist John Ogilby produced an account of the coronation celebrations in 1661 and the next year a luxury edition followed, massively commemorating the event. *The Entertainment of His Most Excellent Majestie Charles II, In His Passage through the City of London to His Coronation* (1662), replete with engravings and source commentary, offers a comprehensive and handy manual of the battery of iconographical motifs applied at the Restoration. The work is of value in documenting the foremost theatrical impulse of the new age, an impulse which grew, in Ogilby's words, out of 'that inexpressible Happiness, which these Kingdoms have received by the glorious Restauration of our Sovereign to his Throne, and of us His Subjects to our Laws, Liberties and Religion, after a dismal Night of Usurpation and Oppression...' (p.1.). The coronation was actual, yet uniquely remarkable, 'the occasion thereof being the most Miraculous, and Joyful of any, that ever happened'.[3] To express the inexpressible Ogilby heaps up precedents in his commentary only to have them surpassed by the here and now: the triumphs may imitate 'the antient *Romanes*, who, at the return of their Emperours, erected *Arches* of Marble', but London's 'far exceed theirs in Number, and stupendious Proportions' (pp. 1-2). London can proudly style itself S.P.Q.L. (p.31). The numerous Virgilian quotations in the inscriptions and mottos on the triumphal arches and in the speeches of the allegorical personifications make unmistakeable the panegyrical claim that Charles has inherited the mantle of empire and brought about a golden age in the state. A painting on the first arch, depicting Charles's arrival at Dover, is captioned '*ADVENTUS AUG.*', an inscription 'often found among the Coyns of the *Roman* Emperours upon a peaceful return' (p.21). Another painting, of the king chasing Usurpation into hell's jaws, has the motto 'VOLVENDA DIES EN ATTULIT ULTRO' (*Aeneid*, IX. 7, used in 1660 by Cowley as the epigraph to his *Restoration Ode*). A picture of 'a Trophy with decollated Heads' is captioned 'ULTOR A TERGO DEUS' said to refer 'more particularly to that History of *Augustus*' who having revenged his father's blood 'consecrated a *Temple*' (pp. 25-6). The upper paintings on the first arch's east side '*are Ruinous, representing the Disorder the Kingdom was in, during His Majestie's Absence*', while those on the west side '*are finished, to represent the Restauration of our Happiness by His Majestie's Arrival; the Motto*, FELIX TEMPORUM REPARATIO' (p. 37). Over the great table on this first arch, which represents the overthrow of Rebellion, Confusion and Usurpation by Monarchy and Loyalty, is that key Virgilian phrase, from the fourth eclogue:

REDEUNT SATURNIA REGNA
  (p.37)

Romanness is established as a characteristic glory of Charles's

Restoration, both as an item of praise for what has been achieved already and as an ideal to be followed. Virgil and secondarily Claudian, the panegyrist of imperial Rome, are claimed as the harbingers of both Charles's poets and Charles's regime.[4] But these parallels are, in an important sense, conditional. It is not simply a matter of grafting Roman attributes on to Charles, the 'PATER PATRIAE', the 'MENS OMNIBUS UNA', the 'UNITAS' (pp. 126, 133-4). Displayed in public, the relationship between Roman glory and the king's return is made to depend on the people. Ogilby openly claims a hortatory purpose in recounting the coronation, '*that the Ingenuous may be instructed, the Malevolent silenced, and Misinformations prevented*'.[5] The first triumphal arch in the parade called on the people to be loyal. As the king passed, a sensational, terrifying figure of Rebellion, 'mounted on a Hydra' (p.13), seized the stage and spoke:

> *I am Hell's Daughter,* Satan's *Eldest Child....*
> *I Sorc'ry use, and hang Men in their Beds,*
> With Common-wealths, *and* Rotas *fill their Heads,*
> *Making the Vulgar in Fanatique Swarms*
> *Court Civil War, and dote on Horrid Arms....*
> (p.41)

The gap between mythological Satanic manipulation and topical reference to Harrington's Rota club is bridged easily here, to warn the people while exculpating individuals of their anti-monarchical crimes. Then Monarchy rises, represented by hierarchically arranged statues of James I and Charles I ('DIVO') and Charles II, and chases Rebellion off. Rebellion had attacked the 'Succession', which is assimilated here to Virgil's 'VOLVENDA DIES', translated by Ogilby as 'Successive Time', because history runs with the dynastic line of succession (pp. 28-47). The little drama urges the people's responsibility to the overall good, illustrated on the arch by a sociably Virgilian bee:

> *a Swarm of Bees, whetting their Stings, the Word,*
> PRO REGE EXACUUNT.
> *Pliny* ha's observed, that of Animals none, but a Bee, ha's a King. Their Loyalty to him he ha's at large described.
> (p.39)

And if the people do their duty, they have a right to ask the king to do his. 'The Second *Arch*, which is *Naval*' (p. 43) urges on Charles the development of the navy and related arts. Charles is celebrated as Neptunus Britannicus and his royal oak appears as Robur Britannicus 'in allusion to His Majestie's Royal *Navy*, those Floating Garrisons made of Oak. For Themistocles ha's observ'd, that *Whosoever desires a secure Dominion by Land, must first get the Dominion of the Sea*' (p.37). Along with the navy 'Arithmetick, Geometry, Astronomy and Navigation' will improve, and, most important of all, trade too. Personifications of Europe, Asia, Africa and America appear, paying tribute to London and '*bearing the* Arms of the *Companies* trading into those parts' (p.67). Immediately above Neptune on the arch appears an image of 'the EXCHANGE', the centre of commerce, so intimately are the two connected. The attached motto contains another reference to industrious bees (from *Georgic* IV, 249-50): 'GENERIS LAPSI SARCIRE RUINAS', which Ogilby '*speaking of the Industry of Bees*', translates 'they strive the Ruins to repair/Of their fal'n Nation, and they fill th' *Exchange...*' (p.66). The appeal is for mercantile aggression to improve the economy and the defence of wide territorial waters is part of this. 'The Dominion of the BRITTISH *Seas*' belongs to 'the *King* of ENGLAND', 'the Antiquity whereof being purposely, and at large declared by MR. SELDEN' (p.52). Ogilby strengthens the argument for *mare clausum* by reprinting large, intensely patriotic sections of *Poly-Olbion*, the Elizabethan-Jacobean poem by Michael Drayton, Selden's friend. The translation of empire from Rome to London is mediated symbolically by ancient British rights and the rollicking upshot is active hostility towards England's rivals. In Charles's name the sailors in the pageant cry:

> *King* CHARLES, *King* CHARLES, *great* Neptune *of the Main*!
> > *Thy Royal Navy rig,*
> > *And We'll not care a Fig*
> *For* France, *for* France, *the* Netherlands, *nor* Spain.
>   (p.107)

Such high expectations of marine supremacy were bitterly dashed in the second Dutch War and the disappointment reflected badly on the ideas of imperial restoration raised in 1660-61. The third arch more amiably depicted the Temple of Concord, representing the return of peace and abstract virtue:

Comes not here the King of Peace,
  Who, the Stars so long fore-told,
From all Woes should us release,
  Converting Iron-times to Gold?
    (p.135)

The fourth arch, the Garden of Plenty, took up this theme hyperbolically in terms of a pastoral vision of an economic paradise, 'the glitt'ring Plenty of this Golden Age' (p.165), made possible by Charles as a worldly messiah. The universal peace 'after the Victory at Actium, about the time of the Nativity of Our SAVIOUR' was matched, Ogilby explained, by 'the fortunate arrival of our Sacred Sovereign into His Kingdome, at what time there was a *GENERAL PEACE* throughout all *Christendom*' (pp.142-3). The propagandist imagination of the coronation triumphs was neither circumspect nor passive.

By contrast the many shows arranged by John Tatham on behalf of City interests are popular and down-to-earth, though a similar repertoire of stock motifs is used to arouse the onlookers' wonder, as Neptune says to Charles

Your *Actions* have created *Wonders* (Sir)...
Convinc'd the *Atheist* in a powerful sense,
Who ne're till now did own a *Providence*....[6]

Touches of low comedy occur, in *The Royal Oake* (1660) when mummerzet-speaking rustics dance around the tree and in *Aqua Triumphalis* (1662) when a waterman frankly urges the king to have legitimate heirs: 'don't take it in dudgeon that I am so familiar with Thee ... though I Thee Thee and Thou Thee, I am no Quaker' (p.6). With naive loyalty, honesty is an old-world virtue too. The merriment of Tatham's Restoration pageants contrasts with the pious sobriety of his pre-Restoration work. Among other wonders Charles had achieved for his people 'Government, and pleasure too'.[7] It sounds like a Utopian election slogan and, indeed, when Tatham celebrates the industry needed in Charles's nation, it is in terms of the pre-lapsarian harmony of work and joy:

  Though *Adam* a Delver was
    Yet *Eve* his wife did Spin,
    No doubt a bonny Lasse

For she brought the knack on't in.
Then fall to your work and sing,

Chorus
    Then fall to your work and sing,
    For when we have done
    None under the Sun
    Shall be merrier than we, but the King.[8]

Tatham used his displays to push the interests of the guildhalls and
the City, but in a manner which complimented the king. His
petition for St Paul's to be rebuilt, for example, was couched in
terms of the good Ethelbert's restoring of the national church,
centuries earlier: 'And *Paul's*, be *Paul's* be you but *Ethelbert*'.[9]
Underlying Tatham's work (and Ogilby's) is a more specific
concern than unthinking support of the king. Tatham is not
reverentially aristocratic. He is chiefly concerned with effective,
virtuous administration, which will help the City. '*Wisdome* and
Magistracy shall be One', he writes, and

A *Magistrate* should have a careful Eye
To see the Poor have Work, not Starve and Dye ....[10]

Finally, in Tatham's last pageant of the period in 1664, the
hortatory vision could take on a rather different perspective, as the
ideal and the reality conspicuously diverged and panegyric
became criticism.

The kinship between Restoration pageantry and verse
panegyric is paralleled by the relationship between stage drama
and pamphlet literature.[11] Both before and after the Restoration
controversialists cast their versions of contemporary history into
the form of plays.[12] These unacted tract plays share the vigorous
satirical energy of the pamphlet writing of the 1640s and 1650s,
presenting an extreme, simplistic, but effective burlesque of the
issues of the day. A royalist pamphlet in 1660 takes the form of a
play called *Cromwell's Conspiracy. A Tragy-Comedy, Relating to our
latter Times*, in which Cromwell is made to caricature his own
political theory:

If Kings do not obey their Subjects, They May imprison, banish
or put them to death.[13]

In such works historical figures and events are converted into sensationalistic, grotesquely distorted stereotypes, establishing the models real playwrights were to follow. *Hell's Higher Court of Justice* (1661) presents a definitive version of Cromwell as the machiavellian, Satanic villain:

> And when hereafter will name a Villaine
> Soaked in all mischeifes call him by his name,
> If you here of a man under the skies,
> Has acted all deceits and told all lies,
> Has killed his Soveraign and inslaved the people
> Destroid the Church and pulled down the steeple
> Acted impieties beyond Lucifer
> Let him be stil'd by his name Oliver....[14]

These tract dramas exemplify the thoroughly polemic ancestry of topical stage plays. One of the first, 'acted Many Times with Great Applause', was Tatham's *The Rump: Or the Mirrour of the Late Times* (1660), which adopted the style of pamphlet satirists.[15] Dramatists readily used qualities, such as reductive lampoon, or masque-like exaltation, or biblical religiosity, which had proved their worth elsewhere in the panegyrical arena. Anything that bound the stage to the new Stuart age could be accommodated: Anthony Sadler, author of *The Subjects Joy for the Kings Restoration*, a masque about David, proclaimed that his piece, wondrously in keeping with the times, was 'Strange, but yet Pertinent; New, but yet Serious; and Theatrical, but yet Sacred'.[16]

Comic dramatists were quick to realise the potential of the opposition between Cavaliers and puritans, and Elizabethan and Jacobean anti-puritan plays provided good precedents. Cowley's *Cutter of Coleman-Street*, acted in December 1661, and Robert Howard's *The Committee*, acted in October 1662, exposed the folly and corruption of fanatics. Tragic dramatists, however, faced a harder task. It was difficult to raise contemporary history above the topical to an heroic level, especially since the key event of recent times, the king's Restoration, was so thoroughly untragic. One solution was to present a story which ran parallel to the rebellion, Interregnum and Restoration in some respects only, allowing the audience to compare and contrast the stage representation with historical experience. John Wilson described his tragedy *Andronicus Comnenius* (written in 1662) in this way:

A Story of the Eastern Empire, between the years 1179 and 1183; and such perhaps, as might not be thought altogether unparalel to what our selves have seen, were not the one, but too fresh in our memories and the other, too far remov'd from our knowledge.[17]

Wilson's appeal to the audience's sceptical intelligence befits a play which persistently attacks the unthinking gullibility of the people, 'constant to nothing, but inconstancie', drunkenly crying for 'anything, but what we are: Liberty — Liberty — Liberty'. They play straight into the hands of the tyrant Andronicus whose divide-and-rule tactics are like those of 1658-60:

> We must have parties,
> And Antiparties; Factions and Antifaction;
> Untill they break to nothing ....

Wilson's play analyses the workings of tyranny, and the description of Andronicus in I.i resembles Clarendon's famous portrait of Cromwell:

> He is a Prince of the most daring soul
> Er'e dropt from Heaven; industrious, vigilant,
> Kind, affable, magnificent: —
> Yet all this good, Nay, all his lusts and passions
> Are slaves to his Ambition: Take him there,
> Nothing can hold him; Lawes, Religion, All
> Sacred, or civil, are no more....[18]

In the end the tyrant is opposed by the noble Lord Constantinus and the true heir Isacius Angelus, symbolically named parallels to Monck and Charles. The state wreaks its revenge on Andronicus and a restoration occurs. But it is a commonsensical, lukewarm restoration — 'though we're not in *Plato's* Commonwealth ... the first stone is laid' — and the ideal of a truly regenerate world seems impossibly remote. Despite the happy ending, Wilson's understanding of politics is cynical and at times grisly:

> Now I see that Nature took a fall when young...
> What's all that noise, and cry of publick good,

> But a conspiracy of the richer sort,
> To grind the poor, and fence themselves with Laws,
> To keep that safely, they've unjustly got?[19]

More's *Utopia* is recalled here in an angrily Rochesterian vein. The triumph of restoration can be espoused only partially — and this must have goaded some members of the audience.[20]

The Usurper by Edward Howard ('foolish Ned'), acted early in 1664, is a more straightforward tragedy of tyranny. Pepys saw it in 1668 when Restoration ecstasies had cooled and found it distasteful, partly because it was naively topical, partly because it was vindictive (he had earlier disapproved of the exhumation of the regicides' bodies): 'there was *The Usurper*; a pretty good play in all but what is designed to resemble Cromwell and Hugh Peters, which is mighty silly'.[21] The play considered itself a kind of exhumation, repeatedly enacting Cromwell's death as an expiation for anti-monarchical sins:

> As now this Play, by some such Magick Call
> Has rais'd a bold Usurper up, to Fall...
>
> Faith let him live, if but to dye agen,
> His Crime was horrid, and it is not fit,
> One death of the Usurper Expiate it....

The concluding restoration here is both literal ('the Secluded Members of the Senate do every minute Creep out of their obscurities to admiration') and ideal, covenanted by a double marriage. As the play's penitential plot is worked out the guilty people receive the king's pardon:

> There shall be an Indemnity for those
> Whose frailty, and not malice, made 'em Act
> Under the Tyrant.

Howard's play depends for its effect on the audience's implication in what has been portrayed on stage.[22]

Another version of the exotic Andronicus story crops up in *The Unfortunate Usurper* (author unknown, probably performed 1662-3). The plot explicitly foreshadows Charles's Restoration when a prophet arises to foretell that not only will the good Isaacus succeed the tyrant, but centuries later 'Great *Britains* Titular Angel' will purge the land, allowing 'great *Charles*' to steer the ship of state away from 'that *Monstrous Whale*', the Rump. It is a neat theatrical moment because the prophecy is seen to be self-fulfilling, taking place on a stage restored by the restored monarchy. The prophet has predicted 'what many years hence should be/Acted on *Englands* Stage'. The audience is asked to recognise that the prophecy has come true literally, on the stage of the theatre, and this leads to the endorsement of the larger claim about the stage of the nation.[23] In these plays it is assumed that the audience's engagement with theatrical effects will be continuous with an involvement in external political concerns. Behind this assumption lies a special relationship between the theatre-going public and the king. Tatham realised there was a crucial difference between his own political pageants and earlier Stuart masques:

> We hope Your Majesty will not suppose
> You're with your *Johnsons* and your *Inigoes*;
> And though you make a Court, y'are in the Citty,
> Whose vein is to be humble, though not witty....
> This day You *shew* as well as *see*, for You
> Are both our *Triumph* and *Spectator* too.[24]

In the Caroline masque, it has been argued, the king was the *primum mobile* and the masque defined and refined the centring all-embracing power of kingship.[25] In Restoration theatrical forms a different concept of kingship was adumbrated. Charles had, technically, been invited back by the English people. He was the people's chosen agent and responsible to the people. Accordingly no longer could a king-centred vision be portrayed in pageants and heroic plays, but rather an insistence that by looking to the public good the king should actively earn his central place. The centripetal power of kingship was represented as contingent. Concretely the organisation of the new Restoration theatres reflected this attitude: rather than at the focal point, the king now sat among the audience, hierarchically related to the public but not dominant. More importantly the plays presented ideas of kingship which were not designed to engulf the spectators, but to be contemplated by them. The audience was far less homogeneous than at Caroline masques. The plays aimed at different sectors of the audience, whose judgement could be independent of the court line.[26] Symbolically speaking, the king's presence in the theatre opened him to the attitudes of independent groups in the community. It was a limited exercise in participatory democracy and Pepys, for one, allowed his frank opinionativeness free rein.

Everywhere in prologues and epilogues these playwrights voice their concern with the audience's judgement, appealing for approval, condemning standards and generally worrying about the nature of the audience's judicial powers. Irresistibly, it seems, the question of judgement is considered in political language. Not only would a verdict often depend on a play's political content, but also, more profoundly, the free exercise of judgement in an effort to arrive at the unprejudiced, unfanatical authority of truth was as important an ideal politically as critically. If judgement was not directed to or by authority, chaos would break out: as Dryden wrote later

> The Plays that take on our Corrupted Stage,
> Methinks resemble the distracted Age;
> Noise, Madness, all unreasonable Things,
> That strike at Sense, as Rebels do at Kings!
> The stile of Forty One our Poets write,
> And you are grown to judge like Forty Eight.[27]

Whether a play's true quality resided in the work innately or lay in the hands of the public was a problem which, typically, worried Dryden. His brother-in-law Sir Robert Howard had glibly claimed that only the public, not the author, could perceive a play's worth, but Dryden, in the *Defence of an Essay of Dramatic Poesy* (1668), resisted: 'The liking or disliking of the people gives the play the domination of good or bad, but does not really make or constitute it such'.[28] Appropriately the disagreement was called '*the civil wars of censure*'.[29] Dryden, although arguing an ultimately absolutist position, was careful to allow for the need of the audience to arrive freely at acknowledgement of the one truth. The successful playwright like the successful ruler is he who can persuade people to submit to his authority freely. 'The poet is then to endeavour an absolute dominion over the minds of the spectators', but the spectators must judge for themselves that the poet's worth warrants his dominion.[30] Finally Dryden defended his critical position against the charge of being 'magisterial': 'my whole discourse was sceptical', containing 'several opinions, all of them left doubtful, to be determined by the readers in general'.[31] The need for freedom of judgement was potentially in conflict with the belief in the absoluteness of truth, but it was precisely this grey area which gave Restoration drama leeway to be politically lively and effective.

Most of the 'serious' plays of the 1660s support the Restoration in a loosely orthodox, popular manner. It is possible to describe a sub-genre, the tragedy of tyranny, which presents vivid, schematic images of history to heighten the audience's gratitude for Charles's return and its own era. *The Unfortunate Usurper*, *The Usurper* and *Andronicus Comnenius* can be grouped with exotic stories, such as *The Indian Queen* by Dryden and Robert Howard, and *The Indian Emperour* by Dryden. To these can be added plays from English history, such as John Caryll's *The English Princess*, and a number of Roman plays. There was a special vogue for translations from Corneille: in Katherine Philip's *Pompey*, acted in 1663, the word 'restore' runs like a *leitmotif*; in *Pompey the Great*, translated by Waller, Sedley, Edward Filmer, Sidney Godolphin and Charles Sackville, acted in January 1664, the martyred Charles is identified with Pompey in a piece of pietistic sensationalism; and a version of *Horace* by Katherine Philips and John Denham was performed in February 1668. The powerful, prescriptive civic ideals of Romanness also inspired original work, including Robert Howard's *The Vestal-Virgin* (acted February 1665) and John Dover's war-mongering *The Roman Generalls* (published in 1667 in the wake of the Dutch war). By amalgamating these plays one can imagine a typical drama of restoration. Their styles usually aim at exalted verse, rhyming or not, and their historical plots, whether exotic, Roman or native, usually have imperial overtones. Generally there is a monstrous, unlawful tyrant who is deposed by a small group of good statesmen, with the help of an ideal hero or heroine who usually turns out to be the rightful ruler. A Restoration occurs, if not of the monarch then at least of law and order, and this is underlined metaphorically by the preservation of a woman's virtue, by which innocence is restored to the state. In *The Usurper*, for example, the true heir marries a virtuous lady who had narrowly escaped being raped by the usurping tyrant.

Dryden and Howard's *The Indian Queen* (acted January 1664) brings many of these features together and links them with Charles. A happy Indian kingdom, formerly ruled by a mild fatherly king, falls victim to the usurping queen Zempoalla and her ambitious adviser. To oppose hereditary monarchy, Zempoalla uses the republican position which refused to recognise authority descending from conquest:

> Let dull successive Monarchs mildly sway:
> Their conquering Fathers did the Laws forsake....
>   (III,i,113-14)[32]

But the villains are defeated by an unknown warrior who turns out to be the old monarch's long-lost son Montezuma. He is 'the gaulless Dove' (II.i.42), a phrase commonly applied to Charles II in Restoration panegyric.[33] His power, resistless 'like the vast seas', ensures his Restoration (I,i,61). Having proved himself in action his place is confirmed by the revelation of his legitimacy:

> King *Montezuma* their loud shouts proclaim,
> The City rings with their new Sovereigns name....
>   (V,i,194)

By the end all the obstacles between Montezuma and his beloved Orazia have been removed and, despite the tragic tones proper to the deaths that have occurred, the conclusion inaugurates a happier age. The mood fulfils the prophetic prologue, where the conquest of the New World by the Old — England's imperial expansion — was seen to initiate a higher stage of beatitude for the Americas: 'Mercy flows' from the explorers' looks, 'more gentle than our Native Innocence' acknowledges an Indian child (15-16)!

John Caryll's *The English Princess*, sub-titled *The Death of Richard III*, is another, more interesting example of the type. Unlike Shakespeare's *Richard III* the emphasis here is on the end of Richard's reign, the king's desperation and the extensive planning by Richmond to replace Richard with Elizabeth, providentially destined to be the true ruler. In Act III a Prior prophesies Richmond's eventual success and from this moment the play has a strong, upward, restorative movement. Richard, who had also styled himself protector, was often associated with Cromwell and with Cromwell's son, 'Richard the Fourth', and the connection made the old historical story newly relevant;[34] as the epilogue points out:

Richard is dead; and now begins your Reign:

Let not the Tyrant live in you again.
For though one Tyrant be a Nation's Curse,
Yet Commonwealths of Tyrants are much worse:
Their Name is Legion; And a *Rump* (you know)
In Cruelty all *Richards* does outgo.

Richard is an eloquent, lascivious monster who has abused the most natural bonds:

Two Paricides did his foul hands imbrue,
When he his Soveraign in his Nephew slew.

His tyranny is aimed at 'the destruction of Mankind' and the rape of 'fairest Innocence'. Princess Elizabeth has the double value of legitimacy and virtue, but Richard is a cynic who cannot conceive of higher values, nor understand how 'frail Woman, Natures slightest thing' could outbrave his force. He tempts virtue like a serpent and virtue's rescue from this violation, the redeeming of 'the Princess sacred Life', is crucial to the working out of the plot. Finally virtue, conquest and legal right combine in the ideal ruling couple, Richard and Elizabeth, and Providence is seen to be in harmony with human organisation as the crown is 'impos'd by us and by the Hand of Fate'. The play shows history put to work. Not only does the historical precedent underline the significance of Charles's restoration, it also provides historical validity. The sequence of succession seems truly to reflect providence's overall plan. In addition the connections of Richard III's downfall with Elizabeth I and the Elizabethan stage suggest further glorious historical precedents to be reachieved and surpassed in Charles's golden age.[35] The Prior's vision of Stuart empire in *The English Princess* is the destined culmination of an historical sequence stretching from Bosworth Field to the Restoration:

Then he describes the Man (and you are he)
Who must redeem this Realm from Tyrannie;
Who after Conquest shall by force of Love
More then by War, our happiness improve...
They shall an Union make of louder Fame,
And of two Kingdoms one great Empire frame.
But after this a Tempest does succeed,
Which Hell shall with contagious Vapours feed;

This Tempest will produce a deed so black,
That Murther then shall an example lack.
But from this dark Eclipse a Prince will rise,
Who shall all Vertues of your Race comprise.
Forreign, and Native Foes he shall o'recome,
With force abroad, with lenity at home.
Though in our sep'rate World, this happy Land
The center of his Power will fixed stand,
Yet here the wide Circumf'rence must not end,
But with the Ocean joyntly shall extend.

Such is the Stuart dream of *renovatio*.[36]

The first new 'serious' drama on the Restoration stage was Sir William Davenant's *The Siege of Rhodes*, in two parts. It had started as an operatic entertainment performed privately in 1656, and combined two distinctly aristocratic influences, the Caroline masque and the new continental music drama.[37] The full post-Restoration version strains for exaltation, the self-conscious expression of a high new age. Davenant's aim is to refine and retail heroic ideals 'nor have I wanted care to render the ideas of greatness and virtue pleasing and familiar', he says in his dedication to Clarendon. The refinement of dramatic poetry signified the change in the nation, freed from those enemies of heroic plays who 'entertain the people with a seditious Farce of their own counterfeit gravity'. Davenant roundly declares his allegiance and his play's political implications:

> it proceeds from the same mind, not to be pleas'd with Princes on the stage, and not to affect them in the throne; for those are ever most inclin'd to break the mirror, who are unwilling to see the images of such as have just authority over their guilt.[38]

Davenant's concern is with the ideals supposed to underlie historical events. In Part One the agent of Christian Rhodes's salvation from the pagan Turks is a virtuous woman who 'is all harmony'. In her reunion with her husband she embodies the sacred, platonic ideal of concord. In Part Two she is 'a high and good example' and the political plot is conceived almost entirely in terms of domestic vicissitudes. The nation's fortunes are seen to be crucially dependent on individual virtue:

Pow'r is an arch which ev'ry common hand

Does help to raise to a magnific height....[39]

Political ideals are established in terms of abstractions and of individual emotions: at the end, though Rhodes remains besieged, the restoration of the lady's innocence is sufficient cause for rejoicing. Dryden inherited Davenant's heroic exaltations and in his tragedies and poetic comedies he translated his ideological thought largely into the language of abstract human experiences such as love, friendship, honour and passion. *The Indian Emperour* (acted 1665), *Tyrannick Love* (acted 1669), and *The Conquest of Granada*, Parts One and Two (acted in 1671), move away from the overthrow of tyranny and the triumph of monarchy to emphasise, instead, the power of ideal virtue in action. Almanzor, the hero of *The Conquest of Granada*, is characteristically the restorer and not the restored. In the course of the action he 'restores' (the word is used each time) two thrones, the liberty of a king's brother and wife, his own troubled spirit, and also promotes Isabella's plans for improving her country:

> At once to freedom and true faith restored,
> Its old religion and its ancient lord.[40]

The ideal hero provides a moral example to the audience rather than an object to be celebrated. More than ever the stress falls on the people's obligation to subject themselves to the agents of divine power. The play was dedicated to James, Duke of York, and in the dedication Dryden expressed his wish 'to restore to you those ideas, which in the more perfect part of my characters I have taken from you'. Almanzor was a portrait of James designed to inspire awe-struck loyalty in the audience and to urge the Duke too to greater virtue: 'the feigned hero inflames the true; and the dead virtue animates the living'.[41] The drama is still in political service (and not all playwrights shared Dryden's views) although the idea of restoration has become disembodied.

The most popular heroic dramatist was Roger Boyle, Earl of Orrery, but, perhaps in sympathy with his public, his weary, wooden plays betray a much more sceptical, half-hearted commitment to idealism than Dryden's. Boyle was a thoroughly political creature, opportunistic, pragmatic, lacking deep ideological allegiance throughout the 1650s and 1660s. His record of political changeability prevented him prospering quite as much as he would have liked under Charles and he played a sordid part in · the attacks on Ormonde during the purging of Clarendonians after the Dutch war. Boyle was one of the new self-interested politicians, neglecting both parliament's rights and the king's prerogative as it suited him.[42] His plays emphasise mechanical plot. Complex, schematic alliances and oppositions are set up, exhibiting a dramatic arithmetic akin to William Petty's political arithmetic so popular with new Restoration social theorists. In *The History of Henry the Fifth* (acted in 1664) the Dauphin loses his crown to Henry and ecclesiastical scholars maintain that, anyway, the Dauphin was a usurper and Henry was the 'Lawful Heir' to 'this Crown' (V.vii.529). The convenient readjustment of history is presented baldly, almost cynically. Naturally, now Henry has won the crown, the nobles and the people all agree that he has heaven's sanction. But the play's forced endorsement of policy drains most of the joy from its vision of restoration:

> A States-man all but int'rest may forget,
> And only ought in his own strength to trust:
> 'Tis not a States-man's Vertue to be just....
>   (II.ii.34-6)

The Black Prince (acted in 1667) repeats the elements of English history even more perfunctorily. Pepys commented that the play's 'contrivance... was almost the same that had been in his two former plays'.[43] The play presents a bland notion of *de facto* sovereignty effectively removed from involvement in and accountability for government: 'Kings partake not Sins which Subjects do' is its summary motto (III.ii. 226). *Mustapha* (acted 1665) is a descendant of *The Siege of Rhodes* in which the virtuous Christian Queen of Hungary just manages to restore her young son to his rightful throne. The Queen is remarkably constant in the play's shifting world, but her absolute value, while making her a powerful *example*, also makes her politically vulnerable. The necessities of policy bring out the precariousness of values like innocence and honour:

> But Honour, Madam, quickly will forget
> And lose it self whilst it does counterfeit....
>   (IV.i.145-6)

Only disillusioned, dictatorial efficiency can maintain political stability. In Orrery's plays values are undermined by policies which resemble those of the Restoration regime. Leaving out the 'sublime', Wilson Knight's description of Restoration tragedy is peculiarly applicable to Orrery's work: 'these dramas are sublime problem plays rather than tragedies. They leave us unrestful; evils were too near and too appalling for acceptance, enjoyment and catharsis....'[44] The wish to idealise is always slightly out of line with the experience and capacity of the 'poor madame-muse'. [45]

The theatrical works of the 1660s expressed localised, polemical opinions across a spectrum ranging from Dryden's vision of omnipotent heroic monarchy to Tatham's stress on the primacy of the City's interests. This circumscribed range was significantly extended by Sir Robert Howard's play *The Great Favourite: or, The Duke of Lerma* (acted in February 1668). In the years immediately before the appearance of his play, Howard had been a central figure in the fall of Clarendon. While Buckingham managed the movement for the Chancellor's impeachment in the Lords, Howard managed it in the Commons. Coventry and Arlington, sharing Howard's anti-Clarendonian feeling, had been instrumental in Clarendon's initial downfall, but stopped short of pressing for an impeachment on treasonous grounds, because they realised the dangerous precedent a concocted impeachment would set. Buckingham and Howard, however, were determined to prevent the Chancellor's possible return to power. Others fell in Clarendon's wake, and when the attack turned to Ormonde (the Lord-Lieutenant of Ireland, one of the least tainted politicians of the time), Orrery joined forces with Buckingham and Howard, fellow playwrights, and the severity of Ormonde's fate was softened only by Arlington's intervention. The force behind these shabby, treacherous, feuding manoeuvres was, above all, Buckingham's ambition and, although others prospered, it was Buckingham's reputation which rose to a height in the aftermath. He was associated with the wits and also with prominent non-conformists, and had popular support. He 'thinks to be another Oliver', wrote a hostile observer. Buckingham's temporary triumph was, however unpleasantly, a victory for parliament and a rekindling of radical politics.[46]

When Pepys saw Howard's *The Great Favourite* he thought it highly controversial:

The play designed to reproach our King with [his] mistress; that

I was troubled for it, and expected it should be interrupted; but it ended all well, which salved all. The play a well-writ and good play; only, its design I did not like, of reproaching the King —but altogether, a very good and most serious play.[47]

Howard's play, as the preface admits, is an adaptation of an older work, possibly a lost piece by Ford or another Caroline dramatist, such as James or Henry Shirley.[48] It was common practice in the Restoration to rework earlier plays: allusion to a 'happier' Stuart world was a means of upbraiding the present and, more importantly, political points could be made more sharply by grafting contemporary characters and situations on to familiar stories and archetypes. Howard's criticism of the king's promiscuousness is no less obvious, though it is less impertinent, when it comes as part and parcel of an old play. For reasons of caution, and to leave room for the audience's judgement, Howard's play, like many others, moves in and out of alignment with contemporary matters. *The Great Favourite*, however, deserves to be called the first opposition drama. It offers a sustained critique of Charles's regime and provides evidence that, by the end of the decade, the theatres freely and even dominantly exercised the right of supporting a new faction and opposing the old-guard architects of the Restoration settlement. As Marvell and the Dutch War satirists applied the rhetoric of restoration to the improvement of government, so in *The Great Favourite* the dramatic form of restoration — the deposition of the tyrant — is turned to justify a change of administration.

The tyrant is deposed and the monarch restored: but this tyrant is no longer a caricature of Cromwell; rather he is the king's favourite and highest counsellor, so bloated with ambition that he has effectively usurped the throne. Howard has summoned up the charged memory of the rebellion in order to point to a new threat to the nation's ancient liberties from within the court itself. The play opens with the death of the old king and the dissident murmurings of the counsellor Lerma: 'These decay'd Out-Houses shew the Chief Building/Wants Reparation'.[49] At the swearing in of the new young king, the situation resembles the Restoration in 1660. All must be judged, punished or rewarded, loyal oaths must be sworn and the government must be put straight: ' 'till all things are dispos'd in better order'.[50] But Lerma has conceived his plans. He will use his virtuous daughter to influence the susceptible king, and he manipulates his allies Caldroon and the Confessor into positions of power, 'the new *Indian* Stars' who use the king's majesty as the 'Pawn of all their Villanies'.[51] The situation is reaching a crisis when the noble Lord Medina reveals the state of affairs to the king: but at the last minute Lerma appears in Cardinal's robes, immune from prosecution. He has bought the position from the Pope and makes a parting speech, ironically inveighing against the unprincipled rapacity of ambition:

> It is your Countreys cause until full grown
> In long sought power, then it proves your own.[52]

The court has been cozened by the great favourite. At the end the nation's purity can only be restored if Lerma's still virtuous daughter will legally marry the king:

> You sav'd us all, preserve your Nation now...
> That Vertue still may flow from you, their Spring.[53]

But she remains undecided at the sober conclusion.

Howard's language, by contrast with the blandness of Orrery's and idealising smoothness of Dryden's, is 'satyrically' rough, bathetic, murky and sensationalistic. Traditional political ideas are grotesquely perverted in strained conceits, for example:

> Such a magnetick Power's in a King,
> Where he but kindly touches, others cling....[54]

The language often approaches Jacobean pastiche, echoing plays such as *Hamlet, Macbeth, Measure for Measure* and *Volpone* which bear on Howard's themes of usurpation and violation of innocence.[55] The style fits the play's concern with the tarnishing and obscuring of truth. In the image which recurs in the painter satires, bad counsellors constitute 'a Cloud that hangs upon [the king's] brightness'.[56] Faulty, flattered, too human monarchs encourage men to have dangerously 'daring Tongues and Eyes'.[57] Instead Howard recommends an impersonal, impartial, remote kingship — in short the parliament's ideal of non-involvement:

> From henceforth, Sir, be everybody's King,
> And then you are your self: lend equal ears

> To what all say, and like a skilful Chymist
> Draw the quick spirit off, from every Counsel,
> And from your wise breast breath it as your own.[58]

Of course Howard's interest in the king's perspicuous representativeness stems from narrower, less noble aims. Lerma the great favourite is a figure of Clarendon and so too is his adviser Caldroon (almost an anagram), described at one point in terms of the current satirical picture of the ex-Chancellor:

> thou ill-drest Puppet of Authority;
> Thou Stalking Property, that walk'st on Screws,
> Which but laid by, thy Honour is unjoynted,
> And grows as bedrid as the Impotent.[59]

Similarly, Lerma's prostitution of his daughter parallels Clarendon's treatment of Anne Hyde, as popularly regarded, but Maria radically contrasts with Anne by preserving her chastity.[60] Nonetheless, despite the play's topical, interested grounding, it powerfully embodies a new apprehension of political evil. The corrupt counsellor, the serpent who whispers in his victim's ear —Satan, Lerma, and, later, Dryden's Achitophel and Pope's Sporus — has replaced the machiavellian, Cromwellian superman as the threat to restored peace and good government.[61]

By the end of the decade plays had ceased to declare any direct relationship with the Restoration of the king. The idea of restoration, having served so many purposes, had become diffuse and uninteresting. The conventions of panegyrical drama had been seriously undermined: the revised *Rehearsal* in 1671 brilliantly caught public disenchantment with the heroic. Writers like Settle and Crowne were experimenting with an excessively spectacular form of drama, aiming at baroque amplitude rather than local relevance, and, most importantly, the comic dramatists had developed a new, tough, witty style. The first comedies of Etherege, Wycherley, Shadwell and Aphra Behn were acted between 1668 and 1671. In these plays the focus has shifted from historical and political mythology to a version of *social* reality, yet the idealised language of Restoration political and religious thought has largely, ironically, been maintained. This allows the playwrights at their best to achieve a disinterested, yet penetrating insight into the complexities of their age, impossible for the apologising or chastising 'serious' plays. In any case the political climate had changed. By the early 1670s Charles's personal power was at a height. He was, comparatively, unchallenged and unchecked. Attention turned to the future — the Catholic question and the succession — but these concerns were as yet too vague to quicken an audience's attention. The wave of anti-Catholic plays did not break until 1679-85.[62]

The plays of the Restoration decade had distinctive political voices, however limited, and this quality was developed by writers over the next century who were excited and engaged by the theatre's scope as a political arena. It is an important part of the restored stage's legacy. A general modern verdict on Restoration heroic drama has been that it is 'factitious', cut off from the life of the time; it has been represented as a victim of the 'dissociation of sensibility', divorced from Elizabethan and Jacobean vitality.[63] My reading of the plays helps explain this feeling. It is not that the audiences were substantially more 'elitist' than in earlier times, nor that the plays were all uniformly and mindlessly royalist.[64] Within a general royalism, playwrights such as Tatham, Dryden, Orrery and Howard could engage with the issues of the day and adopt contrasting positions. The failing of Restoration heroic drama needs to be seen another way. The plays were simply too *close* to the interests of the 1660s, too concerned, in a narrow sense, to abstract and codify contemporary experience. The recent upheavals oppressed the dramatic as much as the poetic imagination. History demanded to be explained and justified, and its demands were very closely tied to the topic of the king's Restoration, which ruled the stage for nearly ten years.

8 *Samson Agonistes* : The Play Turned Upside Down

John Milton was exceptional among his contemporaries for resisting to the end the inevitability of a Stuart Restoration. As late as April 1660, only weeks before Charles II's landing at Dover, he published his revised version of *The Readie and Easie Way to Establish a Free Commonwealth*. The work concluded with a plea which distinguished God's history from the perverse history unfolding at that very moment:

> What I have spoken, is the language of that which is not call'd amiss *the good Old Cause*: if it seem strange to any, it will not seem more strange, I hope, then convincing to backsliders. Thus much I should perhaps have said though I were sure I should have spoken only to trees and stones; and had none to cry to, but with the Prophet, *O earth, earth, earth!* to tell the very soil it self, what her perverse inhabitants are deaf to. Nay though what I have spoke, should happ'n (which Thou suffer not, who didst create mankinde free; nor Thou next, who didst redeem us from being servants of men!) to be the last words of our expiring libertie. But I trust I shall have spoken perswasion to abundance of sensible and ingenuous men: to som perhaps whom God may raise of these stones to become children of reviving libertie; and may reclaim, though they seem now chusing them a captain back for *Egypt*, to bethink themselves a little and consider whether they are rushing; to exhort this torrent also of the people, not to be so impetuos, but to keep thir due channell; and at length recovering and uniting thir better resolutions, now that they see alreadie how open and unbounded the insolence and rage is of our common enemies, to stay these ruinous proceedings; justly and timely fearing to what a precipice of destruction the deluge of this epidemic madness would hurrie us through the general defection of a misguided and abus'd multitude.[1]

Milton draws on language of destruction — 'ruinous', 'precipice', 'epidemic madness' — to characterise the Restoration. The people have been diverted from 'thir due channell' back to Egypt, but Milton still hopes, and reinforces his hopes with his massive rhetoric, that God may not suffer it to happen, that he may redirect history along the path to liberty.

This was Milton's last substantial piece of prose. But after 1660 he published a poetical work which was significantly political in its ramifications. *Samson Agonistes*, licensed for publication in July 1670, is in simple terms a political drama. Samson, unlike Adam in *Paradise Lost* and Christ in *Paradise Regained*, is a public figure and a man of action, and his story was traditionally available for political interpretation. As we have seen, the new Stuart regime 'found' its context in an elaborate ideology of restoration. Such Stuart ideas of restoration, in all pomp and circumstance, provide a natural background for the reading of *Samson Agonistes* and suggest the sort of political interpretation a reader at the time of first publication would have given the work. Milton's play is about a spiritual restoration which counters the political Restoration, falsifying its values and claims.

Such an argument must rest on the traditional assumption that *Samson* was written after the completion of *Paradise Lost*. There is no irrefutable evidence for such a date, or for any other, but although in recent years a case has been put for a much earlier dating, the arguments, circumstantial and biographical in the main, are less persuasive than similar arguments for the late date.[2] The fact that in the later context the drama makes an intensified kind of sense further suggests that, after all, the Restoration is the work's natural home.

In *Samson Agonistes* a twofold restoration is achieved through a twofold destruction. The Israelites are delivered from oppression and Samson once more receives God's inspiration: at the same time the Philistine temple and a large number of Philistines are destroyed, and Samson himself is killed. The work is constructed in terms of many such radical contrasts and oppositions. The most fundamental of these is the opposition between the true God, worshipped by the Israelites, and the false god, Dagon, worshipped by the Philistines. The final action of the drama, the pulling down of the temple while Dagon is being celebrated, represents the vindication of the true God. Where Dagon's attributes are falsity, unreality and weakness, God's are, necessarily, truth, existence and omnipotence. At the opening of the drama · Dagon is in the ascendancy, in terms of worldly support: Dagon seems, illusorily, to exist, to have power and to have expelled God, so far fallen is God's agent, Samson. False resemblances are the counterpoint to oppositions in the play. In traditional treatments of the Samson story, it was possible for Dalila to be a Jewess, not a Philistine, or a harlot and not Samson's wife. Milton makes her both Samson's wife and a Philistine. Within the most intimate bond of marriage the most extreme discord enters. The marriage is a mere shadow of true union and represents the occasion by which God is deserted and Dagon permitted to triumph. Dalila, 'seeming at first all heavenly' is in reality 'a thorn/ Intestine' and 'a cleaving mischief' (1035, 1037-9). 'Intestine' hints that the discord is civil, within what should be a united and virtuous entity. 'Cleaving', meaning both dividing and joining, reminds us of the deceitful resemblance of the true and the true-seeming false.

The opening passages establish in detail the oppositions of the drama. First there is the contrast between Samson's past glory and his present degradation. Samson alludes only slightingly to his heroic achievements: 'Ask for this great deliverer now, and find him/ Eyeless in Gaza' (40-1); but the Chorus and Manoa provide abundant testimony to his former prowess. The cause of his greatness, as deduced by the Chorus, Manoa and Samson himself, was his special inspiration from God. His very birth was 'from heaven foretold' and since then he has been 'prescribed...a person separate to God' (23, 30-1). Formerly the whole creation was instinct with God's presence for Samson. He remembers the plain water he used to drink, which in the early sunlight was touched by 'heaven's fiery rod' and offered him nourishing refreshment (547-52). God's presence was manifested by Samson's strength, and the strength with which he could invest humble objects of the creation, slaying 'the flower of Palestine' with 'the jaw of a dead ass' (143-4). Samson's only duty towards God, his sign of faith, was to keep the secret of his strength, which lay in his uncut hair, his 'capital secret' (394).

Samson's secret represented an inner mystery about God's way of operating, and the keeping of the secret, in the face of temptations, betokened the keeping of God, inviolate, at the centre of Samson's being. Milton does not presume to describe God's actual working in Samson's spirit. Even at the end his description is external: Samson 'stood, as one who prayed' (1637). He does, however, circumscribe Samson's secret power: 'this high gift of strength...in what part lodged' (47-8), 'under the seal of silence' (49), 'the secret gift of God' (201), 'intimate impulse' (223), 'the mystery of God...under pledge/ Of vow' (378-9), 'his holy secret' (497), 'divine instinct' (526), 'my head and hallowed pledge' (535), and others, most expressive of all his 'fort of silence' (236). In these phrases God's power is conceived as existing in a place within Samson. The 'fort of silence' is strong and embattled, and what lies inside is inaccessible and unknowable, unless Samson betrays its secret. This has happened when the drama opens. The 'fort' has been seized and violated. God's former presence in the world, and now his absence, are established in the drama in and through Samson, his privileged agent. Samson is able to know if God is in the world only if He is felt to be present within Samson's 'fort of silence', which, like 'Silo his bright sanctuary' (1674) is a place where God can dwell. For the Chorus, Manoa and the readers, accordingly, God's presence can be known only through Samson's physical actions, and hence the destruction of the temple through Samson's return of strength is the sign that God is again with his people.

But at first the drama is concerned to establish, in contrast, the absence of God. Clearly this could not be true, absolutely, so as we enter the play Milton restricts us to Samson's deprived world. We share his groping uncertainty as the 'guiding hand', identity unknown, leads him to a slightly better place (with 'choice of sun or shade') and leads us into the drama (1-3). Samson's state is extraordinary. He seems divorced from heaven and from the whole created world. At the height of his despair he testifies to his 'sense of heaven's desertion' (632). Although he is properly unwilling to fly in the face of the Almighty, he cannot resist rehearsing what seems a well-worn debate about his history and his fatal gift of strength without strength of mind. At this stage his peace in God's will is no more than bitter resignation:

> But peace, I must not quarrel with the will
> Of highest dispensation...
> Suffices that to me strength is my bane....
> (60-1, 63)

He is in a state of misery and extremity: 'a life half dead, a living death' (100).

At the hands of the Philistines Samson was blinded. His loss of sight comes to be a sign of God's abandonment, depriving him of spiritual as well as physical light:

Light the prime work of God to me is extinct....
    (70)

In the absence of light, Samson is not only lacking God's restoring power, but almost life itself. He is virtually dead, 'dead more than half' (79), because:

    ...light so necessary is to life,
And almost life itself....
    (90-1)

Samson is denied the healing power of nature: 'nature within me seems/ In all her functions weary of herself', he adds later, despairingly (595-6). Being blind, Samson cannot see the external world. As far as he is concerned, it is 'extinct' and 'annulled' (70, 72). No 'breath of vernal air from snowy alp' can soothe him now (628). It is as if a disaster has occurred, destroying the whole creation. Samson is denied God's 'prime work' and 'prime decree' (70,85). The allusion to Genesis, 'let there be light' (84), underlines the point. God's prime work, his first act (and also the prime season, spring, the weather in Eden), has been undone and the world has reverted to chaos. The darkness of the opening is the colour of mourning suitable to Samson's 'grief' and 'wail' (66, 72). But the 'total eclipse' and dark sun (81, 86) also remind us of the end of Christian history, and there is mourning for the creation itself, as yet unredeemed. The removal of the season spring means the end of nature and the play re-echoes with suppressed puns, intimating a longing for now absent spring — the 'day-spring' Samson cannot see at the beginning (11), the denied 'prime' work and decree, and the 'fountain or fresh current' (547) from which once he drank. In this context the 'blaze of noon' resembles a holocaustic fire, anticipating that from which Samson's phoenix virtue will rise at the end. That Samson's loss of sight signifies to him the apocalyptic extinction of the external world is further suggested by the planetary metaphors he uses for his eyes: 'such a tender ball as the eye' (94) and more explicitly 'these dark orbs' (591).[3]

If the creation has been annulled, how and where then does Samson himself exist? This problem is resolved when the intrusion of the Chorus reminds us that Samson has generalised too far in assuming the world's end from his own degradation. His own state, however, as he perceives it is still problematic. His voice, isolated in its darkness, seems to be an entity partaking of a strange semi-existence. Without light and almost life itself, his being is nearly divorced from existence itself. The state is paradoxical and impossible, unaltered 'within doors, or without' (77). Opposites tug at him, 'dark in light' (75), culminating in the essential phrase 'myself, my sepulchre'. The nouns 'self' and 'sepulchre' have opposing meanings but here take on a syntactic and aural equivalence. Samson has made himself 'a moving grave', and has buried himself (102). Samson's obscure psychic state is contradictory, as he both accuses and accepts God's will, and again we are reminded of the desertion of a God, who cannot exist in contradictions. Samson's sense of separation from mortal life, his only possible mode of existence, is suggested when he says that his miseries are so great that each one 'would ask a life to wail' (66). It is as if Samson is quite dissociated from his particular temporal existence so that his voice can offer his whole life, this particular ruined one, in atonement, and then still have other of its lives for further sacrifice. The usage hints at the vastness of things beyond one mortal 'life', and this sense returns beautifully when Samson delivers himself into God's will at the end: 'And for a life who will not change his purpose' (1406). Most beautiful of all as an image of Samson's mode of unbelieved existence is the moon, whose desertion to the vacant cave is reminiscent of Samson's void eyeball and earth:

> The sun to me is dark
> And silent as the moon,
> When she deserts the night
> Hid in her vacant interlunar cave.
>   (86-9)

Samson's sense that he has virtually ceased to be is matched by the Chorus's sense that he has ceased to be himself. They regard him as a man given over to chaos, and a fallen man: their language echoes the language of the fall in *Paradise Lost*:

> See how he lies at random, carelessly diffused,

With languished head unpropped,
As one past hope, abandoned,
And by himself given over....
(118-21, cf. *PL*, IX, 210, 443, 852; X, 717, 995 ff.)

Samson's dark and wretched state is set over against the
triumphant and well-lit state of the Philistines:'O dark, dark,
dark, amid the blaze of noon' (80). But this blaze of noon, the
height of Philistine glory, is only a Satanic parody of the true light,
and the opposition between Samson's degradation and the
Philistines' triumph is a false one. We see then a new sense in which
the creation has ceased to exist because it has been given over to
the false god Dagon. The Philistine world is an intensely visual
world of appearances. The language becomes exceptionally,
gorgeously visual when describing Philistine arms and buildings
(131-4, 147, 1605ff), when describing Dalila's entry, and when
Samson describes Harapha's arms, ironically, unable to see them
(1119-22). The most pictorial imagery in the play, 'Sea, Snake,
Flower, and Flame', is associated with speciousness,[4] and Milton
himself makes the relevant pun: Dalila is a 'specious monster', her
falsehood lies in her face (230). Behind all this lies Dagon, a god
who can be represented pictorially as a 'sea-idol' (13), unlike the
true God whose unknowability irritates the Philistine champion:
he sneers to Samson, 'thy God, whate'er he be' (1156).

Samson is tempted in various ways to acknowledge the false
Philistine world of appearances. Manoa encourages his son in the
interests of self-preservation not to despair (502-20). But of course
for Samson this suggestion is impossible. To make some sort of new
life for himself would be a false action, involving the acceptance of
his degraded form and accommodation to the Dagon-dominated
world. 'As for life,/ To what end should I seek it?' he says (521-2),
implying his belief that he is already severed from life. He describes
his unmanning in sexual terms, how he laid his head in the lap

Of a deceitful concubine who shore me
Like a tame wether, all my precious fleece,
Then turned me out ridiculous, despoiled....
    (537-9)

To accept Manoa's plan of offering a ransom for his son's life, so that Samson could live out his days quietly at home, would be to accept his emasculated, un-Samson-ed state:

> ...to sit idle on the household hearth,
> A burdenous drone....
> (566-7)

Effeminacy was Samson's fault, meaning a susceptibility to Dalila improper for a man (410). He served Dalila (with sexual overtones) instead of serving God (410-16). He holds out obdurately against Manoa's offer, because he wants to find a way of serving his nation again, in recompense (564-5).

Dalila encourages Samson to acknowledge Dagon's victory in different ways. First she tries to make him accept her specious excuses and her sympathy. Then she offers him physical pleasure and again the temptation of accepting some sort of continued life: 'life yet hath many solaces' (915). And like Manoa, she offers to take him home and treat him 'with nursing diligence' (924). With some difficulty he resists all her attempts, again on the grounds that he must not accept his unmanning to 'live uxorious to thy will/ In perfect thraldom...' (945-6). His stubbornness is the residual element of his faith. The dialogue with Dalila contains the most anguished passages in the drama because Samson is confronting the essential and humanly understandable causes of his downfall: 'love seeks to have love' (837). In this most intimate area of experience the natural impulse seems closest to the divine and the illusory material world seems most nearly aligned with God's true world. Yet the Philistine state with Dalila's help has perverted the impulse 'against the law of nature', setting nation above marriage bonds (890). The irreparable rift between divine and natural impulses is revealed, and the chasmal division between the individual spirit and even the closest representative of the external world: 'thou and I long since are twain', says Samson (929).

A further temptation comes from Harapha, representing Philistine military might. His power is thoroughly outward, 'his look/ Haughty as is his pile high-built and proud' (1069). Samson is not daunted for a moment and has no trouble frightening him off simply by brandishing the threat of truly God-given power: 'then put on all thy gorgeous arms...I only with an oaken staff will meet thee' (1119-23).

The final temptation occurs when the Philistine officer summons Samson to entertain at the Philistine feast. Here the former temptations recur in their most grotesquely reduced form. Samson is to be subjected to the most debased servitude imaginable: 'although their drudge, to be their fool or jester' (1338). He is not merely to be degraded. His true status is to be turned upside down, and his God-given power is to be equated with an illusory kind of carnival trickery. The great deliverer is to be set among

> sword-players, and every sort
> Of gymnic artists, wrestlers, riders, runners,
> Jugglers and dancers, antics, mummers, mimics....
>   (1323-5)

Setting Samson amongst the mummers and mimics makes his true God seem false and does honour to Dagon. The way in which Dagon is honoured, with 'sacrifices, triumph, pomp, and games' (1312) is outward, ostentatious and utterly theatrical, as befits this god of appearances. Samson is reduced to a theatrical fool to do honour to the god of worldly show. By celebrating itself in a theatre (1605) and by means of theatre, the Philistine world unknowingly declares its falsity.

At this point, unexpectedly, Samson begins to feel 'some rousing motions' within himself (1382). When the officer returns to repeat his command, Samson can at last reply with superb double reference, confidently in his mind setting true authority over against false:

> Masters' commands come with a power resistless
> To such as owe them absolute subjection....
>   (1404-5)

A process of renewal is adumbrated in a line which tentatively reunites God's interests with those of the individual and the nation. Whatever happens, he says, will not dishonour 'our God, our Law, my nation, or myself' (1425). At this point he disappears from the stage.

Manoa enters, talking of coming to terms with the Philistine world, finding something 'generous...and civil' in it (1467), and Samson's 'liberty' is to be made dependent on mundane political 'success' (1454). But a shout is heard from the Philistine theatre, while Manoa talks of his plan to redeem Samson materially (1472, 1482) and gradually the catastrophe is taken in. Samson has destroyed the theatre and

> all who sat beneath,
> Lords, ladies, captains, counsellors, or priests,
> Their choice nobility and flower....
> (1652-4)

Samson has destroyed the Philistine triumph and overturned the theatre, the place of Philistine self-glorification and the symbol of the false world of appearances. Up to the end of the messenger's speech, the reaction of Manoa and the Chorus hovers between grief and joy. But the messenger's speech conveys the vast and godly nature of Samson's act, and therefore there can be no doubt. 'O dearly-bought revenge, yet glorious!' says the Chorus immediately after the narration (1660), then the semi-choruses celebrate the event with ecstatic language.

A restoration has occurred. During the very death-throes of those in the theatre Manoa had anticipated that 'God will restore him eyesight to his strength' (1503) and the Chorus had echoed the remark, foreshadowing the plot's final turn:

> ...if his eyesight...
>   ...by miracle restored,
> He now will be dealing dole among his foes....
> (1527-9)

If Manoa and the Chorus envisage the restoration of eyesight in rather simple terms, Samson's own speeches earlier in the poem make us realise what a vast restoration is actually involved. Samson is being returned to spiritual life and no longer will the creation be dead to him, or falsely vivified by the values of Dagon: God's prime decree will be re-established. In terms of Christian history, this amounts to a regeneration of the fallen world, which can be restored only through apocalypse. Appropriately, the destruction of the Philistines' empire is depicted in apocalyptic terms. The Chorus had commented on the noise:

> ...universal groan

As if the whole inhabitation perished,
Blood, death, and deathful deeds are in that noise,
Ruin, destruction at the utmost point.
     (1511-14)

And the messenger's speech describes the scene as if the whole creation had cracked: 'with the force of winds and waters pent,/ When mountains tremble...with horrid convulsion' (1647-9). The second semi-chorus adds the equivalent image of a phoenix, a 'holocaust', revived by fire (1699-1707).

As a result of the restoration achieved by destruction, the Israelites have regained 'honour' and 'freedom' (1715) and Samson has achieved a state resembling eternal felicity: 'eternal fame', commemorated by a monument shaded with 'laurel ever green' (1717, 1735). He has become an exemplary inspiration, a renewing force for the young. Most importantly, God's providence has been reasserted:

All is best, though we oft doubt
What the unsearchable dispose
Of highest wisdom brings about,
And ever best found in the close.
     (1745-8)

'Ever best found in the close' as 'death to life is crown or shame' (1579). In *Samson Agonistes* God's history is revealed only in the moment of closing, in Samson's act of ending his life which abruptly precipitates the drama's close and hence reveals its true meaning. The messenger's speech relates the only true action in the drama, which is also the action uniquely embodying God's truth. Paradoxically the drama's one piece of true spectacle occurs in destroying the false spectacle of the Philistine theatre and properly we are prevented from enjoying this as spectacle: the narrated account draws its excitement from relaying the *import* of the event. Once this has happened, dramatic action is promptly abandoned in favour of lyrical, choric and elegiac interpretation. Dramatic time has ceased in witness to the presence of eternity.

Samson's action re-established the course of God's true history, which in turn is an aspect of establishing God as the one true God. Samson, in his despair, had been moved to blame the corruption of the Israelite people, at least in part, for their subsequent oppression:

> But what more oft in nations grown corrupt,
> And by their vices brought to servitude,
> Than to love bondage more than liberty,
> Bondage with ease than strenuous liberty....
>   (268-71)

His attack prompts the Chorus to compare Samson with Gideon and Jeptha, two other divinely inspired heroes who, apparently unlike Samson, had successfully served their people and God's purpose (277-89). Samson had from birth been 'separate to God' but had betrayed his privilege through his submission to Dalila. She is confident that she, not he, will be remembered as the valiant one. Dalila realises that there is more than one version of most events:

> Fame if not double-faced is double-mouthed,
> And with contrary blast proclaims most deeds....
>   (971-2)

She also realises that it is the victor's version of events which becomes received history. By virtue of the victor's power and in the interests of his triumph, those figures which contributed to his victory are accorded Fame, a lasting, ineradicable metamorphosis. Dalila does not care that she will be cursed by 'the circumcised/ In Dan...and the bordering tribes', for that peripheral history will not be underwritten by empire and heeded by posterity. She will be remembered where, to her, it matters:

> But in my country where I most desire,
> In Ecron, Gaza, Asdod, and in Gath
> I shall be named among the famousest
> Of women, sung at solemn festivals,
> Living and dead recorded, who to save
> Her country from a fierce destroyer, chose
> Above the faith of wedlock-bands, my tomb
> With odours visited and annual flowers.
>   (980-7)

This is Philistine history and we recognise it to be a deviation from the Christian history we have received. The feast in the theatre, celebrating the defeat of Samson, is to establish and honour precisely this false history, and at the end it is overthrown. The commemoration and eternal fame Dalila envisages reverts to its true deserver, Samson.

The distinction between opposing versions of the same events, between true and false histories from providence's point of view, is what relates *Samson Agonistes* to England in the 1660s. The quotation from Milton's *Readie and Easie Way* revealed a similar distinction in which the imminent restoration of Charles was seen as a falsification, a deviation from the people's 'due channell'. The idea of true providential history, which might run counter to the fortunes of worldly empire, was common enough. The comprehensive plan of God's providence was frequently pictured as a work of art, for example, a book, or a stage-play, or a painting, or a building. By virtue of its perfected design, the final stage of the work was the part which confirmed the meaning of the whole. Sir Thomas Browne, for example, spoke of history as a stage-play advancing towards 'that one day, that shall include and comprehend all that went before it, wherein as in the last scene, all the Actors must enter, to compleate and make up the Catastrophe of this great peece'. Analogously, in *Samson Agonistes*, the concluding action makes the meaning of the piece. The convenience of this way of seeing history was that it allowed for certain stages when the workings of providence would not be readily apparent. There could be times when the ascendancy of ungodly groups marked an evident divergence from God's scheme. There could be stretches of history which were ungodly and inauthentic — not directly the work of the author 'Providence in her dramatick plot'. Ralph Cudworth described how '*Divine Providence*' did not 'perpetually interrupt the *Course* of *Nature*', but rather followed 'a *Still and Silent Path*': 'the *Deity is Slow or Dilatory, and this is the Nature of it*'. At times the wicked 'have an Uninterrupted Prosperity'. Those who because of this cry out against providence are like spectators who condemn a plot because a villain is 'for a while Swaggering and Triumphing', whereas if they waited to the end, his deserts would come. 'The Evolution of the World ... is ... a *Truer Poem*, and we men Histrionical Acters ... who ... insert something of our *Own* into the *Poem* too; but God *Almighty*, is that *Skilful Dramatist*, who always connecteth that of ours which went before, with what of his follows after, into good *Coherent Sense....*'[5] *Samson Agonistes* is a play which suggests just such a model of providential history, a model applicable not only to plays, but to actual history.

Political events were commonly discussed in theatrical terms in the seventeenth century. In particular, the royalist association with the theatre allowed opponents to play ironically on the disjunction between the tragedy enjoyed on stage and the actual 'tragedy' to which the royalist party was simultaneously succumbing. I suggest that Milton is aware of such theatrical analogies in *Samson Agonistes* and is concerned to measure, and find wanting, Restoration political theatrics in terms of an ultimate, providential reality.

In his preface to *Samson* Milton described tragedy as 'the gravest, moralest and most profitable of all other poems'. *Samson* shares the instructive intention of *Paradise Lost*, to 'assert eternal providence/ And justify the ways of God to men': the Chorus echoes the epic's famous lines (293-4). In the play Samson achieves fame in becoming a lasting example to his people, 'enrolled/ In copious legend, or sweet lyric song' (1736-7), and it is a necessary part of his after-life that the significance of his example should be understood. Milton brings home the meaning of Samson's story to his audience by linking it to the experience of contemporary Englishmen. He does not reduce the noble and eternal scriptural story to a topical allegory. He does, however, allude sufficiently to contemporary England for it to be grasped that the Restoration state is a particular instance of the kind of empire associated with the Philistines: inauthentically imperial, outwardly showy, theatrical, martial and, most importantly, false and transient. To establish the sense of the eternal kingdom as true and unchanging, it is appropriate for Milton to contrast it with a particular, and therefore transient, moment in worldly time. Allusions to the Restoration remind us that the Philistine empire is necessarily a fleeting mortal period. It is hard not to associate the Philistine 'lords, ladies, captains, counsellors, or priests' with those who returned to power at the Restoration. The Philistine flower are given to show, mirth, drunkenness, feasting, licentiousness, lordliness, atheism and idolatry. This matches Milton's description of his nation in his last work, *Of True Religion, Heresie, Schism and Toleration*, published in 1673 not long after the publication of *Samson Agonistes*:

it is a general complaint that this Nation of late years, is grown more numerously and excessively vitious then heretofore; Pride,

Luxury, Drunkenness, Whoredom, Cursing, Swearing, bold and open Atheism every where abounding....[6]

The Philistine nobility derives an especially Restoration tone from its predilection for theatrical forms of display, and from its general association with the theatre. It was only with the return of Charles that theatrical activity was recommenced fully in London and his Restoration was celebrated with a profusion of show. The Philistines celebrated their victory over Samson in a similar fashion, with spectacle. Their 'city rings/ And numbers thither flock' (1449-50). The Philistine triumph is symbolised by the building, both temple and theatre, where the spectacle takes place. Milton provides the main features of this theatre's design. It is 'half round on two main pillars vaulted high' while 'the other side' is 'open' (1606-9). The 'two massy pillars' give 'main support' to 'the arched roof' (1633-4). Except for the two pillars, these details are not in any earlier treatment of Samson's story. Milton's architecture is figurative, not literal, and requires an interpretation. The building is most readily imagined as a classical, Vitruvian amphitheatre, but this does not quite account for the two pillars and arched roof. Vitruvius' account of Roman and Greek theatres was reinterpreted during the Renaissance and a modified design was produced, which attained to the highest principles of proportion. This design featured a large arch, or alternatively two pillars supporting an arch, an early kind of proscenium; and Frances Yates has argued that it influenced Elizabethan theatrical design. Palladio reconstructed Vitruvius' theatre for Barbaro's 1556 edition of Vitruvius, and his illustrations amount to preliminary studies for the Teatro Olimpico at Vicenza, which features a large arch in clearly triumphal form. The two pillars supporting an arched roof can be considered as alluding to a kind of triumphal arch, like those seen in London in 1661 as part of the coronation entertainments. The amphitheatre form, combined with a high arch and a closed ceiling, reappears in a building especially germane to *Samson Agonistes*. Christopher Wren's Sheldonian Theatre, started in 1664 and finished in 1669, and which Milton, of course, can never have seen, was deliberately designed to allude to the glories of the Augustan Roman Empire. Its original designs were modelled on the Theatre of Marcellus at Rome, completed under Augustus. These designs were subsequently abandoned, but in various ways the building maintained its amphitheatrical fiction. The new design in any case resembled a Renaissance reconstruction of Vitruvius. The Sheldonian Theatre was peculiarly representative of early Restoration self-regard. It was a marvel of the age and confirmed the Royal Society's scientific optimism, together with the defeat of destructive fanaticism by enlightenment. The message was made clear by Robert Streater's allegorical painting on the ceiling and Robert Whitehall's panegyrical poem on the theatre's opening.[7] As a classical amphitheatre the building is suggestive of pagan empire. As a Renaissance Vitruvian structure it represents the world itself, but in this context the false world of appearances, as opposed to the true order of God, which would be represented by an unambiguous temple. As a triumphal modern theatre it brings to mind not only the Restoration triumph, but the Restoration theatre too. In overturning this building Samson is overturning an accumulation of Restoration panegyrical claims and by an extension rejecting the Restoration settlement itself.[8]

Samson Agonistes has a peculiar relationship with theatre. Milton wrote in his preface that his work 'never was intended' for the stage, but it is written in the form of a play. We know, not least from the evidence of *Comus*, that Milton had no absolute aversion to theatrical forms if piously and instructively used. It is more likely that the work never was intended for the stage because that stage would have meant the Restoration stage, which Milton found repellent, despite his quite close associations with some of its prominent figures such as Davenant, Robert Howard and Dryden. Ostensibly a play, the work's formal sources lie in Greek drama and in Italian *sacra rappresentazione* and *melodramma*. By comparison with Shakespeare's plays, which are echoed here and there, *Samson Agonistes* lacks characters and action. The main action occurs off-stage and the essential drama occurs in a place inaccessible to us, within Samson, in his 'fort of silence'. The work presents a contrast between the eternal world of God's providence (outside time and therefore untheatrical), and the temporal, physical world where the Philistines reign. It is the Philistine world which has theatrical qualities, and these are signs of falsity. Samson is forcibly given a theatrical identity, while in reality his true being seems divorced from the whole material creation. His very presence on the stage marks his debasement. Milton's work in the end rejects theatrical values, when God's providence makes itself known. When Samson, analogously, pulls down the theatre, the poet anticipates another mode, 'legend' and 'lyric song'. The claim that the work never was intended for the stage is a tactical move in the interests of higher truth.

Did Milton's original readers notice his strategy? There is evidence that at least one of his contemporaries read *Samson Agonistes* as a work engaging in political and literary controversy, 'a lecture in literary art' in Masson's phrase.[9] Milton's play seems to have provoked the only dramatic effort of William Joyner, a devout Catholic who had resigned his fellowship at Magdalen College, Oxford in 1645 on religious grounds and thereafter lived a quiet life until his brief return to the college in the reign of James II. He was acquainted with Cowley, and with Milton — possibly by virtue of earlier Oxfordshire connections.[10] Joyner's play *The Roman Empress* was acted in August 1670, a month after *Samson Agonistes* was licensed for publication, and the two plays have enough similarities to suggest that Joyner had seen Milton's manuscript in its final stages.

Langbaine calls both *The Roman Empress* and *Samson Agonistes* not plays, his customary term, but *dramas*, by which he means a lofty poetic work, particularly one after a Greek model. Milton had 'endeavour'd' to imitate the Tragedy of the Ancient *Greek* Poets' and Joyner had 'propos'd the *Oedipus and Hippolitus* for his pattern'. Langbaine's comments confirm that Joyner considered his work to run counter to contemporary theatrical fashions. In his preface, Joyner censures the contemporary audiences for not attending the theatre 'to learn true history, or religion'. He refuses to tickle the ear with 'gingling Antitheses', but rather will attempt 'the Majestique Grace of a Tragique Theater' by combining what is best in *Oedipus* with a story founded in Roman 'truth and reality'. Joyner's stricture against rhyming couplets resembles Milton's scorn for the 'trivial pleasure' of 'the jingling sound of like endings' in his note to the verse of *Paradise Lost,* and Milton, in his preface to *Samson,* shares Joyner's high sense of tragedy. Both poets aim at the decorous dramatic unity which, in Joyner's words, 'gives the last perfection and beauty to all Subjects moral, as well as natural'. There are internal similarities too. Joyner imitates the language of *Samson Agonistes* superficially, yet more closely than anything else in the period. *The Roman Empress* is in blank verse, often metrically irregular, with occasional interspersions of rhyme; the vocabulary and syntax are latinate, and such figures as inverted word order, long syntactial units and frequent repetition make the language a pastiche of Milton's. Some close parallels with phrases and motifs in *Samson Agonistes* occur. Both plays are concerned with the relationship between true religion and worldly power. Langbaine noted that under the character of his hero Valentius, Joyner 'means *Constantine* the Great'. His power is superhuman, he is 'the soul diffused through the vast body of/ The Empire'; his fault is being 'uxoriously/ Subject to the ill government of women'. He's not unlike Samson.[11]

However, the relationship between the two works only highlights their radical difference in intention. Milton adapted a Greek style to a Hebraic story, to ground his work in truth. Joyner, on the other hand, sought 'truth and reality' by transforming a Greek story into a Roman play. Rome, to the Catholic Joyner, offered the most edifying example, and his hero resembles the Constantine who united church and empire. In 1670, thinking of this holy Roman achievement, Joyner made his pro-Catholic appeal, since already under Charles, he says 'we see restor'd to us the secure felicity of the times of *Augustus.*' In *The Roman Empress* the great man's soul is commensurate with and promotes empire: 'that soul...did not only animate thy body,/ But the whole fabrick of the *Roman* Empire....' Such ideas were radically opposed to Milton's. *His* hero destroys the fabric — the temple — of worldly empire and his spirit is animated only by God. Joyner's play offered imperial Roman history in opposition to Milton's providential anti-Roman history.[12]

The Roman Empress is a reminder that a contemporary could respond to the polemical element in Milton's new style of tragedy. But Milton's obdurate exclusion of Roman elements from his drama, and his dismissal of temporal history in favour of an alternative providential history, sets his play apart from virtually all the 'serious' plays of the Restoration decade. As we have seen, the fashion was for plays dealing with historical, imperial, often exotic themes and, with few exceptions, supporting the Restoration in a simple, largely formulaic way. The plots characteristically depicted the deposition of a usurper and the restoration of a monarch, stability and virtue to the nation.[13] *Samson Agonistes* turns such plays of restoration upside down. In *Samson* the enemy is not a monstrous individual, but the Philistine state itself which identifies its own interests with the good. The dominant figure is not an all-powerful usurper, but a deposed and powerless hero. As a hero he proves not passively merciful (as Charles had done), but violently active and vengeful. The plot works towards destruction rather than reparation. The lords, who characteristically work for a restoration, by bringing the hero into the city's triumphs, achieve their own and the city's annihilation. The ideally virtuous and innocent woman, who characteristically collaborates with the lords, has become corrupt. In other plays it was her marriage to the hero that marked a true restoration. Here her radical divorcement from the hero is a prerequisite for his spiritual restoration. The loyal man of the people — the figure of General George Monck in the dramas of restoration — is now the aristocratic coward Harapha. Characteristically the Stuart plot worked back towards an Augustan peace and a vision of the Golden Age. Milton's plot works forward towards God's peace and a pre-figuring of the end of the world. If Milton considered the restoration plot a perversion of true history, *Samson Agonistes* suggests the shadowy, unschematic ways in which he imagined alternative inversions of that perverse plot.

This is not to suggest that *Samson Agonistes* is a fantasy based on Milton's unfulfilled historical wishes.[14] Rather the reflection in *Samson Agonistes* of the Restoration theatrical plot reminds us that fortune's history is but a shadow, in this case inverted as in a glass darkly, of the true plan of God. The destruction of the Philistine triumph is correlated with the antithetical high-point of fortune's wheel, in recent experience the Restoration in 1660.

The drama provides one clue to this correlation. The climactic moment of the drama for us is the messenger's speech, which reports Samson's act of destruction. This act marks the end of the false Philistine triumph and inaugurates a new era of freedom for the Israelites, with eternal fame for their hero. At this point the plot proper turns, releasing the magnificent choric and semi-choric celebration of God's providence. The line which marks the completion of the narrated action and the commencement of celebration is numbered 1660. Milton has timed the Chorus's entry for line 1660 by inserting a line which, without precedent in any source, clarifies the political dimensions of the tragedy: 'The vulgar only scaped who stood without' (1659). The change involves the political leaders, but in the words of *The Readie and Easie Way* passes by 'the misguided and abus'd multitude'. The line number, 1660, unobtrusively points to the most familiar blessed change of recent times, in the year 1660, which has found its truly divine (because inverse) counterpoint in the blessed change wrought on the theatre by Samson.[15]

To some extent Samson's story had already been gathered into the panoply of panegyric welcoming Charles in the 1660s. In March 1660, Dr Matthew Griffith had compared Charles to an avenging Samson, and was rebuked by Milton for abusing scripture. Another supporter wrote that Charles had reared 'up the broken Pillars of [his] Peers', and Monck too was said to have 'more than *Samson's* strength'. More commonly Charles's enemy, the Good Old Cause, was likened to Dagon, as in the pamphlet *Dagon Demolished* (1660). By 1667 Marvell was able to use such rhetoric to undermine the panegyrical tradition. When the Dutch captured the *Royal Charles*, Marvell made this telling comparison:

> Such the fear'd *Hebrew*, captive, blinded, shorn,
> Was led about in sport, the publick scorn.
> (*The Last Instructions to a Painter*, 735-6)[16]

Many such panegyrical motifs are found in *Samson Agonistes*, transmuted, like the restoration plot, to serve Milton's theme. Samson takes over the role of monarch in Milton's drama. (His name was etymologically associated with the sun, a central symbol of kingship.) When Harapha appears, armed, 'giant and high-built', resembling England's marine enemy described by Waller in his *Instructions to a Painter* — 'the tall Batavian in a vast ship rides,/ Bearing an army' (141-2) — Samson appropriately threatens him with the true English weapon, 'an oaken staff' (1123), which was also a personal symbol for Charles. The king had hidden under an oak when fleeing the battle of Worcester. And if Charles had received his crown in a triumphal spectacle, Samson too receives his 'crown' during the triumphs. 'Death to life is crown or shame', Manoa had said earlier (1579), and Samson's honourable death proves his crown. After his death he is celebrated in monarchical imagery. He is 'an eagle' (1695) when his inner vision is restored, and wields the 'cloudless thunder' of the true king of heaven (1696).

The eagle at once gives way to the phoenix. This startling emblem of regeneration provides the drama's most unequivocal key. Samson is

> Like that self-begotten bird
> In the Arabian woods embossed,

That no second knows nor third,
And lay erewhile a holocaust,
From out her ashy womb now teemed,
Revives, reflourishes, then vigorous most
And when unactive deemed,
And though her body die, her fame survives,
A secular bird ages of lives.
    (1699-1707)

The language flares up, like the image, into a restoration which concludes with fame. The phoenix had been applied to Charles (as to earlier Stuarts), 'this rare and Phoenix King', and was equally available to those who opposed the Restoration settlement.[17] (A seditious pamphlet appeared in 1662 called *The Phenix, or Solemn League and Covenant.*) A reader sensitive to the political shadowings of language could have responded to the controversial connotations of the phoenix. He might have realised that in applying the image to the saintly champion of an oppressed people, Milton was subverting, or at least stripping away, the contemporary Stuart connotations of the image.

A final aspect of the drama's contemporaneity concerns Dalila. The chorus interrupts its moralising to give the odd and arresting description of her arrival. The first picture of Dalila is so vivid, despite the Chorus's evasions, because it has the quality of something recognised. Dalila is seen instinctively as a fashionably dressed seventeenth-century lady, ostentatious in a foolish, even continental style. Recognition is made easy because Dalila, unlike much in the drama, is such a thoroughly outward creature, and because she is at once identifiable as a courtly theatrical heroine: 'bedecked, ornate, and gay...all her bravery on...a damsel train behind'. It has been observed that she takes her place in a line stretching from Cleopatra to Millamant. She has both contemporaneity and theatricality, two defining qualities of the transitory world of appearances. Her other qualities connect her with a particularly Stuart world. She is 'stately', 'rich', 'courted' by the winds, like an especially imperious, mercantile ship from Tarsus (probably Southern Spain), bound for the Ionian isles or Cadiz. (Cadiz was the Spanish port most visited by English ships in the period and its chief export was wine.) She smells of amber, an exotic fragrance originating in whales and procured from the New World. Even in the 1670s the importation of luxury goods could be associated with vice and voluptuousness, attributes of Dalila by implication. And in recent times Spain had been ready to support Charles's government, whereas Cromwell had waged war on Spain, so Dalila's ship can be considered an enemy of the republic. She has *usurped* James Harrington's description of the commonwealth 'with all its Tackling, full sail, displaying its Streamers and flourishing with Top and Topgallant'.[18]

She is a naval creature and the navy, improved by his efforts, was especially associated with Charles in the 1660s. He himself had arrived in England by sea, 'like some huge *Gallyon*...From farthest *Indies* richly laden home' in Richard Flecknoe's words.[19] The development of the navy became a chief claim of Stuart glory, nowhere more spectacularly than in Dryden's *Annus Mirabilis*, and ships were the means both to eastern wealth and to Augustan empire. As such, the ship was an agent of fortune. In Milton's play Dalila's good fortune is Samson's bad fortune. She has 'sails filled' and is able to 'storm' him; he's like a 'pilot' in a 'wreck' (718, 405, 1044). Dalila's splendid ascendancy derives from fortune, not from God's true providence.

Underlying these negative associations of Dalila's ship is the relationship between ships, Leviathan and Satan. In *Paradise Lost* Satan is seen as Leviathan, huge, distended and reptilian, floating on the flood (I, 200-8), and Leviathan is an image of the absolutist state, in Milton's words 'the floating carcas of a crazie, and diseased Monarchy' (*Of Reformation, Complete Prose*, I, 572). Dalila's own god, Dagon, is similarly a sea-monster — in *Paradise Lost* the idol of a 'gay' religion, 'full of pomp and gold' (I, 372, 46) — and she betrays her allegiance by being a gay, gorgeous marine creature. She is the daughter of a particular kind of corrupt state: superficial, secular, imperial, greedily mercantile, crypto-Catholic, absolutist, and hence evil. The context of Milton's image gives Dalila a contemporaneity which makes her hateful qualities applicable to the Restoration regime. She is the product of a state which uses its 'grave authority' to make sure 'that to the public good/ Private respects must yield' (867-8). In seizing the triumph from Dalila, Samson has brought about God's judgement on such a state.

9 Conclusion: Artifice and Scrutiny

Of all the works which address themselves to political concerns in the years after the Restoration, Milton's rugged play is the most profound. One reason for this is Milton's seasoned political intelligence, even if the climate in which he was writing made the hope of influencing political actuality quite vain. *Samson Agonistes* is impressive for its struggle to bring into conjunction, to comprehend in one coherent work, disparate orders of experience: politics and history, the purposes and ways of providence, and the psychology of the solitary man. Going beyond this, what makes *Samson Agonistes* magnificent is its repeated setting at risk of its own enterprise. Its power kindles at point after point from Milton's insistence on the incommensurability of the terms he is dealing with: the drama rises from the gulfs which separate public experience from private, empire from the spiritual commonwealth, the soul from the tribe. The courage of *Samson Agonistes* is the same quality which makes the play disturbing and knotty to many readers today. Milton's mind reaches in almost too many different directions in its attempt to see things whole; what remains (for all that the outcome is a deliverance for the Israelites) is a weighty sense that the world cannot quite be worked round in this way. The play is a tragedy; its final note is an exalted kind of exhaustion. At the heart of *Samson Agonistes* is a tragic recognition of how difficult it is for a man to encounter his own fate; only through catastrophe, at the highest cost, can 'a single life' attain to consciousness of the destiny it longs to be united with. Milton struggles to bridge the gap, and to assert the oneness of a man's individual experience and the larger patterns of providence. But that struggle in art carries with it Milton's tragic consciousness that in life the gap is unbridgeable. It is an ancient awareness. Milton's achievement is to rediscover it in terms of the problems, ideas and images of his time. The wisdom of *Samson Agonistes* is its appreciation of the pain of living within a perplexed consciousness of one's place and responsibility in the world, and Milton arrives at that wisdom in part by including in his work shadows of the imperial dreams, pious hopes, facile orderings and obdurate despairs which men fell back on (as they do habitually) in respect of the new regime in the 1660s. In *Samson Agonistes* Milton understands why men edge towards easy solutions, or closed pessimism, even as he places those impulses within a larger vision of the high potentiality inherent in history, revealed only as it is inevitably betrayed in a fallen world. Milton's is a lone voice. It was scarcely possible for a lesser writer, grappling with such themes, to produce a work of comparable depth and power. No other writer found a way of transmuting his engagement with political and historical anxieties into Milton's mastering detachment from historical confusion.

It is remarkable that the unacted play of an isolated, elderly enemy of the state should be the work which raises historical anxiety to tragic power, thereby giving full moving utterance to an important element in contemporary experience. And to make that observation is to beg the question which underlies this study throughout, as to the relationship between a work of literature and the society from which it originates. Milton's is a lone voice; nevertheless that voice offers a more sensitive response to the concerns of his time than any other. This is not merely to suggest what is obvious, that the greatness of Milton's art can be felt in the quality of its political and historical intelligence. Rather, it is to make the stronger claim that the greatness of the art, when properly judged, educates us in a deeper, truer sense of the potentiality and loss, social and psychological, inherent in a particular human world at a particular moment in time. That is a large claim to make, especially of *Samson Agonistes*, which for modern readers readily floats free of history. My purpose in making it, apart from to praise Milton, is to prepare a way of talking about the failure of lesser writers in the Restoration decade. Their artistic failure can be felt in their failure to achieve any very penetrating understanding of politics and history in action, and that failure of achievement must in turn be explained in terms of their failure to *seek* any such understanding. And their failure to seek can largely be explained in terms of complacency about their own art. A reading of Restoration poetry enlisted in polemic service points to one conclusion. Underlying much of the political poetry of the decade — and the charge must be directed chiefly against royalist panegyrists — is the suspect assumption that the end of poetry is to give form and persuasiveness to a fiction and that the fiction itself is enough. It is a watered-down version of Sidney's argument that poetic fancies shadow forth platonic truths, 'not...what is, or is not, but what should or should not be'. But watered-down, such a view meant selling short the potentiality of poetry, especially in an age which increasingly suspected that platonic truths were so many whimsies of the mind. The poet's first task, in the interests of propaganda, was to present ideal celebratory images of the king, monarchy and the achievements of the regime. Translating that into other terms, one might say that the poet's task was to create a 'myth', or less nobly a fiction, a falsehood. The pressure on the poet was not the pressure of catching reality, but the opposite, the need to glaze over things. Such a pressure produces poetry of artifice. This is paradoxical, given how close the writers were to the material they dealt with. Most royalist panegyric treated actual personages, current events and contemporary history, about which the writers were usually well-informed and in which they were often closely implicated. This paradox can be illuminated, as my discussion in the early part of this book is intended to show, by a consideration of the predicament which panegyrists faced in the years immediately after the Restoration. There was a degree of provisionality and uncertainty at the heart of the Restoration settlement. There was nothing which could be pointed to as 'social reality'. Political exigencies were confused. There was no received version of the immediate past, and hence no established ways of seeing the present or anticipating the future; and the literary conventions to hand were in various ways anachronistic or inappropriate. In such a situation, in answer to a widespread and many-faceted desire for reparation and restoration, the poets engaged in an art of fabrication. A naive craftsman like Sir William Davenant, for example, was concerned to work up a coherent and positive view of the king's return. He made his job straightforward by the exclusion of complicating doubts and alternatives. Davenant's poems were (and are) superficial exercises, in which his artistic complacency betrays his political sophistication. The effectiveness of his poetry is undermined by his facile language, which offers no resistance to his polemical ambitions. The literary historian, alert to contextual nuance, can pick up Davenant's glibness:

You keep with prudent arts of watchful care
Divided Sects from a conjunctive War;
And when unfriendly Zeal from Zeal dissents,
Look on it like the War of Elements;
And, God-like, an harmonious World create,
Out of the various discords of your State.
    (*Poem to the Kings Most Sacred Majesty*, 141-6)

The poetry is unable to isolate itself from the larger current of contemporary language and experience, which brings a devastating pressure and density to bear on Davenant's artifice. For the retrospective reader, the poem is beleaguered with ironies of which it is unaware. This makes it interesting evidence of Davenant's effete social intelligence, but does nothing to improve its literary standing.

In the work of those subtler writers who faced the same predicament, the ironies are not all the privilege of the historian: some at least are incorporated in the poems as part of a more complex and strategically sophisticated sense of the poet's difficulties in presenting an account of contemporary history. One such writer, as we have seen, is Cowley, whose intricate forms and oblique concerns, explored across conflicting frames of reference, enabled him in part to absorb doubts about the political settlement and in part to evade the need to admit such doubts. In particular Cowley recognises, somewhat wistfully, that his view of public events is inextricably bound up with his own peculiar personal fortunes. Cowley's is hardly great poetry either, but its acknowledgement of the problems involved in concocting heroic images of the contemporary world gives it a certain integrity.

Dryden, by comparison, engages directly with the trickiness of his task and turns it to positive advantage. He is the greatest because the canniest of the Restoration panegyrists. The distinctive texture of his verse of the early 1660s shows his responsiveness to the difficulties he faced. More or less absent are the features of his later verse — 'the full resounding line, / The long majestic march', which Pope noticed, the suavely conversational tone and the energetic sweep of paragraph and argument. This is not just a matter of immaturity. Dryden's poems of welcome to the new regime are full of friction, sluggishness, overjudicious and compromising kinds of ingenuity. He persistently admits negative possibilities:

> Frosts that constrain the ground, and birth deny
> To flow'rs, that in its womb expecting lye,
> Do seldom their usurping Pow'r withdraw,
> But raging floods pursue their hasty thaw:
> Our thaw was mild, the cold not chas'd away
> But lost in kindly heat of lengthnd day.
> Heav'n would no bargain for its blessings drive
> But what we could not pay for, freely give.
> The Prince of Peace would like himself confer
> A gift unhop'd without the price of war.
> Yet as he knew his blessings worth, took care
> That we should know it by repeat'd pray'r;
> Which storm'd the skies and ravish'd *Charls* from thence
> As Heav'n it self is took by violence.
>   (*Astraea Redux*, 131-44)

The rhythms here are constrained too, or stretched, and the couplets are twisted. The verse with its 'seldom', 'but', 'not', 'but', 'but what we could not', 'without', 'yet' is full of resistance and forced difficulty, wanting to find something almost unnatural and dangerous in Charles's happy return: 'As Heav'n it self is took by violence'. There is a curious confusion of vehicle and tenor, agent and recipient, as if to perplex explanations of the event. 'The Prince of Peace would like himself confer/ A gift': is Charles the prince of peace here, or merely the gift? Is the gift Charles himself, or the ensuing peace? Blasphemous literalness, clever figurativeness and providential blandness strain together in such lines. Dryden is felt to be grappling with a complex array of pressures here. In 1662 he wrote to Clarendon about the Chancellor's enemies:

> Let Envy then those Crimes within you see
> From which the Happy never must be free;
> (Envy that does with misery reside,
> The joy and the revenge of ruin'd Pride;)
>   (*To My Lord Chancellor*, 119-22)

Here too the abstractness of explanation in which Dryden seeks consolation for a recalcitrant political climate leads to peculiarly involuted verse, where 'Envy', 'Crimes', happiness, 'misery', 'joy', 'revenge', ruin and pride must be thought of in terms of complex interrelating equations. Later in the same poem he adds:

You have already weary'd Fortune so
She can not farther be your friend or fo;
But sits all breathlesse, and admires to feel
A Fate so weighty that it stops her wheel.

Dryden's verse also strains beneath such a weight, as its casual and occasional qualities are stopped by the heavy fate it deals with. One simple but very important aspect of this is Dryden's determination to invest his poetry with a charge of particularity and contemporaneity, even while keeping one eye firmly on the general patterns and values he would reveal. As a result his poetry gains immediacy, but his larger aims are threatened. In *Annus Mirabilis* concreteness is achieved through journalistic details and lush sensuous imagery, but, as I have argued, such inclusive attentiveness to a random world of things subverts the providential order Dryden would assert. At best the poem is a teetering balance act.

From this one is drawn to speculate on a central tug-of-war in Restoration poetry. On one hand the poetry pulls towards order and idealisation, constructing coherent if elaborate patterns in art as it seeks to reveal them in history. In response to the chaos of contemporary life, never felt so keenly as in the moments just before Charles's return, a need arose for stable self-definition, at many levels. To assuage that need poets devised artificial and comforting versions of things. The impetus of such poetry was the will to give substance to an idea — restoration. But by constricting the poet's power to explore the world freely, such an attitude produced attenuated poetry. A logical conclusion of this process can be pointed to in Dryden's funeral-pindaric on the death of Charles in 1685, a generation later. *Threnodia Augustalis* is turgid and vacuous because it is so very wishful. Structure quite overwhelms content, both in terms of the poem's form and also in terms of the pattern Dryden would impose on history by arguing for the inevitability of James's succession. On this occasion Dryden uses the loosely architectural pindaric, as Cowley had done, to evade history. The poem ends by hailing James with a clear echo of Dryden's poem in welcome of Charles, as Neptune 'with a willing hand, restores / The *Fasces* of the Main'. It is as if history has neatly moved in a circle of twenty-five years, rather than forward in a line: we are supposed to be back once again at the momentous point of restoration. But the colourlessness of the language, its stripping of particularity, shows Dryden hardly bothering to give substance to his own claims. It is, after all, contingent on the verdict of posterity:

> For all those Joys thy Restauration brought,
> For all the Miracles it wrought,
> For all the healing Balm thy Mercy pour'd
> Into the Nations bleeding Wound...
> For these and more, accept our Pious Praise;
> 'Tis all the Subsidy
> The present Age can raise,
> The rest is charg'd on late Posterity.

On the other hand there is also in the poetry of the period an opposite pull, in which the pressure of the unruly material world is felt; in which humans have a solid, if atomistic, individuality; in which is registered — to use a later phrase of Rochester's — life's struggle against its tendency to become 'the lumber of the world'. In other places, on less grandiose occasions, Dryden's poetry moves in this direction. It is the impetus behind some of the period's crude satire, as it uncovers the gross materialism behind the elaborate artifices of state. Chiefly, as I have tried to show, it energises Marvell's unwieldy satire, *The Last Instructions to a Painter*. But a vital qualification must be made. What invigorates Marvell's poetry is not merely the vividness, numerousness and specificity of its raw materials. What matters is Marvell's attitude to the world. He is concerned to strip away, to scrutinise, to turn over, to look sharply and closely at and into things. In other words his poetry is powered by a probing, sceptical quality of mind. It is truth-seeking art, the very opposite of the will to give substance to a fiction. The concreteness of Marvell's art, so unusual in the Restoration decade (and yet to become a centrally enlivening feature in the work of Marvell's successors — Swift, Gay, Pope and Johnson), is a consequence of his belief that the chaos and multiplicity of the world can reveal its own meaning — or, at the very least, that the world demands intense open attention, in search of its possible meaning. Marvell immerses himself in the flux of history and politics, appreciating the coagulation of disparate energies, specific material things and distinctive psychologies. Marvell's Restoration poems are very mixed. They remain bound by his polemic commitment, which, although it is to overturn, binds him in turn to the artifices and deceptions he would challenge. The apotheosis of the loyal Scot at the end of *The Last Instructions to a Painter* aspires to an iconic force as awkwardly as does Dryden's idealisation of Charles at the end of *Annus Mirabilis*. There is, however, an affinity between Marvell's polemic and Milton's wresting himself free of polemic in *Samson Agonistes*. Milton also understands, profoundly, that the truth of things can only be discovered by living it in history — calamitously, in Samson's case. In *Samson Agonistes*, as indeed in *Paradise Lost*, Milton struggles with the complex processes of questioning by which the meaning of history can be sought and perhaps grasped.

I am arguing that one legacy of the Restoration's troubled attempts to define itself though fabricated ideas was a countermanding pressure of scrutiny, which turned men's attention back to the intractability of things as they actually were. In the case of literature what begins as an enfeebling problem is gradually turned, by the best writers, into a new source of strength. The writing of the early 1660s is debilitated by its failure to deal with the contradictory ways history can be explained — the mind's conflicting pull towards idealisation, and towards the subversion of its own loftiest dreams. We are uncomfortable, for example, with Dryden's attempt to explain away rebelliousness as a penitential sacrament: 'as those Lees that trouble it, refine / The agitated Soul of Generous Wine' (*Astraea Redux*, 272-3). The incongruity of both his explanation and his image asks to be passed over tactfully by the reader. Twenty years later, in *Absalom and Achitophel*, it is the appreciative play with precisely such incongruity that enlivens the poem. Dryden's wit particularly turns on people's comically bland obscuring of distinctions:

Th' *Egyptian* Rites the *Jebusites* imbrac'd;
Where Gods were recommended by their Tast.
Such Savory Deities must needs be good,
As serv'd at once for Worship and for Food.
    (118-21)

By this stage Dryden has discovered a liberating, critical way of making something from what was problematic earlier.

Such examples of how poetry in the period finds its true life point to some of the larger ways in which English society after the

Restoration found itself. It was a matter not of living up to wistful images but of discovering the potentiality within the new society of the time. As in literature, so in life: the longing for ideology led swiftly to a sense of the fakeness and failure of the ideology offered. This was felt in distinctively Restoration terms, although memories of failed ideology during the civil wars were still about as background shadows. The important factor was the conspicuous failure of the Restoration regime to make good its own ideological claims, a fault lying as much with the grand, ahistorical nature of those claims as with the deficiencies of the regime. Practical shortcomings and mythical self-images do not square. The very act of imagining a splendid all-explaining myth carries with it a degree of disbelief. Almost any subsequent event or new piece of information must bring disillusionment as it requires readjustment of the myth. One might conclude that the quality of scrutinising particularity in which literature finds vitality reflects other qualities of the society, arrived at as part of the same process of cultural change. Pragmatism; empiricism; flexibility; a new 'honesty' of desire and self-determination; a form of government which admits an increasing degree of dynamic, participatory scrutiny — in such terms, very generally, one thinks of the achievements of the age inaugurated with Charles's return. In some measure they follow from the failure of the idea of restoration as it was first uttered in 1660. What happened in Charles II's reign was part of a larger, more complicated, more gradual process of change, of course, but within that process the year 1660 had a catalytic force, I suggest, partly because of the oversimplified, overconfident, overinflated set of assumptions which a confused, unstable society was willing — or forced — to settle for at Charles's return.

I began this investigation of political literature in the 1660s by mentioning Pope's suspicions of the developments that followed Charles's Restoration. Pope's friend Jonathan Swift shows a more marked contempt for the age that saw itself as triumphantly 'modern'. In his *Battle of the Books* Swift lampoons Dryden for setting himself up as the modern match for Virgil, the great imperial poet. To engage with Virgil Dryden rides in on a monstrous gelding in a clattering suit of armour; but when Dryden reveals himself inside the armour, Virgil is suddenly

possessed with Surprize and Disappointment together: For, the

Helmet was nine times too large for the Head, which appeared Situate far in the hinder Part, even like the Lady in a Lobster, or like a Mouse under a Canopy of State, or like shrivled Beau from within the Pent-house of a modern Perewig: And the voice was suited to the Visage, sounding weak and remote. *Dryden* in a long Harangue soothed up the good *Antient*, called him *Father*, and by a large deduction of Genealogies, made it plainly appear, that they were nearly related.[1]

Swift is ruthlessly sensitive here to the cultural and historical pretensions of the poet of the Restoration. The modern anxiety to establish contact with a great ancient tradition is seen by Swift as the merest vanity, when what should be most apparent is the radical discrepancy between ancient values and modern capacities. Virgil's armour is of gold, 'the others but of rusty Iron'. Swift considers it an evasion of self-knowledge, and responsible self-scrutiny in the limited present, to go casting about for large ideals, golden worlds, great traditions and remote utopias. To aspire to find oneself in those terms is not to find oneself at all. And Swift's intuition is right. He focuses on the gap between aspiring rhetoric and what can actually be achieved. As we have seen, within the limited terms of the present study, that gap is central to much of the writing of the Restoration years. Swift, unlike Pope, makes little allowance for the historical pressures which forced such a gap, and is impatient of the kinds of art, or of consciousness, which such historical pressures encouraged. Dryden, like Cowley, like Marvell, like Milton, was troubled about the ways of providence, unsettled by history, and creatively driven by the discrepancy between the two. And to say that is to discover that the major poets of the 1660s were in touch with the central concerns of their time.

It is sometimes said that the emergence of the modern world can be described in terms of the secularisation of history, which made possible the evolving dream (and subsequent disappointments) of unending temporal advance. If so, the Restoration of Charles II is a good place to watch the story in action. When we read the writers of the 1660s, what we feel, explored with vastly different degrees of intelligence and sensitivity, is the pressure of a time which denied the consolations of providence and forced men into the flux of history. The greatest work to appear in the 1660s was *Paradise Lost*. There Milton wrests an epic, a psychological narrative, from the cyclic, redemptive shape which providence wants things to have. The work ends with man's first steps into his own world of mutability and historical time:

> In either hand the hastening angel caught
> Our lingering parents, and to the eastern gate
> Led them direct, and down the cliff as fast
> To the subjected plain; then disappeared.
> They looking back, all the eastern side beheld
> Of paradise, so late their happy seat,
> Waved over by that flaming brand, the gate
> With dreadful faces thronged and fiery arms:
> Some natural tears they dropped, but wiped them soon;
> The world was all before them, where to choose....

No other place could be as movingly right or as appropriately challenging for the humankind we have come to understand and value in the course of Milton's long poem. The discovery of that world, one might say, extending the figure, and the last lingering resistance to it, was the concern of those writers whose work has been examined in this study. It is ironical that the Restoration of a king who claimed divine right should have so shaped men's impulse to restore responsibility to themselves. The political literature of the 1660s illuminates the way men deal with the angel of history, blown into the future while looking towards the past.

NOTES

PREFACE

1. All quotations are from *The Poems of Alexander Pope*, ed. John Butt (reprinted, 1968).

2. Samuel Johnson, *Lives of the English Poets*, ed. G.B.Hill (3 vols, Oxford, 1905), III, 87.

3. Witness John Wain, 'Restoration Comedy and its Modern Critics', *Essays in Criticism*, VI (1956), 367-85, the reply by F.W. Bateson, 'Second Thoughts: II. L.C.Knights and Restoration Comedy', *Essays in Criticism*, VII (1957), 56-67, and subsequent comments by William Empson and Norman Holland in the same journal.

4. Thomas Babington Macaulay, *The History of England from the Accession of James the Second*, ed. C.H. Firth (vol. I, 1913), pp. 160-1.

5. Thomas Babington Macaulay, *Critical and Historical Essays* (2 vols, 1907), II, pp. 414-15, 419.

6. Any investigation of this relationship raises numerous questions of methodology, but to chase them all up would take me far from my primary concerns. I return to some of the issues in my concluding chapter. Michael McKeon has a fine account of the methodological problems in *Politics and Poetry in Restoration England : The Case of Dryden's 'Annus Mirabilis'* (Cambridge, Mass., 1975), pp. 1-43.

7. Theodor Adorno, *Minima Moralia : Reflections from Damaged Life*, trans. E.F.N. Jephcott (1974), p. 219.

CHAPTER 1   THE STATE CHAOS

1. *CSPD*, CCXXI, 428.

2. *Minor Poets of the Caroline Period*, ed. George Saintsbury (Vol.I, Oxford, 1905), pp. 507-8.

3. *The Complete Poems of Dr. Joseph Beaumont*, ed. Alexander B. Grosart (2 vols, Edinburgh, 1880), II, 146.

4. *Astraea Redux*, 236-7;*Britannia Rediviva* (Oxford, 1660), sig.Bb3ᵃ; Rachel

Jevon, *Exultationis Carmen* (1660), p. 6.

5.   Lines 358-69; the poem is reprinted in *POAS*, I, 3-19.

6.   *The Complete Poems of John Wilmot, Earl of Rochester*, ed. David M. Vieth (New Haven and London, 1968), p. 155.

7.   For example, *The Cities Loyalty Display'd* (1661), *Of the Celebration of the King's Coronation-Day, In the famous City of Bath* (1661) and Tatham's London pageants; for Dover and Canterbury, Pepys, I, 158-61.

8.   Pepys, I, 92; *Iter Boreale*, 344-7.

9.   John Collop, *Itur Satyricum* (1660), p. 4.

10. *Astraea Redux*, 285; Collop, *Itur Satyricum*, p. 4; cf. Macaulay, I, 142-3.

11. Carew Reynel, *The Fortunate Change* (1661), reprinted in *Fugitive Tracts*, second series, 1660-1700 (1875), sig. A2ᵇ; Henry Bold, *Poems* (1664), p. 208. Bold was an Oxford don, known for his drinking and castigated by Anthony à Wood for his ready about-face to support of the Restoration, one of those who 'on the change, acted like so many *Protei*", Andrew Clark, *The Life and Times of Anthony Wood, Antiquary, of Oxford, 1632-1695, described by Himself* (4 vols, Oxford, 1891-95, I, 369; *A Poem Upon his Majesties Coronation* (1661, author unknown), p. 9.

12. Masson, V, 415.

13. *The Memoirs of Edmund Ludlow*, ed. C.H. Firth (2 vols, Oxford, 1894), I, 274, 356.

14. For a general discussion of this subject, Alastair Fowler, *Triumphal Forms* (Cambridge, 1970).

15. Richard Bulstrode, *Memoirs and Reflections Upon the Reign and Government of King Charles the Ist and King Charles the IId* (1721), p. 222.

16. Ogg, I, 139.

17. The following paragraphs draw on Austin Woolrych's account of the events leading to the Restoration, given in 'Last Quests for a Settlement, 1657-1660', *The Interregnum: The Quest for Settlement, 1646-1660*, ed. G.E.Aylmer (1972), pp. 183-204, and the historical introduction to Milton, *Complete Prose*, VII, pp. 1-228; supplemented by Davies, pp. 70-363 and the recent account by J.R. Jones, *Country and Court: England 1658-1714* (1978), pp. 113-39. Also in general Masson, V, 414-703; Ogg, I, 1-34, 141-7; and Christopher Hill, *The Century of Revolution, 1603-1714* (1961), pp. 117-18, 142-4. For specific areas, Clements R. Markham, *A Life of the Great Lord Fairfax* (1870), pp. 380-3; J.D. Griffith Davies, *Honest George Monck* (1936), pp. 206-29; David Underdown, *Royalist Conspiracy in England, 1649-1660* (New Haven, 1960), pp. 254-85, 312; Lois G. Schwoerer, *No Standing Armies: The Antiarmy Ideology in Seventeenth-Century England* (Baltimore and London, 1974), pp. 69-71.

18. Edward, Earl of Clarendon, *The History of the Rebellion and Civil Wars in England Begun in the Year 1641*, ed. W. Dunn Macray (6 vols, Oxford, 1888),

XVI, 13. Reference is to book and paragraph.

19.   Davies, p. 101.

20.   George Roberts, *Britannia Rediviva*, sig. Cc1ᵇ.

21.   Woolrych, 'Last Quests', p. 193.

22.   *The Letter-book of John Viscount Mordaunt*, 1658-60, ed. Mary Coate (Camden third series, vol. LXIX, 1945), p. 31.

23.   *Memoirs of Ludlow*, II, 206-8; Markham, *Life of Fairfax*, p. 383; Ogg, I, 20; Underdown, *Royalist Conspiracy*, pp. 275, 312; Davies, p. 131 and n.; Jones, *Court and Country*, 122-3.

24.   Warwick, *Memoires*, pp. 389-90, 399.

25.   Marchamont Nedham, *Interest will not Lie, or, a View of Englands True Interest* (1659), p. 20; J.G.A. Pocock, *The Ancient Constitution and the Feudal Law* (Cambridge, 1957), p. 156.

26.   Milton, *Complete Prose*, p. 22.

27.   Ailesbury reports his own and Bulstrode Whitlock's bitterness at Ashley Cooper's quiet reversal ('being of a great discernment') at this period. *Memoirs of Thomas, Earl of Ailesbury, written by Himself*, ed. W.E.Buckley (2 vols, 1890), I, 19.

28.   *The Poems of John Collop*, ed. Conrad Hilberry (Madison, 1962), pp. 8-13.

29.   *Essays of John Dryden*, ed. W.P.Ker (2 vols, Oxford, 1926), I, 31; James Sutherland, *English Literature of the Late Seventeenth Century* (Oxford, 1969), p.137; *The Restoration*, ed. Joan Thirsk (1976), p. 41.

30.   *Sir William Davenant: The Shorter Poems, and Songs from the Plays and Masques*, ed. A.M. Gibbs (Oxford, 1972), p. 391.

31.   *History of the Rebellion*, XVI, 115; Pepys, I, 87; Milton, *Complete Prose*, VII, 171, 174, also 138; *Letter-book of John Viscount Mordaunt*, p. 174; Griffith Davies, *Honest George Monck*, p. 208, also pp. 207, 209-10; see also Ogg, I, 142 and Davies, pp. 215, 285.

32.   Sutherland, *Literature of the Late Seventeenth Century*, p. 2.

33.   *The Clarke Papers. Selections from the Papers of William Clarke*, ed. C.H. Firth (vol. IV, 1901), p. 112.

34.   *To the Kings Most Excellent Majesty* (1660), p. 5. Lluelyn was appointed the king's physician in 1660, and the same year was made a commissioner of the University of Oxford by the king. He had good cause for writing panegyric. Anthony à Wood, *Athenae Oxonienses* (2 vols, 1691-2), II, 529.

35.   Donald Nicholas, *Mr. Secretary Nicholas (1593-1669) : His Life and Letters* (1955), pp. 294-5.

36.   Moses Wall to Milton, May 1659; *The Life Records of John Milton*, ed. J. Milton French, vol. IV, 1655-69 (New Brunswick, 1956), p. 267.

37. Marchamont Nedham, *A Short History of the English Rebellion* (1661), p. [83], written in 1660.

38. *Memoires*, p. 417.

39. Davies, pp. 121, 175-6, 258; Hill, *Century of Revolution*, pp. 142-4; Schwoerer, *No Standing Armies*, pp. 67-71, 75-78; Pocock, *The Ancient Constitution*, p.156; Milton, *Complete Prose*, VII, 144; Joan Thirsk, 'The Restoration Land Settlement', *Journal of Modern History*, XXVI (1954), 315-28; H.J. Habakkuk, 'Landowners and the Civil War', *Economic History Review*, second series, XIII (1965), 130-51. *The Interest of England Stated* (1659, author unknown), pp.4, 9; Woolrych, 'Last Quests', p.201.

40. 'Epistle Dedicatory to *The Rival Ladies*', 'Preface to *Annus Mirabilis*; *Essays of John Dryden*, I, 1, 14.

41. For example, Cowley's *Restoration Ode*, line 207 and John Locke, *Britannia Rediviva*, sig. Ff3.

42. *Complete Poems of John Wilmot*, pp. 94-5.

43. For example, Etherege's *She Would If She Could* (1668), Sedley's *The Mulberry-Garden* (1668) and Wycherley's *Love in a Wood* (1671).

44. John Fitz-William, *Britannia Rediviva*, sig. Eel[a].

CHAPTER 2   NEW ORDER

1. Thirsk, 'The Restoration Land Settlement', p. 323.

2. H.J. Habakkuk, 'Landowners and the Civil War'; Ailesbury, *Memoirs*, I, 6-7.

3. *Britannia Rediviva*, sig. Ee4[b]; Alexander Brome, *Songs and Other Poems*, the Third Edition enlarged (1668), pp. 322-3, written in 1660; Thomas Higgons, *A Panegyrick to the King* (1660), pp. 6-7. Higgons was an MP from January 1659 until the middle 1660s.

4. C.V.Wedgewood, *Poetry and Politics Under the Stuarts* (Cambridge, 1960), p. 196; Lawrence Stone, 'Literacy and Education in England, 1640-1900', *Past and Present*, 42 (1969), pp. 69-139.

5. Barbara Everett has a fascinating essay on Milton's use of ancient names, 'The End of the Big Names: Milton's Epic Catalogues', *English Renaissance Studies, Presented to Dame Helen Gardner in honour of her Seventieth Birthday* (Oxford, 1980), pp. 254-70; Christ's rejection of Greek philosophy in *Paradise Regained* is suggestive in this context; see also my discussion of *Samson Agonistes's* anti-Romanness in Chapter 8 below.

6. J.G.A.Pocock, *Politics, Language and Time* (1972), p. 199.

7. 'T.G.' in *Britannia Rediviva*, sig. Ff1[a].

8. Joan Thirsk, 'The Fantastical Folly of Fashion: the English Stocking Knitting Industry, 1500-1700', *Textile History and Economic History*, ed. N.B.

Harte and K.G. Ponting (Manchester, 1973), pp. 50-73; also Joan Thirsk, *Economic Policy and Projects: The Development of a Consumer Society in Early Modern England* (Oxford, 1978), pp. 106-32; for an illustration, see scene 1 of *The Man of Mode* where Dorimant's fruit is a sign of status.

9. *Brome*, Songs, p. 323.

10. *Commons Journals*, VIII, 172 (September, 1660).

11. *The Life of Edward Earl of Clarendon, Lord High Chancellor of England, and Chancellor of the University of Oxford* (3 vols, Oxford, 1759), I, 96.

12. Ibid., pp. 96-7.

13. I.M. Green, *The Re-establishment of the Church of England 1660-1663* (Oxford, 1978), p. 200 and *passim*. This work thoroughly re-examines the available evidence on this difficult topic and makes important distinctions between the changing policies of Charles, Hyde and the other parties involved.

14. Robert S. Bosher, *The Making of the Restoration Settlement, 1649-1662* (Dacre Press, Westminster, 1957), p. 274. Formerly the standard account, this book emphasises the coercive imposition of the Anglican settlement.

15. Green, *Re-establishment of the Church*, p. 210; also pp. 1-2, 203-36.

16. Ibid., p. 200; Anne Whiteman, 'The Re-establishment of the Church of England, 1660-1663', *Transactions of the Royal Historical Society*, fifth series, 5 (1955), p. 130.

17. Green, *Re-establishment of the Church*, p. 180.

18. Reprinted in *The Restoration*, ed. Thirsk, p. 156.

19. *The Downfall of Mercurius Britannicus, Pragmaticus, Politicus, That Three Headed Cerberus* (1660, author unknown), title page.

20. David Hume, *The History of England, From the Invasion of Julius Caesar to the Revolution in 1688* (8 vols, 1807) VII, 368-9.

21. 'G.V.', 'T.G.', W. Portman, in *Britannia Rediviva*, sigs. Aa2[a], Ff1[a], Ff1[b]; Joseph Beaumont, *Psyche*, canto XI, stanza 138.

22. Collop, *Itur Satyricum*, pp. 8-9.

23. *Britannia Rediviva*, sig. Ee4[a].

24. Masson, VI, 332-3.

25. For example, Pepys, II, 174.

26. For examples see the notes to lines 89-92 and 144 of *Heroick Stanzas* in the Clark Dryden, vol.I; also James D. Garrison, *Dryden and the Tradition of Panegyric* (Berkeley and Los Angeles, 1975), pp. 129-40.

27. *A Letter from a Person of Quality, To His Friend in the Country* (1675), p. 2. Ashley Cooper and Locke are possible authors of this pamphlet. Also, Ogg, I, 139.

28. Ogg, I, 139-40.

29. Hume, *History of England*, VII, 373.

30. Ibid., p. 377.

31. Davies, p. 363; Thirsk, 'Younger Sons', pp. 358-77; E.A. Wrigley, 'A Simple Model of London's Importance in Changing English Society and Economy, 1650-1750', *Past and Present*, 37 (1967), 44-70.

32. Masson, VI, 224.

33. Nedham, *A Short History*, p. 54.

34. *Letter from a Person of Quality*, p. 3.

35. Stone, *Causes of the English Revolution*, p. 114.

36. *To the Kings Most Excellent Majesty*, p. 6.

37. *A Panegyrick to the King, p. 8.*

38. [Samuel Tuke?,] *A Character of Charles the Second* (1660), p. 6.

39. *A Poem to His Most Excellent Majesty Charles the Second* (1660), p. 5. Beeston became a Doctor of Law at New College, Oxford, in 1660 (Wood, *Athenae Oxonienses*, II, 805).

40. *Englands Joy For the coming in of our Gratious Soveraign King Charles the II* (1660), broadsheet.

41. *Modern Policy Compleated* (1660), p. 55. Lloyd left his rectory at Ibstone in 1659 to become reader in the Charterhouse, until 1663.

42. Davies, pp. 340-1.

43. See, generally, R.H. Tawney, *Religion and the Rise of Capitalism*, 1926, pp. 228-73.

44. Ailesbury, *Memoirs*, pp. 6-7.

45. *A Poem Upon His Majesties Coronation* (1661, author unknown), p. 6.

46. Reynel, *The Fortunate Change*, sig. B1ª.

47. *Eikon Basilike, or, The True Pourtraicture of his Sacred Majesty Charls the II* (1660), Book I, p. 60.

48. Harold Fisch, *Jerusalem and Albion: The Hebraic Factor in Seventeenth-Century Literature (1964)*, p. 166; French R. Fogle, 'Milton as Historian', *Milton and Clarendon*, Clark Library Seminar (Los Angeles, 1965), pp. 1-20.

49. Sir Charles Firth's remark is quoted and discussed by H.R. Trevor-Roper, 'Clarendon and the Practice of History, *Milton and Clarendon*, pp. 42-3.

50. Macaulay, I, 134, also p. 143.

51. Masson, VI, 343.

52. Tawney, *Religion and the Rise of Capitalism*, pp. 250, 268.

53. *Century of Revolution*, pp. 188-9.

CHAPTER 3   IDEAS OF RESTORATION I : THE PANEGYRIC
TASK

1. Memoirs, I, 9-10.

2. *The Interest of England stated*, p. 13.

3. Nedham, *Interest will not Lie*, p. 20.

4. J. Walker, 'The Censorship of the Press During the Reign of Charles II',*History*, new series, XXXV (1950), 219-38; Sutherland, *English Literature of the Late Seventeenth Century*, p. 271; Masson,VI, 326-30.

5. Roger L'Estrange, *Considerations and Proposals in Order to the Regulation of the Press* (1663), p. 8; *DNB* entry 'L'Estrange'.

6. Milton, *Complete Prose*, VII, 462.

7. Howard, *Poems on Several Occasions* (1696), p. 9.

8. *Minor Poets of the Caroline Period*, I, 297.

9. Joseph Beaumont, *Psyche*, canto XX, stanza 46.

10. *Memoires*, pp. 410-11.

11. Cf. W. Portman who rejoiced to be 'suddenly transformed', *Britannia Rediviva*, sig. A2ᵃ, and John Collop who saw the nation 'converted', chains changed to gold, *Itur Satyricum*, p. 4.

12. *Heroick Portraits*, sig. B3ᵃ.

13. Dryden, *Astraea Redux*, 212; Warwick, *Memoires*, p. 399.

14. *Memoires*, p. 429.

15. Richard Bulstrode, *Memoirs and Reflections*, p. 324.

16. 'T.G.', *Britannia Rediviva*, sig. Ff1ᵃ.

17. *Memoirs*, II, 326.

18. In many respects it was a version of patriarchalism (although Filmer had died a decade earlier and *Patriarcha* was not to be published until 1680). Filmer had wanted 'a principle that would make it impossible for people to defend change of any sort and he evidently believed that he had hit upon such a principle in patriarchalism', *Patriarcha and Other Political Works of Sir Robert Filmer*, ed. Peter Laslett (Oxford, 1949), p. 31.

19. Jane Lang, *Rebuilding St. Paul's after the Great Fire of London* (1956), pp. 6-10.

20. In Sir Robert Howard's *The Great Favourite* (1668) 'the Chief Building' (the king) needed 'Reparation' (*Five New Plays*, 1692, p. 209); see also the broadsheet *Rebuilding the City* (1669) in which the nation's ancient virtues are seen to need rebuilding; also *POAS*, I, 20-156, 266-83.

21. Cf. Erwin Panofsky's comment, that the Renaissance regarded the classical

past 'as a totality cut off from the present', *Renaissance and Renascences in Western Art* (Paladin edition, 1970), p. 113.

22. *Rare Prologues and Epilogues, 1642-1700*, ed. A.N. Wiley (1940), pp. 8-12; the text here is from *The Poetical Works of Sir John Denham*, ed. T.H. Banks (New Haven, 1928), pp. 94-5.

23. Cf. Kantorowicz, *The King's Two Bodies*, pp. 84, 273-84; and Frank Kermode, *The Sense of an Ending* (Oxford, 1966), pp. 67-74.

24. *Eikon Basilike*, Book II, p. 4.

25. For example, John Ogilby, *The Relation of His Majesty's Entertainment* (1661), p. 10; Robert Wild, *Iter Boreale*, 322-3; *Montelion, 1661*, sig. C3a.

26. James I had written: 'that which concernes the mysterie of the Kings power, is not lawfull to be disputed; for that is to wade into the weaknesse of Princes, and to take away the mysticall reuerence, that belongs unto them that sit in the Throne of God', *The Political Works of James I*, ed. C.H. McIlwain (New York, 1965), p. 333.

27. *To the Kings Most Excellent Majesty*, p. 6.

28. Cowley, *Restoration Ode*, 11-23; *The Works of John Dryden*, vol. I, *Poems 1649-1680*, ed. E.N. Hooker and H.T. Swedenberg, Jr. (Berkeley and Los Angeles, 1956), pp. 232-3.

29. *Heroick Portraits*, sig. B2a.

30. Sig. A4b; reprinted in *Fugitive Tracts* (1875).

31. *Poems on Several Occasions*, p. 2.

32. *To the Kings Most Excellent Majesty*, p. 8.

33. *Eikon Basilike*, Book II, p. 5.

34. Nedham, *Interest will not Lie*, p. 45.

35. [Richard Overton,] *A Remonstrance of Many Thousand Citizens* (1646), reprinted in *Tracts on Liberty in the Puritan Revolution, 1638-1647*, ed. William Haller (3 vols, New York, 1934), III, 363.

36. Quentin Skinner, 'History and Ideology in the English Revolution', *The Historical Journal*, VIII (1965), 151-78, esp. p. 165.

37. *To the Kings Most Excellent Majesty*, p. 4; *Minor Poets of the Caroline Period*, I, 302.

38. Warwick, *Memoires*, p. 437; Collop, *Itur Satyricum*, p. 5.

39. Henry Beeston, *Poem to His Most Excellent Majesty*, p. 7.

40. Lloyd, *Eikon Basilike*, Book III, p. 63.

41. Cf. Reynel, *The Fortunate Change*, sig. A3a.

42. *Exultationis Carmen*, p. 6; *Restoration Ode*, 44.

43. *Memoirs and Reflections*, p. 221.

44. N. Hodges, *Britannia Rediviva*, sig. Dd3ᵃ; [Tuke?,] *A Character of Charles the Second*, p. 6; for a general discussion of this *topos*, Larry Carver, 'The Restoration Poets and Their Father King', *HLQ,* 40 (1977), 333-51.

45. *Iter Boreale*, 134-5; also *A Poem Upon His Majesties Coronation*, p. 5.

46. Rachel Jevon, *Exultationis Carmen*, pp. 4, 7; *Astraea Redux*, 258-9.

47. *The Letters of John Dryden*, collected and edited by Charles E. Ward (Duke University Press, 1942), p. 9.

48. Mircea Eliade, *The Myth of the Eternal Return, or, Cosmos and History*, trans. Willard R. Trask (Princeton, 1954), p. 142.

CHAPTER 4   IDEAS OF RESTORATION II : LOOKING BACK AND LOOKING FORWARD

1. *Itur Satyricum*, p. 8.

2. Reynel, *The Fortunate Change*, sig. Bbᵇ; Edward Littleton, *Britannia Rediviva*, sig. Bb1ᵃ.

3. Reynel, *The Fortunate Change*, sigs. B1ᵃ⁻ᵇ; Collop, *Itur Satyricum*, p.8; [Thomas Flatman,] *A Panegyrick to His Renowned Majestie, Charles the Second* (1660), broadsheet.

4. Other similitudes of Charles to Augustus are found in Henry Bold, *Poems*, p. 218; Higgons, *A Panegyrick to the King*, p. 5; *A Poem Upon His Majesties Coronation*, p. 11.

5. *Britannia Rediviva*, sig. Ff3ᵇ.

6. For instance, *Essays of John Dryden*, ed. Ker. I, 7, 44, 177; this theme is discussed generally by Howard Erskine-Hill, 'Augustans and Augustanism: England, 1655-1759', *Renaissance and Modern Studies*, XI (1967) 69-73. For an important qualification of the Augustan 'ideal', Howard D. Weinbrot, *Augustus Caesar in 'Augustan' England: The Decline of a Classical Norm* (Princeton, 1978), *passim*.

7. For example, Isaac Barrow uses '*reditum*' as equivalent to 'restored', as do numerous others, in varying forms, in the same volume, *Academiae Cantabrigiensis SOSTRA* (Cambridge, 1660).

8. Charles was compared to Aeneas by Sir Robert Howard, *Poems on Several Occasions*, p. 8; and by Thomas Higgons, *A Panegyrick to the King*, p. 10. He was compared to Jupiter descending by Robert Whitehall, *Britannia Rediviva*, sig. Ff4ᵃ; and Dryden, *To My Lord Chancellor*, 100-4.

9. Collop, *Itur Satyricum*, p. 4.

10. John Ogilby (trans.), *The Works of Publius Virgilius Maro* (1654), p. 19; for the significance of purple, Ogilby, *The Entertainment of His Most Excellent Majestie Charles II* (1662), pp. 17-18.

11. Frances A. Yates, *Astraea: The Imperial Theme in the Sixteenth Century* (1975),

pp. 29-87; Jevon, *Exultationis Carmen*, p. 5.

12.   For example, Lucian, *Saturnalia*, Loeb edition (vol. VI, Cambridge, Mass., 1959), p. 99. Poems by Wild, Collop and Pordage refer, like Cowley's, to such abundance.

13.   *A Panegyrick to the King*, p. 11.

14.   Yates, *Astraea*, p. 39.

15.   'The Prince of Poets crowns the King of Kings' wrote John Ogilby as preface to his translation, *The Works of Publius Virgilius Maro*, p. 19.

16.   For example, in *Cymbeline*; see Emrys Jones, 'Stuart Cymbeline', *Essays in Criticism*, 11, (1961), 87-99.

17.   Stone, *Causes of the English Revolution*, p. 116.

18.   Eugenius's argument in *Of Dramatic Poesy* (1668) exemplifies this belief, *Essays of John Dryden*, I, 43-4.

19.   Erwin Panofsky, *Renaissance and Renascences in Western Art* (Paladin edition, 1970), pp. 30, 42.

20.   Christopher and Stephen Wren, *Parentalia* (1750), p. 335.

21.   *Urania* (1669), p. 7.

22.   The context of the Sheldonian Theatre and of Streater's painting is provided by E.H. Gombrich, who uses it for a different argument, *Art History and the Social Sciences* (Oxford, 1975), *passim*.

23.   Ker, I, 177.

24.   Ibid., p. 176.

25.   *Rare Prologues and Epilogues*, pp. 16-17.

26.   John Shearman, *Mannerism* (Harmondsworth, 1967), p. 42.

27.   The son had incestuously taken the murdered father's place in the 'long-widow'd Realm', Alexander Brome, *Songs and other Poems*, p. 317.

28.   *The Poems of Edmund Waller*, ed. G. Thorn Drury (2 vols, London, 1901), II, 39, 109-18.

29.   Johan Huizinga, 'The Problems of the Renaissance', reprinted in his *Men and Ideas*, trans. J.S. Holmes and H. van Marle (1960), pp. 274-5, 277.

30.   B.S. Capp, *The Fifth Monarchy Men : A Study in Seventeenth-Century English Millenarianism* (1972), pp. 19-20, 28-45, 229-32; Norman Cohn, *The Pursuit of the Millennium: Revolutionary millenarians amd mystical anarchists of the Middle Ages* (revised Paladin edition, 1970), pp. 287-300; Christopher Hill, *The World Turned Upside Down: Radical Ideas During the English Revolution* (revised Penguin edition, Harmondsworth, 1975), pp. 33-5, 96-7, 174, 190.

31.   There had also been royalist millenarians during the 1640s and 1650s, Capp, *Fifth Monarchy Men*, p. 41.

32. Thomas Saunderson, *A Royall Loyall Poem* (1660), p. 7.

33. *Ratts Rhimed to Death* (1660), pp. 15, 84.

34. Collop, *Itur Satyricum*, p. 4; for aspects of the general content of millenarian thought relevant here, Ernest Lee Tuveson, *Millennium and Utopia* (Berkeley and Los Angeles, 1949), pp. 22-70; Cohn, *Pursuit of the Millennium*, pp. 84-8, 106, 113; Capp, *Fifth Monarchy Men*, p. 41.

35. *Itur Satyricum*, p. 8; also Jevon, *Exultationis Carmen*, p. 6; Brome, *Songs and other Poems*, p. 319.

36. Wild, *Iter Boreale*, 194-223; *Ratts Rhimed to Death*, p. 84; Higgons, *A Panegyrick to the King*, p. 5. Also, Henry Oxinden, *Charls Triumphant* (1660), p. 2; cf. p. 111 below, and Cowley, *Essays*, p. 362.

37. Charles Webster, *The Great Instauration: Science, Medicine and Reform, 1626-1660* (1975); Hill, *World Turned Upside Down*.

38. Beeston, *Poem to His Most Excellent Majesty*, p. 3. Cohn, *Pursuit of the Millennium*, discusses Adam-cults, pp. 126, 176-7, 181, 283.

39. Cohn, *Pursuit of the Millenium*, pp. 63, 98-107, 156-62; Hill, *World Turned Upside Down*, pp. 39-56.

40. *Some Considerations Offered to publique View, in Behalf of the many thousand Persons interested in publique Sales* (1660), p. 8.

41. *The Armies Vindication of This Last Change* (1659), p. 20, quoted by Woolrych, in Milton, *Complete Prose*, VII, 126.

42. Quoted by James Sutherland, *English Literature of the Late Seventeenth Century*, pp. 21-2.

43. Margaret Whinney and Oliver Millar, *English Art, 1625-1714* (Oxford, 1957), pp. 33, 132-7, 145-8.

44. *History of the Royal Society*, ed. J.I. Cope and H.W. Jones (St Louis and London, 1959), pp. 122, 124.

45. Davies, p. 289.

46. *Seventeenth-Century Economic Documents*, ed. J. Thirsk and J.P. Cooper (Oxford, 1972), pp. 65-95; C.H. Wilson, *England's Apprenticeship*, p. 171.

47. 'G.M.', *The Citizens Complaint For Want of Trade* (1663), p. 3, reprinted in Fugitive Tracts, second series, 1600-1700 (1875).

48. (Anon.) *Poem Upon His Majesties Coronation* (1661), p. 9.

49. R.H. Davis, *The Rise of the English Shipping Industry in the Seventeenth and Eighteenth Centuries* (1962), pp. 306-7; Hill, *Century of Revolution*, pp. 156-9.

50. Pepys, II, 189.

51. E.R. Wasserman, *The Subtler Language*, (Baltimore, 1959), pp. 13-33, offers a seminal reading of the poem in its immediate political context; helpfully modified by Alan Roper, *Dryden's Poetic Kingdoms* (1965), pp. 141-8.

52. Bold, *Poems*, p. 218; Edwards, *To His Sacred Majesty, Charles the Second, On His Happy Return* (1660), pp. 1-2. For other occurrences of this phenomenon, Yates,*Astraea*, p. 55 and Cohn, *Pursuit of the Millennium*, pp. 13, 20.

53. Pordage, *Poems upon Several Occasions* (1660), sig. B4ᵃ; also Collop, *Itur Satyricum*, pp. 3-5; Brome, *Songs and other Poems*, p. 320.

54. Pordage, *Poems upon Several Occasions*, sig. B4ᵃ; Dryden, *Astraea Redux*, 129-36, 235-49, 284-7; Dryden, *To His Sacred Majesty*, 1-24, 25-32 (line 32 quoted); Davenant, *Poem to the Kings most Sacred Majesty*, 42-3; Robert Howard, *Poems on Several Occasions*, p. 9; Collop, *Itur Satyricum*, p. 4; Wild, *Iter Boreale*, 348-69.

55. *Minor Poets of the Caroline Period*, I, 298; Also Lluelyn, *To the Kings Most Excellent Majesty*, p. 5.

56. Pepys, III, 266-7; also Capp, *Fifth Monarchy Men*, pp. 195-215 and Hill,*World Turned Upside Down*, pp. 348-60.

57. *1661* and *1662* were probably written by John Phillips or Thomas Flatman or both. Both were rather dubious royalists at the time. Anthony à Wood attributes them to Flatman, and is followed by Masson; the *Cambridge Bibliography of English Literature* grants some involvement to Flatman; *STC* attributes them to Phillips. Internal evidence is inconclusive.

58. *Montelion, 1661*, sigs. B5ᵃ, B6ᵃ, C1ᵃ, C2ᵃ, C4ᵃ, C5ᵃ;*Montelion, 1662*, sig. B6ᵃ.

59. *Eikon Basilike*, Book I, p. 2.

60. Pepys, I, 129.

61. *Exultationis Carmen*, p. 9.

62. Alexander Brome, *Songs and other Poems*, p. 348.

63. Warwick, *Memoires*, pp. 403, 437; Lloyd, *Eikon Basilike*, Book I, p. 2, Book III, p. 63; cf. J.G.A. Pocock's discussion of the Hobbesian heaven located 'in the infinite future of the material world', *Politics, Language and Time*, p. 175.

64. My discussion of Dryden's Restoration panegyrics is concerned with how the poet shapes his material, and not with detailed explication of figures, most of which occur elsewhere in Restoration panegyric and most of which are explicated in the notes to Kinsley's edition and in the indispensable commentary and notes to the Clark edition (vol. I, *Poems, 1649-1680*, ed. E.N.Hooker and H.T.Swedenberg); for *Astraea Redux* also H.T.Swedenberg, 'England's Joy: *Astraea Redux* in its Setting', *Studies in Philology*, 50 (1953), 30-44; Jacob Leed, 'A Difficult Passage in *Astraea Redux*', *English Studies*, 47 (1966), 127-30; and Larry M. Maupin, 'Dryden's *Astraea Redux*, 163-8'. *The Explicator*, 31 (1973), No.64.

    As well as the Clark edition, any reading of Dryden's public poems must be indebted to Stephen N. Zwicker, *Dryden's Political Poetry: The Typology of King and Nation* (Providence, 1972); Garrison, *Dryden and the Tradition of Panegyric*; and George McFadden, *Dryden: The Public Writer* (Princeton,

1978); and behind them all, the introductory chapter 'An Allusion to Europe: Dryden and Poetic Tradition' in R.A.Brower, *Alexander Pope: The Poetry of Allusion* (Oxford, 1959), pp. 1-14.

CHAPTER 5 IDEAL RESTORATION AND THE CASE OF COWLEY

1. C.A.Patrides, 'The Salvation of Satan', *Journal of the History of Ideas*, XXVIII (1967), 467-78.

2. R.P.C.Hanson, *Allegory and Event: A Study of the Sources and Significance of Origen's Interpretation of Scripture* (1959), pp. 267-88, 333-56; C.A.Patrides, *The Grand Design of God; The Literary Form of the Christian View of History* (1972), pp. 13-14.

3. H. De Lubac, *Histoire et Esprit: l'intelligence de l'Écriture d'après Origène* (Paris, 1950), p. 199.

4. Henry More, *An Explanation of the Grand Mystery of Godliness* (1660), pp. 514-15.

5. H. Koch, *Pronoia und Paideusis* (Berlin and Leipzig, 1932), p. 158.

6. Henry More, *The Immortality of the Soul* (1659), pp. 371-2.

7. More, *An Explanation*, p. 145.

8. Ibid., pp. 302-3.

9. J. Loosen, 'Apokatastasis',*Lexikon für Theologie und Kirche* (Freiburg, 1957), I, 708-12; Hanson, *Allegory and Event*, pp. 333-56.

10. *The Works of Sir Thomas Browne*, ed. Geoffrey Keynes (4 vols, 1928), I, 16.

11. Cudworth, *The True Intellectual System*, p. 328. This was probably written in the late 1660s as part of a campaign to counter the irreligion seen spreading in the nation under Charles II.

12. More, *The Immortality of the Soul*, pp. 528, 532-3.

13. Gardiner, IV, 23-4; *DNB*, 'Whichcote'.

14. Hanson, *Allegory and Event*, pp. 348-51.

15. Cudworth, *The True Intellectual System*, pp. 805, 818.

16. Benjamin Whichcote, *Selected Discourses* (4 vols, 1701-7), I, 323; II, 412-13. Whichcote's discourses were written between 1636 and 1660, mainly in the 1650s.

17. Ibid., I, 78; II, 107; III, 229.

18. Ibid., II, 381.

19. *John Donne: The Elegies and The Songs and Sonnets*, ed. Helen Gardner (Oxford, 1965), p. 112.

20. 'An Epithalamium, Or mariage Song on the Lady *Elizabeth*, and *Count Palatine* being married on St. *Valentines* day' (1613); *The Poems of John Donne*, ed. H.J.C. Grierson (2 vols, Oxford, 1912), I, 130.

21. *Selected Discourses by John Smith*, ed. H.G. Williams (Cambridge, 1859), pp. 395, 452. Smith was writing between 1650 and 1652 as Dean of Queens' College, Cambridge.

22. Ibid., p. 453.

23. Thomas Hobbes, *Leviathan*, ed. C.B. Macpherson (Harmondsworth, 1968), pp. 516-17.

24. Ibid., p. 442.

25. Ibid., p. 480.

26. Arthur H. Nethercot, *Abraham Cowley, the Muses' Hannibal* (Oxford, 1931), pp. 55-8. Cowley's extensive notes to the *Davideis* reveal his familiarity with patristic writing. Whichcote was ordained by John Williams, Dean of Westminster while Cowley was at Westminster School and the subject of a poem; Henry More admired Hobbes.

27. An exception is David Trotter, who shows fascinatingly how 'history penetrated the "form"' of Cowley's work, *The Poetry of Abraham Cowley* (1979). But Trotter stops short of the Restoration. Generally Cowley has received very little attention. Robert B. Hinman, *Abraham Cowley's World of Order* (Cambridge, Mass., 1960) is a good introduction to his thought and work.

28. *Critical Essays of the Seventeenth Century*, ed. J.E. Spingarn (3 vols, Oxford, 1908), II, 84.

29. Panofsky, *Renaissance and Renascences*, p. 43n.

30. *Critical Essays*, ed. Spingarn, II, 84.

31. Ibid., vol.II, p. 125.

32. Ibid., pp. 124-5; also Nethercot, *Cowley*, pp. 158-60 and Jean Loiseau, *Abraham Cowley: Sa Vie, Son Oeuvre* (Paris, 1931), pp. 116-22, 130-5, 139-40.

33. *Calendar of the Clarendon State Papers*, vol. III, 1655-1657, ed. W. Dunn Macray (Oxford, 1876), pp. 119, 124, 129; Nethercot, *Cowley*, pp. 160-3; Loiseau, *Sa Vie*, pp. 117-18.

34. David Underdown has suggested that they are by the royalist agent John Cooper, *Royalist Conspiracy*, p. 207n.

35. First expressed in a letter from Hyde to Ormonde, 10 May, 1656, *Calendar of the Clarendon State Papers*, III, 128.

36. Letter from Ormonde to Jermyn, 21 February 1660, and letter from Jermyn to Ormonde, 19 February 1660. Reprinted by C.H.Firth, 'Abraham Cowley at the Restoration', *The Academy*, 7 October 1893, p. 296.

37. Ibid., Letter from Cowley to Ormonde, 26 December 1659.

38. Cowley wrote poems about Scarborough and Buckingham in the late 1650s and later a prologue to Tuke's play *The Adventure of Five Hours* (1663). By 1656 Tuke was 'using all the arts he can to get leave to goe into England' from France, Winifred Gardner, Lady Burghclere, *George Villiers, Second Duke of Buckingham, 1628-1687* (1903), pp. 73-4; *The Letters of Dorothy Osborne to William Temple*, ed. G.C. Moore Smith (Oxford, 1928), pp. xli-xliii, pp. 169-70.

39. Quotations from *To the Duke of Buckingham, upon his Marriage with the Lord Fairfax his Daughter* (1657) incorporate emendations derived from the more authoritative text described by Allan Pritchard in his edition *Abraham Cowley : The Civil War* (Toronto, 1973). This text, from a newly discovered MS, does not follow the politically circumspect revisions made to produce the first published version (in 1700), which Waller reprints in his standard edition of Cowley. For background to the marriage, Burghclere, *George Villiers*, pp. 91-8 and Brian Fairfax's 'Account of Buckingham', reprinted in *George Villiers: The Rehearsal*, ed. E. Arber (1868), pp 6-7.

40. Wood, *Athenae Oxonienses*, II, 30; *The Civil War*, ed. Pritchard, pp. 12-23.

41. *Critical Essays*, ed. Spingarn, II, 83.

42. Clarendon, *History of the Rebellion*, VII, 217.

43. Gilbert Burnet, *History of His Own Time* (new edition, 1857), I, 69; Burghclere, *George Villiers*, p. 35; Letters from Cowley to Henry Bennet, 11 June, 18 November 1650; 13 September 1653, printed in *Miscellanea Aulica*, ed. T. Brown (1702) pp. 139, 152, 160; 13 March 1650, printed by J. Simmons, 'An Unpublished Letter from Abraham Cowley', *MLN*, LVII (1942), 194-5.

44. For Cowley's depressed mood at the time, see his letter to Henry Bennet, 28 May 1650, *Miscellanea Aulica*, p. 137; Hilton Kelliher, 'Cowley and "Orinda": Autograph Fair Copies' *The British Library Journal*, 2 (1976), 102-4.

45. Despite Sprat's whitewashing claim that the poem was written while Cowley was still at Cambridge its real date is certainly post-1650, Frank Kermode, 'The Date of Cowley's *Davideis*', *RES* XXV (1949), 154-8. Dorothy Osborne's notice of a David and Jonathan piece by Cowley in 1654 confirms this, as does the excessive annotation, Cowley's habit only in the 1650s. Internally much of the language has an 'Interregnum' tone: for example, the Israelites 'never recovered their ancient liberty, but continued under the yoke' (p. 320.)

46. Page references are to the text in Waller's edition of Cowley's *Poems*.

47. In this period Hobbes too had come to accept the Cromwellian regime. In 1680 Cowley's poem was reprinted, but this time each item of praise was attacked, rebutted and satirised by the anonymous editor, in polemical

defence of the 'true' but shaky Stuart order.

48.   Cf. T.R.Langley, 'Abraham Cowley's "Brutus": Royalist or Republican?', *Yearbook of English Studies*, 6 (1976), 41-52. This detailed account of the poem's possible complexity of intention moves towards a different conclusion: Cowley's 'Republican smokescreen [was] altogether too thick for his Royalist intentions'.

49.   From Cowley's Latin poem on the civil war (first published in 1668, though most likely written much earlier), translated by Aphra Behn, *Of Plants, Book VI, SYLVA* (1689).

50.   Page references are to Abraham Cowley, *Essays, Plays and Sundry Verses*, ed. A.R. Waller (Cambridge, 1906).

51.   It is comparable, for example, to the displacement of Fury by the Good Genius of Great Britain and Concord, in William Davenant and Inigo Jones's *Salmacida Spolia*, performed in 1640. Ed. T.J.B. Spencer in *A Book of Masques* (Cambridge, 1967), pp. 347-52.

52.   G.A.E. Parfitt (ed.), *Silver Poets of the Seventeenth Century* (1974), p. 260.

53.   Nethercot, *Cowley*, pp. 196-200, 215; Loiseau, *Sa Vie*, pp. 140-3.

54.   Samuel Butler, *Hudibras*, ed. John Wilders (Oxford, 1967), pp. xviii-xx. Quotations are from this edition of the poem.

55.   Pepys, III, 294.

56.   Samuel Butler, *Characters and Passages from Notebooks*, ed. A.R. Waller (Cambridge, 1980), p. 371; Ian Jack, *Augustan Satire* (Oxford, 1952), p. 41.

57.   Catholic worship was re-established in the chapel of Somerset House in 1662; another of Cowley's friends, Sir Samuel Tuke, was a prominent Catholic; John Miller, *Popery and Politics in England, 1660-68* (Cambridge, 1973), pp. 21-2, 96-7; Whinney and Millar, *English Art*, 1625-1714, p. 137n.

58.   Ogg, I, 199-208; Miller, *Popery and Politics*, p. 95; K.D.H. Haley, *The First Earl of Shaftesbury* (Oxford, 1968), pp. 161-6.

59.   *Critical Essays*, ed. Spingarn, II, 143.

60.   The classic study is Robert K. Merton, *Science, Technology and Society in Seventeenth Century England* (first published 1938, reprinted New York, 1970), pp. 59-119; also Ogg, II, 611-13; G.N. Clark, *Science and Social Welfare in the Age of Newton* (Oxford, 1937), pp. 4-17, 118-46; Webster, *The Great Instauration*, pp. 88-9, 484-520; and, for a revised version of the theory, Hill, *Intellectual Origins*, pp. 125-30. Hill refers to Cowley's Ode, p.130n, but his hypothesis that the revolutionary imagery may be unconscious can probably be discounted.

61.   'Verses on the Death of Mr. Abraham Cowley, and his Burial in Westminster Abbey', *The Works of Abraham Cowley* (1700), sig. d2a. Cf. R[ichard] P[eers], *Poems* (1667), pp. 11, 18.

62.   Thomas Higgons, 'Ode Upon the Death of Mr. Cowley', *The Works of*

Abraham Cowley (1700), sig. d3ᵇ.

CHAPTER 6   THE POETRY OF THE SECOND DUTCH WAR

1. Clayton Roberts, *The Growth of Responsible Government in Stuart England* (Cambridge, 1966), pp. 151-83.

2. Ogg, I, 311.

3. *Commons Journals*, IX, 5-8, 11-14, 18-20, 27, 40, 49-53, 55, 58, 69, 72, 77, 81-2, 85-6, 88, 91-6; Pepys, VI, 122-3, 195-7, 205, 223-4, 287, 320, 320n; Ogg, I, 284-90 ,298-313, 326-30; P. Fraser, *The Intelligence of the Secretaries of State and Their Monopoly of Licensed News 1660-1688* (Cambridge, 1956),pp. 78-85; J.R. Jones, *Britain and Europe in the Seventeenth Century* (1966), pp. 56-8, 60; Roberts, *Growth of Responsible Government*, pp. 155-78; K.H.D. Haley, *The First Earl of Shaftesbury* (Oxford, 1968), pp. 171-201, 266-8; Graham Greene, *Lord Rochester's Monkey* (1974), pp. 47-54; Michael McKeon, *Politics and Poetry* , pp. 79-131.

4. Abraham Cowley, *Poemata Latina* (1668), pp. 313-64.

5. *Poems*, ed. J. Hunt (1870), p. 61. Cf. *Iter Boreale*, line 363.

6. Mary Tom Osborne, *Advice-to-a-Painter Poems 1633-1856* (University of Texas, 1949), pp. 14-17.

7. Sig. B7ᵃ.

8. One of Charles's particular aims was to preserve young William of Orange's claims against the opposition of de Witt, the Grand Pensionary of the republican States General; Feiling, pp. 85-93.

9. The edition of the poem used is found in *POAS*, I, 34-53. Discussion of the authorship of the *Second* and *Third Advices*, and further relevant references can be found in *POAS*, I, 21, and Margoliouth I, 347-50. The present study accepts Marvell's editors' reasoning and rejects an attribution to Marvell. In particular, the author of *The Last Instructions* has an altogether more sophisticated sense of the relationship between contemporary history and his literary mode than the author(s) of the earlier *Advices*. Some details of the *Second Advice's* answering burlesque of Waller's *Instructions* are given by Warren L. Chernaik, *The Poetry of Limitation: A Study of Edmund Waller* (New Haven and London, 1968), pp. 186-92.

10. For the text, *POAS*, I, 54-66.

11. For the background to unrest at this time, McKeon, *Politics and Poetry*, pp. 79-98.

12. For the text, *POAS*, I, 67-87, and see note 9 above.

13. John Locke, *Two Treatises of Government*, ed. P. Laslett (Cambridge, 1967), p. 433.

14. Ibid., p. 155.

15. Kinsley, I, 48.

16. Dryden's poem shows awareness of the tradition of painter poems: lines 133-6 and 389 probably derive from Higgons's translation, sigs. C5ᵃ, C6ᵃ; but the painter device had been degraded through largely satirical usage by the time Dryden was writing and in any case its conventions would have hampered his more ambitious aims.

17. James Kinsley, 'The "Three Glorious Victories" in *Annus Mirabilis*', *RES*, n.s., VII (1956), 30-7.

18. Roberts, *Growth of Responsible Government*, pp. 151-5, 171; Ogg, I, 320-1. The situation was so delicate that an argument in terms of balance was necessary to dispel fears of absolutism: J.R. Jones, *Britain and Europe*, pp. 57-8; Schwoerer, *No Standing Armies*, pp. 90-1. Dryden used the apparently unobjectionable notion of moderation in a parallel situation later: Charles E. Ward, *The Life of John Dryden* (Chapel Hill, 1961), pp. 123-6.

19. Charles's balance stood over against the motive for the war, the fact that the Dutch had violated *mare clausum* and upset the balance of power and trade internationally; Feiling, pp. 140-50, 98-100; Ogg, I, 246. Cf. *Annus Mirabilis*, 5-6, 25-6, 37-8, 666.

20. Kinsley, I, 44.

21. Superstition flourished in various forms in the middle 1660s and both royalists and dissenters indulged in prophecies about 1666. These phenomena are well documented by McKeon, *Politics and Poetry*, pp. 190-257. He maintains that like many other contemporary writers, Dryden used prophecy and eschatology seriously, but to his own particular ends (pp. 151-3).

22. For example, Evelyn, III, 457.

23. Bruce A. Rosenberg has discussed the poem's alchemical language: '*Annus Mirabilis* Distilled', *PMLA*, LXXIX (1964), 254-8.

24. Kinsley, I, 43.

25. Other painterly elements in the poem are discussed by Michael Gearin-Tosh, 'The Structure of Marvell's "Last Instructions to a Painter"', *Essays in Criticism*, 22 (1972), 48-57.

26. For example, Pierre Legouis, *Andrew Marvell: Poet, Puritan, Patriot* (second edition, Oxford, 1968), pp. 163-92; Ruth Nevo, *The Dial of Virtue: A Study of Poems on Affairs of State in the Seventeenth Century* (Princeton, 1963), pp. 173-9. The balance is redressed by John M. Wallace, who covers the poem's background and emphasises, rather exclusively, the poem's hopeful endorsement of loyalism in the interests of an anti-French foreign policy: *Destiny His Choice: The Loyalism of Andrew Marvell* (Cambridge, 1968), pp. 145-83; see also David Farley-Hills, *The Benevolence of Laughter: Comic Poetry of the Commonwealth and Restoration* (1974), pp. 72-98. More sympathetic is Elsie Duncan-Jones, 'A Great Master of Words: Some Aspects of Marvell's Poems of Praise and Blame' (*Proceedings of the British Academy*, 1975). In her

brilliant 'The Shooting of the Bears: Poetry and Politics in Andrew Marvell', *Andrew Marvell, Essays on the Tercentenary of his Death*, ed. R.L. Brett (Oxford, 1979), pp. 62-103, Barbara Everett appreciates Marvell's reluctance (or incapacity) to 'subsume the minutiae of [his] time into a largely unjust but vital artistic harmony'.

27. Albermarle in fact led the attack on Pett, presumably to prevent an investigation into his own conduct: Roberts, *Growth of Responsible Government*, p. 178. It suits Marvell, however, to blame Hyde and the Court for the impeachment of Pett.

28. The idea of true and false sovereignty in the poem is dealt with by Joseph H. Summers, 'Andrew Marvell: Private Taste and Public Judgement', *Stratford-upon-Avon Studies*, 11 (1970), 181-209.

29. In *The Statue in Stocks-Market*, written about 1675; Margoliouth, I, 394.

CHAPTER 7   THEATRICAL RESTORATION

1. John Tatham, *The Royal Oake With Other various and delightfull Scenes presented on the Water and the Land* (1660), sig. A1[a].

2. Evelyn describes the *impromptu* pageantry of 1660, III, 246; Denham 'Prologue to His Majesty' and Davenant, 'Poem to the Kings Most Sacred Majesty' (1663) link the theatre's restoration with the monarch's. The speeches made by representatives of the guildhalls in March and April 1660 anticipate the resemblance between verse panegyric and public display, for example, *A Speech Spoken to his Excellency the Lord General Monk ... at Drapers-Hall* (1660) and others at Skinners', Goldsmiths', Clothworkers', Vintners' and Fishmongers' Halls. For the tradition of emblematic pageantry, G.R. Kernodle, *From Art to Theatre: Form and Convention in the Renaissance* (Chicago, 1944), pp. 58-76, 90-3; Glynne Wickham, *Early English Stages*, vol. II, Part I (1963), pp. 206-44; L.J. Morrissey, 'English Street Theatre: 1655-1708', *Costerus*, 4(1972), 105-38; Frances A. Yates, *Astraea: The Imperial Theme in the Sixteenth Century (1975)*, pp. 29-87, esp. p. 41.

3. John Ogilby, *The Relation of His Majesty's Entertainment* (1661), p. 2 (the humbler first version).

4. For the contemporary importance of Claudian, James D. Garrison, *Dryden and the Tradition of Panegyric* (Berkeley and Los Angeles, 1975), pp. 22-7, 63-82, 87-99.

5. Ogilby, *The Relation of His Majestie's Entertainment* (1661), p. 2.

6. John Tatham, *Neptunes Address* (1661), p. 7.

7. John Tatham, *Londons Triumphs* (1662), p. 18.

8. Ibid., p. 10.

9. Ibid., p. 17. Cf. for the full significance of the rebuilding, Lang, *Re-building St. Paul's*, pp. 1-6.

10. John Tatham, *London's Triumphs* (1664), pp. 14-16.

11. Harold Love, 'State Affairs on the Restoration Stage, 1660-1675', *Restoration and 18th Century Theatre Research*, 19 (1975), 1-9. Most of the available information about the theatre of this period has been assembled in *The London Stage 1660-1800* (11 vols, Carbondale, 1960-8), Part I, ed. William Van Lennep, with a Critical Introduction by Emmett L. Avery and Arthur H. Scouten (1965). Details of extant plays and performance dates (if any) derive from this work and, unless otherwise stated, from two other standard works, Alfred Harbage, *Cavalier Drama* (New York and London, 1936) and Allardyce Nicoll, *A History of English Drama 1660-1900* (revised edn., 6 vols, vol. I, *Restoration Drama 1660-1700* (Cambridge, 1952).

12. Allardyce Nicoll, 'Political Plays of the Restoration', *MLR*, XVI (1921), 224-42. Nicoll provides an extensive list of examples.

13. *Cromwell's Conspiracy. A Tragy-Comedy, Relating to our latter Times. Beginning at the Death of King CHARLES the First, And ending with the happy Restauration of KING CHARLES The Second. Written by a Person of Quality.* (1660), p. 6.

14. *Hell's Higher Court of Justice; or, The Triall of the three Politick Ghosts, Viz., Oliver Cromwell, King of Sweden, and Cardinal Mazarine* (1661), sigs. C4[b], D1[a].

15. John Tatham, *The Rump: Or The Mirrour of the late Times. A New Comedy* (1660), sig. A1[a]; Love, 'State Affairs', p. 1

16. [Anthony Sadler,] *The Subjects Joy for the Kings Restoration, Cheerfully made known in A Sacred Masque: Gratefully made publique for His sacred Majesty* (1660), sig. A2[b].

17. John Wilson, *Andronicus Comnenius* (1664), sig. A3[a-b].

18. Cf. Clarendon, *History of the Rebellion*, XV, 147-9.

19. Wilson, *Andronicus Comnenius*, p. 86, p. 75, p. 29, p. 5, p. 87, p. 9.

20. Cf. *The Complete Works of St. Thomas More*, vol. 4, ed. Edward, Surtz, S.J. and J.H. Hexter (New Haven and London, 1965), pp. 240-1.

21. Pepys, IX, 381; also II, 29, 31.

22. Edward Howard, *The Usurper* (1668), p. 72, p. 65, p. 70.

23. *The Unfortunate Usurper* (1663), pp. 64-5, p. 61.

24. John Tatham, *London's Triumphs* (1664), pp. 7-8.

25. Stephen Orgel, *The Illusion of Power: Political Theater in the English Renaissance* (Berkeley and Los Angeles, 1975), *passim*.

26. Glynne Wickham, 'The Restoration Theatre', *English Drama to 1710*, ed. Christopher Ricks (1971), pp. 370-4; and note 64 below. An important general study of changing ideas of kingship in Restoration drama is Susan Staves, *Players' Scepters: Fictions of Authority in the Restoration* (Lincoln and London, 1979), Ch. 2, 'Authority and Obligation in the State', pp. 43-110, includes discussion of early Restoration tragedy.

27. Prologue to Nahum Tate's *The Loyal General* (1680): the Stuart succession was then under its next major threat.

28. Sir Robert Howard, *Four New Plays* (1665), sig. a2ᵃ; *Essays of John Dryden*, I, 120.

29. *Essays of John Dryden*, I, 119.

30. Ibid., p. 155; cf. p. 121, 'they cannot be good poets, who are not accustomed to argue well'.

31. Ibid., p. 124; Bruce King discusses philosophical scepticism in *Dryden's Major Plays* (Edinburgh and London, 1966), pp. 7-19.

32. Citations refer to the edition of the play in *The Works of John Dryden*, vol. VIII, ed. John Harrington Smith, Dougald MacMillan, Vinton A. Dearing *et al.* (Berkeley and Los Angeles, 1962).

33. Cf. Cowley's *Ode Upon His Majesties Restoration*, line 44, and Rachel Jevon, *Exultationis Carmen*, p. 6.

34. Cf. Shakespeare's *Richard III*, I.iii.14; *Cromwell's Conspiracy*, p. 4; Robert Wild, *Iter Boreale*, 61.

35. Emrys Jones, 'Bosworth Eve', *Essays in Criticism*, 25 (1975), 38-54.

36. [John Caryll,] *The English Princess, or, The Death of Richard the III* (1667), p. [66], p. 11, p. 8, p. 26, p. 61, p. 64, p. 33.

37. Edward J. Dent, *Foundations of English Opera: A Study of Musical Drama in England During the Seventeenth Century* (Cambridge, 1928), pp. 41-77; Stephen Orgel, 'The Masque', *English Drama to 1710*, ed. Christopher Ricks (1971), p. 366. Davenant had worked with Inigo Jones on the last true Caroline masque.

38. *The Dramatic Works of Sir William Davenant*, ed. James Maidment and W.H. Logan, vol. III (Edinburgh and London, 1873), pp. 257-8.

39. Ibid., p. 278, p. 332, p. 314.

40. *The Dramatic Works of John Dryden*, With a Life of the Author by Sir Walter Scott, Bart., ed. George Saintsbury (8 vols, Edinburgh, 1882), IV, 124. For other usages of 'restore', pp. 71, 95, 104, 107, 162.

41. Ibid., pp. 11-12.

42. Born an aristocrat and royalist, Boyle changed to support Cromwell in Ireland and became President of Munster; by switching to Monck in time he kept the position across the Restoration; [Winifred Gardner,] Lady Burghclere, *The Life of James First Duke of Ormonde 1610-1688* (2 vols, 1912), vol. I, p. 363; vol.II, pp. 10-11, 144-59, 288; *The Dramatic Works of Roger Boyle, Earl of Orrery*, ed. W.S. Clark II (2 vols, Cambridge, Mass., 1937), vol. I, pp. 3-60 (citations from plays use this edition); *DNB* entry 'Boyle, Roger'.

43. Pepys, VIII, 487.

44. G. Wilson Knight, *The Golden Labyrinth: A Study of British Drama*

(1962), p. 170.

45.   Epilogue to Davenant's *Siege of Rhodes*, Part Two, *Dramatic Works*, III, 365.

46.   *Commons Journal*, IX, 21-2, 25, 28, 30; *Lords Journal*, XII, 147-52, 180-4;
       Burghclere, *George Villiers, Second Duke of Buckingham*, pp. 184-8; Burghclere,
       Life of Ormonde, II, 138-51, 155-63; J.H.Wilson, *A Rake and His Times: George
       Villiers 2nd Duke of Buckingham* (1954), pp. 58, 80-3, 86-92, 97-100, 106-9,
       116-17; Roberts, *Growth of Responsible Government*, pp. 158-9, and Ch. 5,
       passim.

47.   Pepys, IX, 81; for his own attitude to the king's mistress, see, for example,
       IX, 19-20.

48.   Howard, *Five New Plays*, p. [203]; Alfred Harbage, 'Elizabethan-
       Restoration Palimpsest', *MLR*, XXXV (1940), 287-319, argues for Ford's
       substantial authorship, pp. 297-304; H.J. Oliver, *The Problem of John Ford*
       (Melbourne, 1955), pp. 131-4, introduces the Shirleys as candidates for
       authorship; cf. H.J. Oliver, *Sir Robert Howard (1626-1698): A Critical
       Biography* (Durham, North Carolina, 1963), pp. 140-1.

49.   Sir Robert Howard, *Five New Plays* (1692), p. 209.

50.   Ibid., p. 213.

51.   Ibid., pp. 226, 229.

52.   Ibid., p. 251.

53.   Ibid., p. 252.

54.   Ibid., p. 220.

55.   Oliver, *Sir Robert Howard*, pp. 142-3, adduces some Shakespearian echoes.
       Also, Lerma's Macbeth-like speeches, pp. 212-13, and his Volpone-like
       'Ha! dost thou swell, that art my creature?', p. 234.

56.   Howard, *Five New Plays*, p. 230.

57.   Ibid., p. 237.

58.   Ibid., p. 230.

59.   Ibid., p. 227; cf. Marvell's *Last Instructions*, 469-76; *The Kings Vowes*, 16-18.

60.   Cf. *Third Advice to a Painter*, 246-52.

61.   Howard's *The Duell of the Stags: A Poem* (1668) fabricated a Clarendonian
       scare to warn against the favourite's resurgence and to promote
       Buckingham (sig. A2ᵇ, pp. 1-3, 7, 13); Charles E. Ward, 'An Unpublished
       Letter to Sir Robert Howard; *MLN*, LX (1945), 119-21, testifies to the
       poem's contemporary political reading. My interpretation differs from that
       of Wilson, *A Rake and His Times*, p. 109, and Oliver, *Sir Robert Howard*, pp.
       161-5. In 1669 Buckingham inserted a scene into Howard's new comedy
       The Country Gentleman, ridiculing Coventry; Robert D. Hume, *The
       Development of English Drama in the Late Seventeenth Century* (Oxford, 1976), pp.
       260-2.

62. Roberts, *Growth of Responsible Government*, p. 183; Miller, *Popery and Politics in England*, pp. 90, 106-7, 119-20; Allardyce Nicoll, 'Political Plays of the Restoration', 231-8. The wave was heralded as early as 1671 by *The Religious-Rebell, or The Pilgrim-Prince*, about Hildebrand the tyrant Pope.

63. L.C. Knights, *Drama and Society in the Age of Jonson* (1937), p. 299; 'Restoration Comedy: The Reality and the Myth' (1937), reprinted in *Explorations* (1963), pp. 132-3; Raymond Williams, *The Long Revolution* (1961), pp. 252-4.

64. Williams, *The Long Revolution*, p. 254 and A.S. Bear, 'Criticism and Social Change: The Case of Restoration Drama', *Komos II* (1969), 23-31; countered by *The London Stage*, I, clxii-v, and Harold Love, 'Bear's Case Laid Open: Or, a Timely Warning to Literary Sociologists', *Komos II* (1969), 72-80.

CHAPTER 8 *SAMSON AGONISTES* : THE PLAY TURNED UPSIDE DOWN

1. Quotations from Milton are from *The Poems of John Milton*, ed. John Carey and Alastair Fowler (1968), and Milton, *Complete Prose*. In a slightly altered form this chapter appeared in *Essays in Criticism*, 30 (1980), 124-50. Its title alludes both to Ian Donaldson, *The World Upside Down* (Oxford, 1970) and to Hill, *World Turned Upside Down*.

2. For a recent summary of the debate, Christopher Hill, *Milton and the English Revolution* (1977), pp. 428-48, 481-6.

3. Cf. *Annus Mirabilis*, 53. Externality is a defining characteristic of the physical world and can be considered a function of our visual experience: sight is the most important sense, for example, Adrian Stokes, *The Quattro Cento* (1932), pp. 156-8.

4. John Carey, 'Sea, Snake, Flower, and Flame in *Samson Agonistes*', *MLR*, LXII (1967), 395-9.

5. *The Works of Sir Thomas Browne*, ed. Geoffrey Keynes (1928), vol. I, p. 57; Henry More, *Divine Dialogues* (1743), vol. I, p. 249; Ralph Cudworth, *The True Intellectual System of the Universe* (1678), pp. 878-9.

6. *The Works of John Milton* (Columbia University Press), vol. VI (1932), p. 178. For two important accounts of the play's historical context, which differ in approach to mine, David Masson, *The Life of John Milton* (1880-1894), vol. VI, pp. 673-4 and Hill, *Milton and the English Revolution*, pp. 428-48.

7. Vitruvius, *De Architectura*, V, iii – ix; Frances A. Yates, *Theatre of the World* (1969), pp. 112-35; John Ogilby, *The Entertainment of His Most Excellent Majesty Charles II* (1662), figures opposite pp. 13, 43, 111, 139; E.H. Gombrich, *Art History and the Social Sciences* (Oxford, 1975), pp. 18-21, 48-9; Robert Whitehall, Urania (Oxford, 1669), pp. 1-7.

8　　Robert Boyle had written 'I esteem the World a Temple', *Some Considerations touching the Usefulness of Experimental Naturall Philosophy* (Oxford, 1663), p. 57; imagery of pulling down, in contrast to rebuilding, had been used to oppose the Restoration, for example, 'It is a time of breaking and pulling down all worldly Constitutions', *The Armies Vindication of This Last Change* (1659), p. 20.

9.　　*Life of John Milton*, VI, 666.

10.　　*DNB*; Nethercot, *Cowley*, p. 131; W.R. Parker, *Milton: A Biography* (Oxford, 1968), pp. 1090-1, 1142-3.

11.　　Gerald Langbaine, *An Account of the English Dramatic Poets* (1691), pp. 308-9, 375; William Joyner, *The Roman Empress, A Tragedy* (1671), sigs. A2ᵃ, A3ᵃ, A4ᵃ, pp. 38, 59.

12.　　*The Roman Empress*, sig. A1ᵇ, p. 67, cf. references to restoration, pp. 9, 45, 54. *The Roman Empress* loosely dramatises the mysterious court scandal in which Constantine (here Valentius) put to death his son and heir (here Florus). Valentius's wife Fulvia, the empress of the title, is the chief villain. She loves Florus, Valentius's general (not yet known to be his son), but he scorns her in favour of Aurelia, daughter of an enemy general. Aurelia in turn rejects him, because he has killed her brother. When Valentius declares Florus his heir, the women, in vengeful fury, plot to undermine him. The emperor comes to suspect him of treachery and ingratitude and orders his execution. Aurelia and Fulvia, now remorseful, also choose death, and Valentius, realising how he has been deceived, takes his own life.

Parallels to *SA* in *The Roman Empress* include 'my soul, my self' (p. 8, cf.*SA*, 102), 'our maturity/ Should change this bondage into liberty' (p. 23, cf. *SA*, 270-1), 'feel within me secret motives'(p. 50, cf.*SA*, 394, 429, 1382), 'as a ship seeming with her ful-blown sails...So I methinks now ardently pursuing/ Revenge' and

> The earth doth many monsters generate;
> So does the sea; yet nothing can produce
> So mischievous in nature, as a woman,
> Pursuing her revenge...

(pp. 50, 52, cf. *SA*, 230, 710-24), death the 'ease of troubled minds', 'safe port of the virtuous' (p. 53, cf. *SA*, 18, 459-60), 'my soul...never felt eclipse but in thy absence' (p. 57, cf. *SA*, 879, 936, 1037-8). Both works associate love with imprisonment and servitude (pp. 23-4), and love with hate, 'the only object of/ My love, as now of hatred' (p. 47). Joyner's latinisms include 'compassionate' and 'conditionate' as verbs (pp. 52, 62). Examples of pseudo-Miltonic style include:

> where we suffer
> Defeats upon defeats, no funerals see
> Of Parents, Friends, Allies; which make not up
> Their horrid train with funerals of others...(p. 2)

and

> were I not (what thou
> Seems't to deny here) an indulgent Father,
> Thou from these hands at present shouldst receive
> Chastisement proper to thy insolence,
> Which now falls on thee mitigated onely
> Into admonishment; thy error is
> Th'error of love, which is excusable
> In younger age, confined within limits
> Excusable...(p. 4).

13. Such plays include *The Unfortunate Usurper* (1663), John Wilson, *Andronicus Comnenius* (1664), John Caryll, *The English Princess* (1667), Edward Howard, *The Usurper* (1668), adaptations of Corneille's Roman plays, and works by Dryden and Robert Howard.

14. Cf. Mary Ann Radzinowicz, *Toward 'Samson Agonistes' : The Growth of Milton's Mind* (Princeton, 1978), pp. 167-79 and *passim*; an intelligent and comprehensive account of the work and its place in Milton's development.

15. In the first edition the line numbers were inadvertently set one line too high: even so, '660' (as it was given) aligns with the conclusion to the messenger's speech. See also Hill, *Milton and the English Revolution*, pp. 438-9.

16. Matthew Griffith, *The Fear of God and the King* (1660), p. 9; Milton, *Complete Prose*, VII, 201-2, 476; Thomas Mayhew, *Upon the Joyfull and Welcome Return of His Sacred Majestie* (1660), p. 8; Samuel Pordage, *Poems upon Several Occasions* (1660), sig. B2[b].

17. Mayhew, op.cit., p. 10.

18. John Dover Wilson, 'Shakespeare, Milton and Congreve', *TLS*, January 16 1937, p. 44; Ralph Davis, *The Rise of the English Shipping Industry in the Seventeenth and Eighteenth Centuries* (1962), pp. 228, 230, 316; Carew Reynel, *The True English Interest* (1674), pp. 6, 10 ('where a Nation Imports by its voluptuousness more than it Exports, it must needs come to ruine'); James Harrington, *The Oceana and Other Works* (1737), p. 468.

19. *Heroick Portraits* (1660), sig. B2[a].

CHAPTER 9   CONCLUSION: ARTIFICE AND SCRUTINY

1. Jonathan Swift, *A Tale of a Tub, With Other Early Works, 1696-1707*, ed. Herbert Davis (Oxford, 1939), p. 157.

Index

Act of Uniformity *1662*   11, 93
Ailesbury, Thomas, *Earl of*   29,
   31, 177
Albermarle, George Monck,
   first Duke of   3, 8, 9, 10-13,
   26, 28, 55, 62, 64, 89, 97,
   102, 160, 193
Anglicanism   xiii, 20-1,
   22, 69, 77, 93
Anne, Queen   xii
apocatastasis   68-9
architecture   55
   see also Saint James's Park;
      Saint Paul's Cathedral;
      Sheldonian Theatre;
      Somerset House
Aristotle   19
Arlington, Henry Bennet,
   Earl of   98, 137
Armorer, Nicholas   75
the army   8, 12, 13
   disbanding of, *1660*   36
Augustanism   xii, 45, 48,
   52, 63, 183

Bacon, Francis   94, 95
Barrow, Isaac   183
Bath   4
Beaumont, Joseph   71
Beeston, Henry   28, 54, 180
Behn, *Mrs* Aphra   140
Bennet, Henry
   see Arlington
Bold, Henry   5, 58, 176
Booth, Sir George   7, 9
Bosher, Robert S.   179
Boyle, Roger
   see Orrery
Braganza, Catherine of   4

Breda, *Holland*   2, 21
Brome, Alexander   18
Browne, *Sir* Thomas   68, 154
Buckingham, George Villiers,
   second Duke of   76, 78,
   137, 189, 196
Bulstrode, Richard   41
Butler, James
   see Ormonde
Butler, Samuel
   Hudibras   92-3

Cambridge   77
   Platonists   67, 69, 71
Canterbury   3, 4
Cary, Lucius
   see Falkland
Caroline
   courtliness   11, 76, 100
   masques   129
   theory of government   20
Caryll, John   131
   The English Princess   132-4, 199
Catholics and Catholicism
   21, 78, 89, 93, 141,
   158, 163, 190
Cavaliers   21-2, 98, 110, 126
Cavendish, William
   see Newcastle
Chamberlayne, William   34,
   40, 59
Charles I   3, 29, 40, 41,
   44, 53, 87, 122
Charles II   xi, xii, xiii,
   xiv, 1, 10, 18, 24-5, 31, 41,
   44, 50-2, 53, 97, 118, 161,
   179, 183, 191
   and settlement   21, 28
   coronation   4, 5, 65, 121

200

Dutch War 97, 98
powers 24, 27, 28, 87-8
proclaimed king 2
returns to England 2-4, 6, 60
Charleton, *Dr* Walter 57
Christianity 11, 40, 44, 48,
 64, 67, 69, 71, 84
see also New Testament
Church of England
see Anglicanism
Cibber, Colley xii
civil wars 13, 17, 26, 29, 98
Clarendon, Edward Hyde,
 first Earl of 1, 7, 12,
 17, 19-20, 21, 22, 29-30, 36,
 65, 76, 78, 97, 98, 100,
 101, 110-11, 119, 137,
 168, 179
 Clarendon Code 21
 State Papers 75
classical allusions 19, 36
 see also Rome
Claudian 122
Collop, John 11, 12, 23,
 44, 54, 181, 184
 Itur Satyricum 10
commerce 30, 123
Committee of Safety 8
commonwealth 23, 35, 98
Cooper, Anthony Ashley
 see Shaftesbury
Cooper, John 188
Corneille, Pierre 131, 199
Council of State 7
Coventry, *Sir* William 98,
 137, 196
Cowley, Abraham 11, 48,
 55, 73-96, 169, 173, 188,
 189, 190
 Brutus 80, 81-3, 85
 The Civil War 77
 The Complaint 91
 Cutter of Coleman-Street 126
 Davideis 78-80, 188, 189
 Destinie 80
 A Discourse by Way of Vision 83
 Hymn. To Light 93
 Ode Upon His Majesties
 Restoration and Return 10,
 36, 41, 46, 54, 121

On the Death of Mr Crashaw 78
On the Queens Repairing
 Somerset House 93
Plantarum 98
Proposition for the Advancement
 of Experimental
 Philosophy 95
The Puritan and the Papist 77
To Mr Hobs 80
To Sir William Davenant 78
To the Royal Society 94,
 95, 97, 190
Cromwell, Oliver 5, 6-7, 20, 24,
 27, 53, 64, 65, 74, 76,
 81, 106, 112, 138
Cromwell, Richard 7, 8,
 13, 83, 132
Crowne, John 140
Cudworth, Ralph 67,
 68, 69, 154, 187

Dante 52
Davenant, *Sir* William 11-12,
 22, 157, 166-7, 190, 195
 Poem to the Kings Most
 Sacred Majesty 22, 35, 40,
 42, 45, 167
 The Siege of Rhodes 134
 'To His Excellency the
 Lord General Monck' 11
decadence xi
 see also immorality; pornography
declaration of Breda 1
Denham, *Sir* John 37-8, 44, 131
Donne, John 70
Douglas, Archibald 116-17
Dover 2, 3, 4, 60
Dover, John
 The Roman Generalls 131
drama
 see theatre
Drayton, Michael 44, 123
Dryden, John xii, xiv, 4,
 11, 24, 42, 48, 55, 57,
 59, 60-6, 97, 130, 131,
 137, 139, 141, 157, 167-73,
 186, 192, 199
 Absalom and Achitophel 50, 171
 Annus Mirabilis 24, 47, 55,

Dryden, John *(continued)*
  103-9, 110, 163, 169, 171,
  192
  Astraea Redux xii, 2, 10,
    15, 34, 41, 42, 45, 54, 56,
    60-5, 99, 168, 171
  The Conquest of Granada 135
  *Defence of an essay on
  Dramatic Poesy* 130
  *Essay on the Dramatic Poetry
    of the Last Age* 48, 184
  The Indian Emperour 135
  The Indian Queen 131-2
  Threnodia Augustalis 169
  To His Sacred Majesty 42, 65
  To My Lord Chancellor 65, 168
  Tyrannick Love 135
Dutch War 96, 97, 108,
  114, 123, 136, 138

education 18-19
Edwards, Thomas 58
Eliade, Mircea 43
Elizabeth I 44, 46, 47, 133
Enlightenment 50
Erasmus, Desiderius 67
Erskine-Hill, Howard 183
Etherege, *Sir* George 42, 140
  The Man of Mode 179
  She Would If She Could 178
Evelyn, John 3-4, 193
Everett, Barbara 178, 193
Excise Bill 113

Fairfax, Maria 76
Fairfax, Thomas, *third Baron* 8
Falkland, Lucius Cary,
  Viscount 77
Fifth Monarchists 59
Filmer, *Sir* Robert 181
Firth, *Sir* Charles 180
Flatman, Thomas 186
Flecknoe, Richard 34, 39, 163
  Heroick Portraits 36
Fletcher, John 49
Ford, John 196

Gay, John 170
General Council of Officers 8
Glorious Revolution 29
Gombrich, E.H. 184

government xiv, 84, 105,
  108, 112, 119
  see also parliament
Green, I.M. 179
Griffith, *Dr* Matthew 161
guilds 4, 193

Ham House xiv
Harrington, James 122, 163
  Oceana 7
Henrietta Maria 12, 74,
  76, 78, 88-9, 93
Henry VIII 39
Herbert, George 70
Higgons, *Sir* Thomas 27,
  47, 96, 99, 178
Hill, Christopher 30, 190, 197
Hinman, Robert B. 188
Hobbes, Thomas 19, 40,
  72, 73, 78, 81, 95,
  186, 188, 189
  Leviathan 27, 72
Holland 2
  see also Breda; Scheveling
Horace 51
House of Commons 11
Howard, Edward
  The Usurper 128, 199
Howard, *Sir* Robert 33,
  39, 58, 130, 131, 141,
  157, 196, 199
  The Committee 126
  The Indian Queen 131-2
  The Vestal-Virgin 131
  The Great Favourite 137,
  138-9, 181
Huizinga, Johan 52
Hume, David 22, 25, 30
Hyde, Anne
  see York, Anne Hyde *Duchess of*
Hyde, Edward
  see Clarendon

immorality xiii, 116
Independents 15
industry 19
Interregnum 17, 33, 54

James, *Duke of York* 25,
  97, 100, 119, 135, 158

James I 122, 182
James II
  see James, *Duke of York*
Jermyn, Henry 76, 115, 116
Jevon, Rachel 41, 46, 55, 59, 60
  Exultationis Carmen 32, 39, 41
Johnson, Samuel xii, 170
Jones, Inigo 190, 195
Jonson, Ben 46, 49
Joyner, William 158
  The Roman Empress 158-9, 198

Knight, G. Wilson 137

Lambert, John 8
Land Tax Bill 113
Langbaine, Gerald 158, 159
Laud, William *Archbishop* 77
L'Estrange, Roger 32
the Levellers 54
literacy 18
Lloyd, David 28, 29, 33,
    38, 39, 60, 180
  Eikon Basilike 33, 36
Lluelyn, Martin 13, 27,
    38, 39, 40, 177
Locke, John 45, 50, 102, 179
London 3, 4, 10, 12, 36,
    56, 57, 109, 119
  Great Fire 98, 105, 106, 108
  insurrections 8
  street pageantry 120
Lord Mayor's Day 4, 120
Louis XIV, King of
    France 116, 118
Lucan
  Pharsalia 77
Ludlow, Edmund 5, 35

Macaulay, *Lord*
    Thomas Babington xiii-xiv,
    30
McKeon, Michael 175, 192
Marvell, Andrew 20, 24, 71,
    138, 170, 173, 192
  Clarendon's House-Warming 119
  First Anniversary ... 24, 65, 112
  Further Advice to a Painter 119
  Horatian Ode upon Cromwell's

  Return from Ireland 12, 65,
    69
  *The Last Instructions
    to a Painter* 98,
    109-19, 170, 171
  Upon Appleton House 76
Masson, David 5, 23-4,
    26, 30, 158, 186
Michelangelo 48
millenarianism 54, 55, 57,
    59, 60, 72, 184
Milton, John 14, 18-19, 29,
    33, 142, 171, 173-4
  Comus 157
  Of True Religion ... 155
  Paradise Lost 49, 147,
    163, 172, 173-4
  Paradise Regained 178
  *The Readie and Easie
    Way ...* 29, 142-3, 160
  Samson Agonistes xv,
    143-63, 164-5, 171, 178
monarchism 13, 17
Monck, *General* George
  see Albemarle
Montelion, 1661 and *1662* 59-60
Mordaunt, John 12, 115
More, Henry 67, 68, 72, 73, 188
More, *Sir* Thomas
  Utopia 128

Navy 56, 99, 104, 110,
    118, 123, 163
Nedham, Marchamont 14,
    26, 32
New Testament 52-3, 84
Newcastle, William
    Cavendish, *first Duke of*
    21, 22
Newton, *Sir* Isaac 50
Nicholas, *Secretary* Edward 14

Ogg, David 6, 25
Ogilby, John 44, 45, 120
  The Entertainment ... 120-4, 183
Origen 67, 68, 69, 72
Ormonde, James Butler,
    first Duke of 76, 137
Orrery, Roger Boyle,
    first Earl of 135-6,

Orrery, Roger Boyle *(continued)*
137, 139, 141, 195
The Black Prince 136
*The History of Henry the
Fifth* 136
Mustapha 136
Osborne, Dorothy 76, 189
Oxford 48, 77, 158

pageantry 5
see also theatre
Palladio, Andrea 156
pamphlets 125, 161, 162
Panofsky, Erwin 48, 181-2
parliament 1, 3, 8, 13, 55,
89, 97, 105, 110, 137
Cavalier 21, 25
dissolution of *1659* 7
see also House of
Commons politicians
Pepys, Samuel xiv, 2, 4,
5, 29, 56, 59, 60, 92,
128, 136, 137, 196
Petrarch 52, 96
Pett, Peter 112, 193
Petty, William 136
Philips, Katherine
'Arion on a Dolphin...' 2, 42
Pompey 131
Phillips, John 186
Pindar 80
the Plague 98
Plato, Platonism 19,
35, 48, 69, 71
Pocock, J.G.A. 186
Pope, Alexander xi-xiv,
73, 170, 172
The Dunciad xii-xiii
Essay on Criticism xiii
Imitations of Horace xi, xii
Windsor Forest xii
Pordage, Samuel 58, 184
pornography xiii
Portman, W. 181
presbyterianism 11, 13, 21
property 14, 17
Protectorate 5, 7, 8, 24,
74, 75, 79, 81, 83
Purcell, Henry xiv
Dido and Aeneas 50

puritanism 5, 25, 29, 30,
69, 81, 95, 126

Queen Mother
see Henrietta Maria

Radzinowicz, Mary Ann 199
religion 53, 64, 86
see also Christianity
Renaissance 48, 49, 52, 156
republicans 7, 79
Restoration settlement
see settlement
Reynel, Carew 4, 39
Richard III 132, 133
Rochester, John Wilmot
Earl of 3, 15, 41,
42, 170
Rome 4, 36, 44, 47, 52,
63, 119, 121, 123
Roper, Alan 185
Royal Society 19, 55,
56-7, 94-5, 97, 157
royalists 2, 7, 53, 60, 75, 79
and land 17
the Rump
see parliament
Ruyter, *Admiral* Michael de
111, 114

Sadler, Anthony 126
Saint Augustine 67
Saint Paul's Cathedral
36, 49, 125
Scarborough, *Dr* Charles 76, 189
Scheveling 2, 3, 62
Scotland 8
Scottish Covenanters 78
Second Advice to a Painter 100-1
Sedley, *Sir* Charles
The Mulberry-Garden 178
Settle, Elkanah 140
settlement 6, 17, 21, 28, 162
Shadwell, Thomas 140
Shaftesbury, Anthony
Ashley Cooper, *first
Earl of* 177, 179
Shakespeare, William 49,
70, 157, 196
Shearman, John 49

Sheldonian Theatre,
    Oxford 48, 156-7, 184
Shirley, James and Henry 138
Sidney, *Sir* Philip 166
1660 1, 19, 21, 25,
    28, 31, 42, 154, 172
Smith, John 71, 188
Somerset House 55, 93
Sprat, Thomas 75, 93, 95, 189
    History of the Royal Society 55,
    56-7
Staves, Susan 194
Stokes, Adrian 197
Stone, Lawrence 18
Stonehenge 57
Streater, Robert 48, 157, 184
Stuart destiny, regime xii,
    19, 22, 46, 98, 103, 105, 162
Stubbes, Richard 17-18, 23
Summers, Joseph H. 193
Swift, Jonathan 170, 172-3

Tatham, John 124-5, 126, 137,
    141, 176
Tawney, R.H. 30
theatre 24, 120-41, 154, 156, 157
Third Advice to a Painter 101-2
trade 14, 50, 55-6, 98, 123
    see also commerce; industry
Trotter, David 188
Tuke, *Sir* Samuel 76, 189, 190

The Unfortunate Usurper 128-9,
    199

Villiers, George
    see Buckingham
Virgil 45, 46, 47, 51,
    52, 103, 121, 172
    Aeneid xii, 45

Vitruvius 156

Wallace, John M. 192
Waller, Edmund 24, 50-2,
    55, 76, 97, 99-100
    Instructions to a Painter 99, 101
    On St James's Park 36, 51-2
    To the King 34, 40, 50, 99
Warwick, Sir Philip 9, 15, 34,
    35, 36
Wase, Christopher
    Divination 101
Wasserman, E.R. 185
Weinbrot, Howard D. 183
Westminster Abbey 29, 51, 96
Whichcote, Benjamin 69,
    70, 71, 73, 187, 188
Whitehall, Robert 48, 157
Whitlock, Bulstrode 177
Wild, Robert 4, 11, 12,
    41, 55, 98-9, 184
    Iter Boreale 2-3, 11
William of Orange 191
Williams, John 188
Wilson, John
    Andronicus Comnenius 126-8, 199
Winstanley, Gerard 67
    Diggers 54
Wood, Anthony à 176, 186
Woolrych, Austin 9, 176
Wren, *Sir* Christopher 48,
    49, 55, 156
Wycherley, William 42, 140
    Love in a Wood 178

Yates, Frances 156
York, Anne Hyde, *Duchess
    of* 100, 101, 116, 140
York, *Duke of*
    see James, *Duke of York*